THREE GENERATIONS

OF

CHILEAN CUISINE

THREE GENERATIONS

OF

CHILEAN CUISINE

BY

MIRTHA UMAÑA-MURRAY

Lowell House
Los Angeles

Contemporary Books
Chicago

Library of Congress Cataloging-in-Publication Data
Umaña-Murray, Mirtha.
      Three generations of Chilean cuisine / by Mirtha Umaña-Murray.
         p. cm.
      Includes biographical references and index.
      ISBN 1-56565-467-6
      1. Cookery, Chilean. 2. Food habits—Chile. I. Title.
  TX716.5983—dc20   96-34515
                                                             CIP

Requests for such permissions should be addressed to:
Lowell House
2020 Avenue of the Stars, Suite 300
Los Angeles, CA 90067

Lowell House books can be purchased at special discounts when ordered in bulk for premiums and special sales. Contact Department TC at the address above.

Photographs courtesy of Mirtha Umaña-Murray
Map of Chile by Gwen Van Ark

Publisher: Jack Artenstein
Associate Publisher, Lowell House Adult: Bud Sperry
Managing Editor: Maria Magallanes
Text design: Laurie Young

Manufactured in the United States of America
10 9 8 7 6 5 4 3 2 1

CONTENTS

I dedicate this book to my American family and friends.

ACKNOWLEDGMENTS

I depended on many people to write this book. My mother and her sister Emma lovingly gave me their culinary knowledge. My husband, always supportive and enthusiastic, tasted every recipe and edited and reviewed my early manuscripts. My step-daughter Debra encouraged me and edited the first draft. Bob and Joy Marks, my wonderful friends, expertly guided me into the publishing world. Theresa Park, my wonderful and dedicated agent, trusted and encouraged me every step of the way. My dear friend Emily Speagle inspired me and suggested the title. My friends Hugo and Nora Castillo helped me with the historic information. Bud Sperry and Maria Magallanes, my editors at Lowell House, edited the book with great skill and competence. Over the years, many friends and family members encouraged me to complete this book. Many, many thanks to all of them.

PREFACE

This book was inspired by my longing to share the many flavors and varieties of authentic Chilean cuisine. To this end, I have translated my Chilean family's hand-written recipes. In these recipes, three generations of Chilean cooking traditions and customs are collected and preserved, from my grandparents' contemporaries, through my mother's generation, to me.

I am a native of Santiago, Chile. Some of my ancestors were Spaniards who journeyed to Chile during colonial times. My paternal grandparents, the Umaña Durán family, were farmers near the northern town of Quillota, a town famous for its *palta* (avocado), *chirimoya* (custard apple), and papaya groves. Like many of his generation, my father left the farm and moved to Santiago at the age of seventeen to become a successful businessman. My mother's grandparents, the Silva Guzmán family, were landowners and industrialists in the southern province of Curicó, a region rich in vineyards and abundant agricultural produce. In the 1930s this side of the family also moved to Santiago where my mother's generation became middle class urban professionals.

As part of my training to become a properly educated Chilean woman, I learned to cook in my mother's kitchen and in school. During my studies in Europe, and since, I have learned much about classic French, Italian, English, and other regional cuisines. I have lived and traveled in South America and the Caribbean, and at every stop my curiosity has led me to learn about the cuisines and customs of the lands I visited. Since 1974 I have lived in the United States, although I have traveled frequently to Chile to visit family and collect new recipes.

Throughout her life, my mother, Aida Bascuñán Silva, collected recipes from family members and developed a cooking style of her own—delicate and flavorful, with an emphasis on sweets and desserts. A few years ago, she gave me her hand-written cookbooks. In these books I found recipes such as *Porotos Granados* (Summer Bean Stew, p. 97), *Caldillo de Erizos* (Sea Urchin Soup, p. 72), *Leche Asada* (Flan, p. 232), and *Turrón de Vino* (Wine Meringue, p. 225).

My grandfather, Agusto Bascuñán Aldunate, was known in his time as a "grand gourmand," a handsome devil and a connoisseur of good food, good wines, and good times. My aunt Emma Bascuñán has told me of my grandfather's culinary abilities. It was very unusual for a man of his time and position to know about the art of cooking. His specialty was *Arroz a la Valenciana* (Rice Valencia Style, pp. 92–93), which he prepared with *congrio* (conger eel) and *locos* (Chilean abalones) as written in my mother's notebooks.

I also inherited my Great-aunt Julia Silva de Neale's cookbook. Great-aunt Julia was a renowned cook in the classic Chilean *criolla* style. This style was developed during colonial times as a blend of the Spanish and local Mapuche cuisines and before the influence of other European cultures made their mark. Great-aunt Julia married an Irishman, Guillermo (William) Neale, who died young due to his fondness for excellent Chilean wines. Great-aunt Julia always wore brown. When I asked my mother why, she explained that it was the result of a *manda,* a promise to the *Virgen del Carmen,* in an attempt to save her husband's soul from eternal damnation. Some of her recipes include *Caldillo de Congrio* (Conger Eel Soup, p. 71), *Gallina en Escabeche* (Pickled Hen, p. 123), and *Riñones al Jerez* (Kidneys in Sherry Sauce, p. 151).

Through my mother's cookbooks and by word of mouth, I also obtained recipes from several other aunts, including Emma Bascuñán de Ghilardi, Ema Neale Silva de Welt, and Erika Leopold. Aunt Emma Bascuñán, my mother's elder sister, received my grandfather's culinary knowledge and passed it on to my mother and me. Her special recipes include *Empanadas Chilenas* (Chilean Meat Turnovers, pp. 52–53), *Machas al Horno* (Broiled Razor Clams, p. 51), and *Corvina al Horno* (Baked Chilean Bass, p. 112).

Aunt Erika Leopold was my mother's best friend from the time they were young women. Aunt Erika is of German descent and received from her mother the culinary traditions of her native land. I can remember as a child visiting aunt Erika and enjoying the most wonderful sweets and pastries at teatime. Some of her recipes include *Cujen (Kuchen) de Fresas* (Berry Tart, pp. 250–251), *Pan de Pascua* (Christmas Fruit Cake, pp. 256–257), and *Torta de Cumpleaños* (Birthday Torte, p. 257).

Many years ago, I married Great-aunt Leonie Boisier de Llona's step-grandson, my first husband Juan Allende Llona. As a wedding present Great-aunt Leonie gave me a cookbook written by her sister, Laurie Boisier. In that book I found recipes such as *Canapés de Mariscos* (Shellfish Hors D'oeuvres, p. 33), *Champaña con Frutillas* (Strawberry Champagne, p. 271), and *Galletas Picantes* (Spicy Crackers, p. 39).

Most of the recipes in my mother's and my Great-aunt Julia's cookbooks did not specify precise measurements or cooking time. These recipes are the result of generations of experience and personal knowledge. By studying and testing them, I have tried to recapture their essence and provide sufficient directions to allow even a novice to prepare them.

I have also collected recipes from friends, from regional restaurants in Chile, and from old Chilean publications. Some recipes are my family's version of very traditional *cocina criolla,* such as *Chupe de Mariscos* (Shellfish, Bread, and Cheese Casserole, pp. 110–111), *Pastel de Choclo* (Corn and Beef Casserole, pp. 84–85), *Humitas* (Chilean Tamales, pp. 58–59), *Alfajores* (Chilean Pastries with Caramel Spread, p. 238), and *Sopaipillas* (Pumpkin Fritters with Molasses Syrup, p. 241).

Finally, the many years I have lived in the southern United States, married to a southerner, Royce W. Murray, have also left their impression on my way of cooking. Therefore, I have included my own version of Fresh Berry Pie (p. 253), Aunt Jennie Herd's Tea Cake (p. 254), Royce's Breakfast Biscuits (p. 26), and Beer Batter (p. 214).

Enjoy!

Mirtha Umaña-Murray
Chapel Hill, North Carolina

THE ORIGINS OF CHILEAN CUISINE

❖

Chilean cuisine is distinctive among the foods of South America. It is a wonderful blend of Old World Spanish and New World cuisine. We call this blend *cocina criolla Chilena.*

You will find from my family's recipes that Chilean food is neither "nouvelle" nor "light," but most dishes promote good health and nutrition. They are high in complex carbohydrates and low in animal fat. Chilean food is sometimes spicy, and always flavorful. We commonly use *Ají* (a very hot yellow pepper), *ají de color* (Chilean sweet paprika), and garlic for strong tastes. Herbs such as cilantro, parsley, oregano, sweet basil, thyme, mint, and lemon balm and spices such as black pepper, cumin, saffron, vanilla, cinnamon, cloves, and nutmeg are used for milder and more subtle flavors. There is enormous variety in Chilean meals. Some dishes are elegant, even extravagant, and appropriate for sophisticated dinner parties. Others are simple and homey and have their origins in the kitchens of the Chilean peasant. Both kinds have been part of my family's cooking traditions.

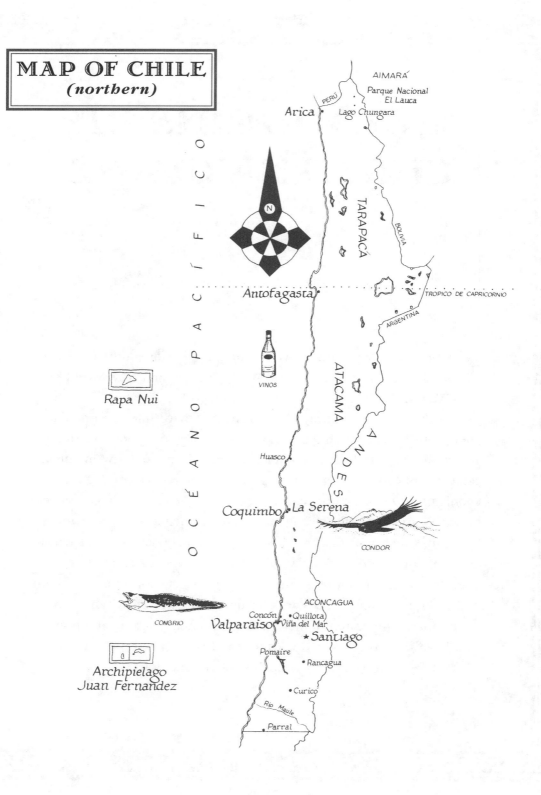

MAP OF CHILE
(northern)

OCÉANO PACÍFICO

AIMARÁ

PERÚ

Arica

Lago Chungara

Parque Nacional
El Lauca

TARAPACÁ

BOLIVIA

Antofagasta

TRÓPICO DE CAPRICORNIO

ARGENTINA

VINOS

ATACAMA

ANDES

Rapa Nui

Huasco

Coquimbo · La Serena

CONDOR

ACONCAGUA

CONGRIO

Concón · Quillota
Valparaiso · Viña del Mar

★ Santiago

Pomaire

· Rancagua

Archipielago
Juan Fernandez

· Curico

Rio Maule

Parral

Concepción

Río Ñuble
Chillán

• Los Angeles

ARAUCO REGION

CONGRIO

× VILLARICA

Valdivia

Osorno •

Puerto Montt

Chiloé

OCÉANO PACÍFICO

PATAGONIA

ARGENTINA

N

Parque Nacional
Torres del Paine

Puerto Natales

ESTRECHO DE MAGALLANES

Punta Arenas

ESTRECHO DE MAGALLANES

Porvenir

TIERRA DEL FUEGO

CENTOLLAS

MAP OF CHILE
(southern)

CHILE'S GEOGRAPHY

Chile is a remote place and has always been hard to reach, even by today's standards of modern jet transportation. The name *Chile* has its origins in the Aimará language of the native peoples of the Bolivian high plateau near lake Titicaca; they called our land *Chilli*, which means, very appropriately, "the land at the end of the world." Because of this isolation, our way of cooking is different from the Mexican, Caribbean, and Brazilian cuisines that may be more familiar to many North Americans and Europeans. Another influence on Chilean cuisine is the shape of the country.

My country is a narrow sliver of land on the southwest end of South America about 4,800 km long. That's roughly the distance between San Diego, California, and Fairbanks, Alaska, or between Miami, Florida, and the Hudson Bay in Canada. The northern part of the Chilean "sliver" is sealed off by 1,000 km of the stunning and impenetrable Atacama Desert, and its nearest neighbor to the south is the frozen Antarctic. Chile's eastern flank is held by the breathtaking granite peaks of the Andes, and on the west it is bordered by the southern Pacific Ocean, which still inspires romance and adventure. About 3,000 km west of central Chile lie the islands of Rapa Nui (Easter Island) and Juan Fernandez Archipelago, where the Scot Alexander Selkirk, alias Robinson Crusoe, lived from 1704 to 1709.

Chile's Pacific coast stretches from the northern port of Arica, where the turquoise blue waters are warm and the golden beaches inviting, to the southern port of Punta Arenas on the Straits of Magellan, where the waters are icy and the wind is a constant reminder that the South Pole is close by. This long coastline, with its many protected coves, sandy beaches, and rocky cliffs, is an incredible fishery because the Humboldt current carries in a wealth of rich nutrients from the cold Antarctic waters. The abundance of fish and shellfish from Chile's coastal environment has endowed Chilean cuisine with diverse and plentiful seafood.

As you might guess, Chile's climate is dramatically different between its northern and southern extremes. In the north the hot, dry Atacama desert is rich in mineral deposits. My adventuresome uncles Miguel Neale Silva and Agustín Bascuñán Silva worked most of their lives there, mining for copper, gold, and other riches. But there are other treasures in this desert. If you are lucky enough to travel through the Atacama in the rare year when there is a little rain, you are in for a spectacular treat. For a few short weeks the desert transforms itself into a brilliant and colorful garden. The desert wildflowers rush to bloom and make seeds that will wait dormant for the next rain, perhaps a decade later. The Atacama also contains oasis valleys watered by streams fed by Andean snow melt. These valleys support some trees such as the native Peumo and provide good farming; today fresh produce is grown there year round. In my recent trips to Chile it has been a delight to find juicy, sun-ripened tomatoes in the markets in Santiago even in August, which is the middle of winter in the southern hemisphere.

In central Chile, where I grew up, the climate is Mediterranean, with warm dry summers and cool rainy winters. The Central Valley, between the Andes and the coastal range, offers extremely fertile, volcanic soil. This is where my family's farms and vineyards used to be. On a clear day, you can admire the majestic, snow-capped Andes from almost anywhere in the valley, and from the air, flying into Santiago, the imposing Aconcagua peak will thrust itself into your view. At over 8,000 meters, the Aconcagua is the tallest mountain in the world outside the Himalayas. Originally, the Central Valley was covered with grasses; shrubs such as *boldo, maitén, espino* (hawthorn), and *litre*; and some trees such as the *encina* (live oak) and *palmera Chilena (Jubaea chilensis)*. Today the Central Valley is Chile's breadbasket blessing the country with a nearly self-sufficient food production. In fact, Chile has exported grains, fruits, vegetables, and wine since colonial times.

The geography of Chile thus provides its cooks with choices from a diverse bounty of fresh fish, meats, fruits, and vegetables. The European small-shop tradition is alive and well there. My mother goes daily to the neighborhood shops and street markets to handpick the freshest, ripest seasonal fruits and vegetables for the meals of the day. On the coast between Valparaíso, Viña del Mar, and Concón, the local people gather at the coves where the fishermen bring in their small boats after a night out at sea. There, cooks expertly choose their next meal from the freshest bounty of the sea. This scene repeats itself along Chile's coast, from La Serena in the north to Concepción, Valdivia, and Puerto Natales in the south. The enjoyment one obtains from choosing food this way can never be found in the supermarket shopping experience!

The south-central part of Chile is cool and wet. The vegetation turns into moist, rich forest where gigantic trees grow. These include the native *Pehuén* (*Araucaria araucana*), *Canelo* (*Drimys winteri,* ritual Mapuche tree), *Coigüe* (*Nothofagus dombeyi*), *Lingue* (*Persea lingue*), *Raulí* (*Nothofagus alpina*), *Roble* (*Nothofagus obiqua,* oak), *Mañío* (*Saxegothaea conspiqua*), and *Alerce* (*Fitzroya cupesssoides,* larch or native sequoia). In these forests grows the *Copihue* vine (*Lapogeria rosea*) with its delicate pink, red, and white blossoms that are the Chilean national flower. This is the lake district, where my husband Royce and I have spent many glorious summer vacation days in the shadows of the volcanos Villarica, Osorno, and Calbuco. These pristine southern lakes are ideal habitat for trout and salmon and are a paradise for fishing and outdoor activities.

Further south, the weather turns cold and the vegetation becomes hardy grassland where transplanted sheep thrive, and then, in the extreme south, the vegetation turns into tundra. These are the regions of Patagonia, Magallanes, and Tierra del Fuego. This part of Chile is a region of unspoiled beauty where there is a fabulous National Park called Torres del Paine. The native wildlife includes *guanaco* (*Lama guanicoe*), *Huemúl* (*Hippocamelus bisuscus,* Andean deer), *coypu* (*L. nutra,* nutria), *ñandú* (*Pterocnemia pennata,* Patagonian ostrich), *flamenco chileno* (*Phoenicopterus chilensis,* flamingo), *cisne de cuello negro* (*Cygnus melancoryphus,* black-necked swan), *cóndor* (*Vultur griphus*), *puma* (*Felis concolor patagonica*), and *Culpeo* (*Dusicyon culpaeus,* Andean wolf). These otherwise unusual animals are easy to find in the spectacular setting of snow-covered granite peaks and glacial lakes. If you have any love for nature at all, this place can capture your heart. It has ours.

CHILEAN PEOPLE AND THEIR CUISINE

This remote and beautiful land has been home to many people for at least 12,000 years. Who are the people of Chile, and who are their ancestors? In pre-Columbian times, the northern desert was populated by sedentary farmers, the *Atacameños* and *Diaguitas.* The northern part of Chile was, for a short time (less than forty years in the fifteenth century A.D.), a distant and almost forgotten part of the highly developed Inca empire. The fertile center and the south of Chile were originally populated by seminomadic tribes who were part-time farmers and hunter-gatherers. These peoples included the *Mapuches* (or *Araucanos*), whom the Spaniards never conquered, and the *Pehuelches* and *Tehuelches* in the south. They cultivated crops of potatoes, beans, corn, pumpkins, and quinoa. These tribes, together with the Spanish conquistadors, are my proud ancestors and the ancestors of most of the modern Chilean population. Fishermen settled the northern and central coastal regions, and further south were nomadic canoe sailors, such as the *Alacalufes, Yaganes,* and the now extinct *Onas.*

Sadly we know little of the culinary traditions of the pre-Columbian Chileans. We know they hunted the native land animals and harvested the bounties of the ocean. They left mounds of mollusk shells along the coast that are up to 12,000 years old. The shells found include *Locos* (*Concholepas concholepas,* Chilean abalones), *Machas* (*Mesodesma donacium,* razor clams), and *Choros* (*Mytilus chorus,* mussels), for which I have included several recipes. Some of the pre-Columbian preparations survive to this day. One example is *Curanto* (pp. 118–119) which is similar to the New England clambake and the Hawaiian luau. *Curanto* can still be found on the southern islands of Chiloé and Tenglo. It consists of seafood, potatoes, beans, and a whole suckling pig, baked in a pit lined with hot rocks and covered with leaves. In Puerto Montt, I remember tasting smoked, dried seafood as prepared in nearby Angelmó using the ancient procedures. In the Arauco region *Milcao* (Mapuche Potato Bread, p. 194) and *Pulmay* (Mapuche Seafood Casserole, pp. 118–119) are still prepared. *Charqui* (jerky) was prepared with *guanaco* (Andean camel) and *huemúl* (Andean deer) meat and today is made of beef. In school, I was fed weekly the inevitable and unforgettable *Charquicán de Cochayuyo* (pp. 103–104) an ancient seaweed casserole. My grandmother Elena used to prepare *Chuño* (Potato Starch Breakfast, p. 17) which is still a common breakfast meal in Chilean villages. In a fashionable restaurant in Santiago, you can find *Ceviche* (pp. 47–48), which is raw seafood marinated according to a recipe probably inherited from the Inca empire. Another ancient recipe is *Ulpo* or *Ulpud* (p. 18), a thick maize porridge prepared with hot water, which today is made of roasted wheat flour and milk.

From the sixteenth century until the middle of the nineteenth century, those who came to Chile were mostly Spaniards: first Castilians and Andalusians, and later Basques. Most of them came by sea, via the dangerous sea passage through the Straits of Magellan to our Pacific coast. Others came by land through Atacama, the driest desert in the world. Most of these intrepid explorers came in search of land, a new life away from the constraints of the Old World, and perhaps new loves. The Spaniards that colonized Chile in those early times mixed (as did their cuisine) with the native population. The modern Chilean population and its foods are a true marriage of the New and Old Worlds.

Our Spanish forefathers brought with them their cooking techniques, crops, and foodstuffs. Old World imports to Chile included grapes, olives, walnuts, chestnuts, rice, wheat, citrus fruits, sugar, garlic, and spices. The Spanish immigrants also brought livestock, including chicken, beef, cattle, sheep, pigs, and rabbits, and their byproducts, including milk, cheeses, and *chorizos* (sausages). Many identifiable Spanish and Moorish dishes can be found in my family recipes, including *Escabeche* (pickled fish and hen, pp. 49, 50–51, and 123), *Estofado* (Beef or Rabbit Stew with Vegetables and Port Sauce, p. 145), *Empanadas* (Chilean Meat Turnovers, pp. 52–53), *Tortilla* (omelets, pp. 56 and 57), *Fricandelas* (Spicy Fried Meatballs, p. 147), *Chorizo* (Sausage), *Leche Asada* (Flan, p. 232), and *Manjar Blanco* (Caramel Spread, p. 245).

MODERN CHILEAN CUISINE

Chile declared independence from Spain in 1810 and from that time on many recipes came to us from other parts of Europe. Beginning in the late 19th century, many German immigrants settled in the south of Chile. Wonderful German beers are common in Chile, as are recipes such as *Pan de Pascua* (Christmas Fruit Cake pp. 256–257), *Guiso de Repollo Morado* or *Choucrute* (Red Cabbage and Apple Stew, p. 173), smoked sausage, *Cujen* (*Kuchen*) (fruit tarts, pp. 250–253), and *Bavarois* (Bavarian Fruit Custard, p. 227).

Modern transportation and communications gradually lessened Chile's isolation in the 20th century, and Chilean chefs began to be influenced by classic French, Italian, and English cuisines. And inevitably, new immigrants began to marry into the Chilean population. For example, my Great-aunt Julia married her beloved Irishman William Neale; my aunt Ema Neale married the handsome

German Arturo Welt; my aunt Emma Bascuñán married a dashing Italian Oscar Ghiraldi; and so the story goes. Consequently, we often find included in our menus dishes like consommés (p. 64), soufflés (p. 109), mayonnaise (p. 206), béchamel sauce (p. 208), risotto, pasta, bread pudding (p. 228–229), and scones (p. 27). Never think, however, that the Old World recipes are preserved entirely intact in Chilean kitchens; the European recipes have been modified to suit the local customs and ingredients. And our superb Chilean wines always accompany these wonderful foods.

CHILEAN WINES

I simply must praise the Chilean wines, because they are beyond doubt the best in South America and compete very well in the international wine market. Chilean vineyards are among the oldest in the Americas. In the sixteenth century, Chile began its tradition of exporting wines, first to the Peruvian Viceroyalty. In the 1850s, noble French rootstocks were introduced by Chileans such as Don Silvestre Ochagavía. When *Phylloxera vastatrix,* an insect pest that bores into the roots of grape vines, devastated European and Californian vineyards in the 1870s, Chile was spared because of its isolation. Today some vineyards still grow the original ungrafted French stocks. The types of grapes currently used to produce the superior Chilean wines include Cabernet Sauvignon, Merlot, Pinot Noir, Semillón, Sauvignon Blanc, Riesling, and Chardonnay. Along the Maipo River Valley, my husband Royce and I have visited several of the most famous vineyards and wine cellars where you can admire the old oak barrels and taste the fine vintage wines.

I remember as a child accompanying my father to buy wine by the 10-liter carafe at the Dominican monastery near the Cerro Calán, which is today the suburb of Santiago called Los Dominicos. Although the friars would not allow women in the monastery, I was young enough to be allowed into the ancient cellars to see this fascinating operation. Back at home we would bottle the wine, lay it down for a while, and have an ample supply for the rest of the year. Every generation in my family has had a wine connoisseur and gourmand. In my generation this honor falls to my dear cousin Álvaro Welt Neale, a fun-loving bachelor and international pilot of a Chilean commercial airline.

CHILEAN EATING HABITS

In Chile as in Spain, people take dining seriously. Those who can afford it take it very seriously indeed. The dining schedule is quite unlike that in America and more like that of old Spain. Our day usually begins with a simple *Desayuno* (continental breakfast): coffee or tea, with milk and toast. *Almuerzo* (lunch) is the principal meal of the day. It begins at about 1 P.M. Working hours in Chile are traditionally from 9 A.M. to 1 P.M. and from 4 P.M. to 8 P.M., which allows a gracious time for luncheon dining and a siesta. This schedule is gradually being abandoned in the large urban centers where American working hours are being adopted.

After Sunday Mass our family lunches were elaborate affairs lasting two or three hours. We began with *Aperitivos* (cocktails) and *Bocadillos* (hors d'oeuvres), followed by several courses moistened with a variety of wines. These courses may have included an *Entrada* (appetizer or first course), a *Sopa* (soup or second course), a *Plato de Fondo* (main course with meat or fish) with an *Ensalada* (salad), a *Postre* (dessert), *Café* (coffee) or *Aguita Caliente* (herbal tea), and a *Bajativo* (liqueur). After a meal like this, the very civilized custom of a siesta is inevitable!

Sometimes, at 5 P.M. we have *Onces* (afternoon tea) consisting of hot tea, *mate,* or *chuño* with some sweet bread, *cujen (kuchen),* cookies, cake, or small sandwiches. *Cena* (dinner or supper) is usually a minor meal served around 9 P.M. or later, consisting of perhaps a soup or a vegetable casserole, and a dessert. On special occasions, however, the Chilean dinner can become the main meal of the day, starting around 9 P.M. with drinks. Such affairs can easily last well past midnight.

I have organized the recipes in this book by the Chilean dining schedule. The collection starts with breakfast, followed by the principal midday meal, and the afternoon tea. In North America the principal meal is in the evening, so the recipes for the midday meal can easily be used for the evening meal. I have changed my dining pattern to that of North America, and the Chilean foods fit into this routine just fine. Occasionally, however, at about 5 P.M., I still yearn for a cup of hot tea and something sweet. Old habits are hard to break. I have included some suggested menus (see pp. 12–14) to help you plan your Chilean-style meals. I hope that this collection of recipes will allow you to capture a little of Chile's spirit and culture through its marvelous cuisine.

Salud y Buen Provecho!

SOME SUGGESTED MENUS

These suggestions include menus for *Desayuno* (breakfast), *Almuerzo* (lunch), *Onces* (teatime), and *Cena* (dinner or supper). The lunch menus are bigger than the dinner menus as is customary in Chile; but you can simply reverse the menus to accommodate North American customs. Two more menus are intended for special occasions and for a birthday party at teatime. Menus have also been arranged according to summer and winter seasons. At one time local fresh produce was available only at harvest time. Therefore, cooks adapted their menus accordingly. This is no longer the case, but traditions are hard to change, so I still like to plan my menus according to the seasons. Desserts usually consist of fruits, custards, or puddings, while pastries and tortes are served mainly at teatime.

A good Chilean wine should accompany the lunch and dinner menus.

Desayuno Diario
WEEKDAY BREAKFAST

Café con Leche (Coffee with Milk)

Toasted Bread with Butter

Dulce de Membrillo (Quince Preserve, pp. 22–23)

Desayuno Para Un Dia Especial
BREAKFAST FOR A SPECIAL DAY

Té con Leche (Tea and Milk, p.19)

Huevos a la Copa (Soft-Boiled Eggs)

Pan Rápido Dulce (Sweet Quick Bread, p. 25) with butter

Dulce de Melón (Melon Preserve, p. 23)

Almuerzo Diario de Verano
WEEKDAY SUMMER LUNCH

Marraquetas (French Style Rolls, pp. 193–194)

Crema Quillotana (Avocado Soup, p. 69)

Pastel de Choclo (Corn and Beef Casserole, (pp. 84–85)

Tomates a la Chilena (Chilean Tomato and Onion Salad, p. 161)

Chirimoya Alegre (Merry Chirimoya, pp. 220–221)

or

Pan Amasado (Kneaded Yeast Bread, p.190)

Tomates Rellenos con Choclo (Corn-Stuffed Tomatoes, p. 45)

Costillar a la Parrilla (Grilled Rack of Pork, p. 149)

Puré de Porotos Picantes (Spicy Bean Purée, p. 182)

Apio con Palta (Avocado and Celery Salad, p. 165)

Bavarois de Frutas (Bavarian Fruit Custard, p. 227)

Almuerzo Diario de Invierno
WEEKDAY WINTER LUNCH

    Pan Favorito (Favorite Herb Bread, p. 197)

    Ajiaco (Beef and Potato Soup, pp. 74–75)

    Chupe de Mariscos (Shellfish, Bread, and Cheese Casserole, pp. 110–111)

    Dulce de Alcayota (Spaghetti Squash Preserve, p. 20)

or

    Pan Candeal (Bakery-Style Yeast Bread, p. 195)

    Ensalada de Porotos (Bean Salad with Lemon Herb Dressing, p. 164)

    Arroz a la Valenciana (Rice Valencia Style, pp. 92–93)

    Turrón de Vino (Wine Meringue, p. 225)

Onces
TEATIME

    Té con Leche (Tea and Milk, p. 19)

    Queque (Jennie Herd's Tea Cake, p. 254)

or

    Café Helado (Coffee with Ice Cream, p. 278)

    Cujen de Frutas (*Kuchen*, Fruit Tart, p. 251)

Cena
DINNER

    Tortilla de Verduras (Vegetable Omelet, p. 57)

    Budín Porteño (Bread Pudding, pp. 228–229)

    Aguita Caliente (Hot Herbal Tea, p. 277)

or

    Valdiviano (Jerky Soup, pp. 79–80)

    Maicena con Leche (Cornstarch Pudding, p. 235)

    Apiado (Celery Liqueur, p. 276)

Cena para una Ocasión Especial
DINNER FOR A SPECIAL OCCASION

    Vaina (Egg and Port Cocktail, p. 274)
    Canapés de Mariscos (Shellfish Hors d'oeuvres, p. 33)

    Palta Porvenir (Avocado with King Crab, p. 53)

    Pan Fino (Fine Dinner Rolls, p. 196)
    Caldillo Marinero (Sailor's Fish Soup, pp. 73–74)

    Salmón con Alcaparras (Salmon with Capers, p. 117)
    Arroz Amoldado (Molded Rice, p. 184)
    Zapallitos Saltados (Sautéed Zucchini or Summer Squash, p. 171)

    Papayas en Almibar (Papayas in Syrup, p. 222)
    Aguita Caliente (Hot Herbal Tea, p. 277)
    Licor de Frambuesas (Raspberry Liqueur, pp. 276–277)

Onces De Cumpleaños
BIRTHDAY PARTY AT TEATIME

    Café Helado (Coffee with Ice Cream, p. 278)
    Té con Leche (Tea and Milk, p. 19)
    Ponche (Berry Punch, p. 268)

    Canapés de Palta (Avocado Hors d'oeuvres, pp. 32–33)
    Chancho en Piedra (Chilean Salsa, p. 36)
    Galletas Picantes (Spicy Crackers, p. 29)

    Pancitos Ingleses (Chilean-Style Scones, p. 27)
    Manjar Blanco (Caramel Spread, p. 245)
    Camotillos (Sweet Potato Candy, pp. 234–235)

    Alfajores (Chilean Pastries with Caramel Spread, p. 238)
    Empolvados (Dusted Pastries with Caramel Spread, p. 239)
    Cujen Millahue (Apple *Kuchen*, pp. 252–253)
    Torta de Cumpleaños (Birthday Torte, p. 257)

DESAYUNO

BREAKFAST

In Chile the first meal of the day is rather simple. It consists of a hot beverage such as *Café con Leche* (Coffee with Milk) or *Té con Leche* (Tea and Milk, p. 19) with toasted bread and marmalade. In the provinces and in rural areas, however, it is still possible to find other choices, such as *Chuño* (Potato Starch Breakfast, p. 17), *Ulpo* (Toasted Flour Beverage, p. 18) or *Mate* (Herbal Tea, pp. 18–19).

Tea was introduced to Chile in the nineteenth century by English merchants. Coffee is a more recent, twentieth century, introduction to our menus. Coffee and tea are not native to Chile, but today they have become the most fashionable beverages in the cities. Coffee beans are not that common, but instant coffee is popular in Chile, especially in the home. For *Café con Leche* the coffee powder is not usually diluted with water, instead it is dissolved in hot (whole, unhomogenized) milk. When the coffee and sugar are stirred together with a bit of water until creamy and hot milk is added, a foam forms on top, and the beverage is called *café batido.* Santiago has several excellent coffeehouses where you can drink espresso coffees like those found in Brazil or Colombia. I will never forget my first taste of this rich black delicacy. As teenagers trying to act like grownups, my best friend Marcela and I once went to Café Santos in downtown Santiago and asked for a coffee. The waiter smiled (as if to say, "I will teach you") and brought us two thick, dark espressos. We took our first sip acting as if we were used to it. After choking on the first taste, we poured so much sugar into it to make it drinkable that it turned into syrup. After a while, unable to finish our drinks, we sneaked out of the café and never returned. Genuine espresso coffee, Brazilian style, is definitely an acquired taste!

Occasionally, a cup of hot chocolate may also be served for breakfast. Chocolate originated in tropical America and was found by the Spaniards in Mexico. The conquistadors brought it to Chile and made it a popular drink among the wealthy in colonial times. Several eighteenth century and nineteenth century accounts mention chocolate as the preferred beverage among the Santiago socialites of the time. Today it is a rarity, but as a child I would occasionally get a cup of hot chocolate as a special treat on a cold winter afternoon.

Breakfast beverages are accompanied with toasted bread and marmalades. In Chile preserves made with apricots, peaches, pears, blackberries, and strawberries are very common. The recipes to make them are the same as the ones you find in any general cookbook, so I have not included them here. On the other hand, the more unusual preserves such as *Dulce de Melón* (Melon Preserve, p. 23), *Dulce de Membrillo* (Quince Preserve, pp. 22–23), *Dulce de Alcayota* (Spaghetti Squash Preserve, p. 20), and *Dulce de Camote* (Sweet Potato Preserve, p. 21) are worth including in this book. The breads are usually purchased at the local bakery, but for special occasions a home-baked bread may be used such as *Pancitos Ingleses* (Chilean-Style Scones, p. 27) or *Pan Rápido Dulce* (Sweet Quick Bread, p. 25).

For a day of pampering, perhaps some eggs may be added to breakfast such as *Huevos a la Copa* (soft-boiled eggs in a glass) or *Paila de Huevos con Jamón y Tomate* (Eggs with Ham and Tomato, p. 24). Chileans serve their 4-minute soft-boiled eggs out of the shell in a stemmed glass, the yolk soft, whole, and unbroken, and the white fully cooked. Bread is used to soak into the soft yolk and the rest is eaten with a spoon. This is a breakfast treat for special occasions; it is sometimes served at other times instead of a full meal. When I was very young, before I went to kindergarten, I used to get two fresh soft-boiled eggs at midmorning to ensure that I would grow up healthy. It worked!

Chuño
POTATO STARCH BREAKFAST

Serves 1

When I was a child, my grandmother, Elena Silva de Bascuñán, used to prepare a cup of *chuño* for me as an after-school treat. This is a pre-Columbian beverage of Andean origin, known in Peru and Bolivia as well as Chile. *Chuño,* or potato starch, was manufactured high in the Andes by crushing potatoes and allowing them to freeze-dry during the cold, dry winter nights. It has the appearance of cornstarch or arrowroot, very white and finely ground. When cooked, it thickens to the consistency of light cream and is semitransparent. Without flavorings it is used as baby food or is served to sick people. In fact my mother was allergic to milk as a baby, her grandmother raised her on *chuño* alone.

1   tablespoon *chuño* or potato starch
1   teaspoon granulated or caramelized sugar
1   cup water or milk, boiling
1   pinch cinnamon powder (optional)
1   pinch orange rind, grated (optional)

In a coffee mug mix *chuño* and sugar well to help dissolve the *chuño.* Pour in boiling water or milk and stir. Continue to stir until the mixture thickens to a light creamy texture. Add optional flavorings and drink hot.

Ulpo
TOASTED FLOUR BEVERAGE

Serves 1

Ulpo was the name given by the Mapuche to a beverage prepared with cornmeal and water. Later, probably during colonial times, the ingredients for *ulpo* changed to toasted wheat flour and milk. Until sometime during this century, *ulpo* was the beverage of choice for breakfast. Today people in the big cities drink tea or coffee instead, but in the provinces you can still find people who prefer *ulpo*. This recipe is the one I remember having at my cousin's farm during summer vacations.

- 1 **tablespoon flour**
- 1 **teaspoon granulated or caramelized sugar**
- 1 **cup water or milk, boiling**

In a nonstick pan toast the flour until lightly golden. Put flour and sugar in a coffee mug and mix well to help dissolve the flour. Add boiling milk and stir vigorously, the mixture will thicken. Drink hot with cake or biscuits.

Mate
HERBAL TEA

Serves 1

Mate was drunk by the pre-Columbian peoples of Paraguay, Uruguay, Argentina, and Chile. *Yerba Mate* is the dried leaves of a shrub of the holly family that grows wild on the banks of the upper Paraguay River. Like coffee and tea, *mate* contains caffeine. In Chile, *mate* has been popular since colonial times. In the big cities, though, it has been replaced by coffee or tea. *Mate* can be drunk any time of day, often as a social ceremony. Traditionally, the *yerba mate* is placed in a dried, hollowed gourd also called *mate*. Boiling water (or milk) is poured in and it is allowed to steep. After a while, sugar is added and the liquid is sipped through a *bombilla,* a metal straw with a strainer at the bottom. Then it is passed around as the conversation and social hour continue. The *mate* gourd can be elaborately decorated and mounted on a silver stand, and the *bombilla* can also be made of decorated silver, so the two utensils often become heirlooms.

> 1 tablespoon *yerba mate*
> 1 teaspoon granulated or caramelized sugar
> 1 cup water or milk, boiling

Place the *yerba mate* in a *mate* gourd or coffee mug. Pour in a small amount (about 2 tablespoons) of boiling water, wait a minute, and drain off the liquid. Pour in the milk and wait 5 minutes. Add the sugar, stir, and drink hot, preferably through a *bombilla.*

Té con Leche
TEA AND MILK

Serves 6

Té con Leche as a breakfast beverage is accompanied with just toast and marmalade. At *Onces,* tea is usually accompanied with sweet pastries, cake, *cujen (kuchen),* or sandwiches. The most common tea in Chile is from Ceylon (Sri Lanka), but other teas can also be used. The milk used in Chile is the whole, unhomogenized type that forms the *nata* (a separated creamy top layer) when boiled. This is the best part of the milk.

> 6 teaspoons Ceylon tea (or 6 bags)
> 4 cups boiling milk
> 6 teaspoons sugar (or to taste)

Put the tea in a preheated porcelain teapot, and pour 2 cups of boiling water over it. Let the tea steep for about 5 minutes, keeping the pot warm. The result should be very dark, strong tea. Pour the tea through a sieve into teacups, filling only one-third of the cup. Fill the rest of the cup with boiled, very hot milk. Add sugar to taste.

DULCES Y JALEAS
PRESERVES AND JELLIES

Dulce de Alcayota
SPAGHETTI SQUASH PRESERVE

My mother is very fond of this preserve and used to make it every fall for winter use. She would serve it at breakfast or at teatime, or in a glass as a dessert with cream on top. There are about 25 different squash and pumpkin species, all members of the *Cucurbita* genus and all native to the New World. *Alcayota* is a member of the pumpkin family and is very popular in Chile. It is an oblong fruit about 12 inches long, with green skin and whitish pulp. It is known in the United States as spaghetti squash due to the long fibers of its pulp.

- 1 **large spaghetti squash (3 to 4 pounds)**
- 3 **pounds sugar (same weight as squash pulp)**
- 1 **tablespoon orange rind, julienned**
- 6 **whole cloves**
- 1 **cup walnuts, chopped**

Bake whole squash in a 500 degrees oven for 15 minutes to loosen the tough skin. Cut the squash lengthwise, discard the seeds, remove all the pulp into a heavy saucepan, and separate the strands of fibers. Pour sugar over it and allow to marinate for about 30 minutes so that the juices are released. Add orange rind and cloves, bring to a gentle boil, and simmer for 30 minutes. Let sit overnight. The following day, simmer again for another 30 minutes, stirring constantly to keep the preserve from sticking to the bottom, add the chopped walnuts, and serve cold.

Dulce de Camote
SWEET POTATO PRESERVE

Sweet potatoes are a New World root crop and are not related to yams, which are of African origin. Sweet potatoes have a high sugar content, between 3 and 6 percent, and it increases with storage at warm temperatures. The preserve will solidify and acquire the shape of its container so you can store it in decorative containers and unmold it when ready to use.

2 pounds sweet potato, cooked, peeled, and puréed
½ pound sugar

Make sure the sweet potato purée is perfectly smooth. Dissolve the sugar in 2 tablespoons of water and bring the mixture to a boil. Add the sweet potatoes to the syrup and cook over low heat until the mixture easily separates from the walls of the pan. Pour the mixture into molds and store covered in the refrigerator.

Serving Suggestions:
Serve as a spread on toast or as a dessert with a scoop of ice cream.

Dulce de Membrillo
QUINCE PRESERVE

Every fall my mother would make enough quince preserve and jelly to last all year long. Quince is a tree of the rose family that bears a pear-shaped fruit with yellow skin and white flesh. It originated in Asia Minor and was transplanted to Chile via Spain in the early colonial days. In Chile two kinds of quince are grown: a tart one for preserves and jellies, and a sweet one for eating raw. I prepared this preserve using quince grown by the North Carolina Botanical Garden, at the University of North Carolina at Chapel Hill campus, compliments of the Coker Arboretum curator, Diane Birkemo. The preserve is very solid and keeps its form, so it can be molded into fancy and decorative shapes.

> 8 cups quince, peeled, diced, seeds separated
> 5 cups sugar, approximately

1. Quince should not be too ripe, slightly green and acidic is better. Peel and dice the fruit, put the seeds in a cheesecloth bag, save peels for *Jalea de Membrillo* (Quince Jelly; recipe follows).
2. Simmer the quince and seeds in 8 cups of water until tender, about 10 minutes. Remove the fruit and seeds from the water, discard the seeds, and save the cooking water (extract) for *Jalea de Membrillo.*
3. Purée the fruit pulp by passing it through a sieve. Measure the volume of purée and add the same amount of sugar.
4. Simmer the fruit pulp, stirring vigorously to avoid sticking. Boil for 15 to 20 minutes. The final color should be golden brown.
5. Pour the preserve into molds. Keep uncovered for three to four days to form a crust on top. Then cover tightly and store indefinitely.

Serving Suggestions:
Serve as a spread for toast or as a dessert with a slice of soft cheese.

Variation:
Jalea de Membrillo (Quince Jelly)

> 6 cups quince extract from the preserve
> 5 cups sugar, approximately

Add the quince peels to the quince extract and boil for about 10 minutes. Strain and measure the volume, add the same amount of sugar. Bring back to a boil and simmer for about 40 minutes, until a syrup of the desired consistency is formed. When ready, the jelly will have a ruby red color. Store in sealed, sterile jars.

Dulce de Melón
MELON PRESERVE

My mother used to make this delicious preserve in the summer to have in winter. She served it at breakfast or teatime on toast. The chunks of melons have a crystalline, transparent quality after cooking. You can use any kind of melon, including cantaloupe, honeydew, and watermelon (called *Dulce de Zandía*).

1   **large ripe melon, diced**
2   **cups sugar (equal in weight to fruit)**

Separate the melon's ripe pulp from the seeds, green pulp, and skin. Save the seeds, green pulp, and skin for *Miel de Melón* (Melon Syrup, p. 243). Add the sugar to the diced melon pulp in a saucepan and allow to soak for about two hours until the juices are released. Cover the pan and bring to a simmer. Cook, stirring occasionally, for about an hour or until a thick, golden syrup is formed. If the syrup is too runny, reduce for about 15 minutes. Serve cold. This preserve will last a long time at room temperature if it is stored in a sterile, sealed container.

HUEVOS
EGG RECIPES

Paila de Huevos con Jamón y Tomate
EGGS WITH HAM AND TOMATO

Serves 1

Paila is a small frying pan with two hook handles rather than one long one like an omelet pan. The *paila* is used to fry the eggs as well as to serve them at the table.

When I lived in Chile I always prepared this dish as a snack and savored it with toasted bread. You can serve this egg preparation for breakfast, as a sandwich filling, a snack, an appetizer, or a light meal.

½   **cup smoked ham, diced**
2   **tablespoons olive oil**
1   **large plum tomato, peeled, seeded, and diced**
    freshly ground black pepper, to taste
2   **large eggs**
    salt, to taste

Sauté the ham in the oil until crisp and brown. Add the tomato and cook down until almost dry. Add pepper to taste. Lightly beat the eggs to mix and pour over the ham mixture. Mix well and cook the eggs until barely set. Salt to taste. Serve hot with toasted bread.

Pan Rápido Dulce
SWEET QUICK BREAD

Serves 8

This is an easy bread adapted from my mother's cookbook. I use it for breakfast with butter and marmalade. The adaptation consisted of replacing milk with buttermilk and butter with oil, clearly a southern United States influence on my cooking.

1	cup buttermilk
½	cup honey
1	teaspoon vanilla extract
½	cup corn oil
2	cups all purpose flour
2	tablespoons baking powder
1	cup raisins or chopped almonds or walnuts
1	teaspoon lemon rind, grated
1	pinch nutmeg, freshly grated

Preheat oven to 450 degrees.

In a bowl mix the buttermilk, honey, vanilla, and oil. In a separate bowl, mix flour, baking powder, nuts or raisins, lemon rind, and nutmeg. Stir the wet and dry ingredients together with a wooden spoon, do not overmix. The batter should be relatively thin. Pour the batter into a greased and floured loaf pan. Bake for 5 minutes, reduce heat to 325 degrees, and bake for another 35 minutes. Check with a toothpick for doneness. Allow to cool on a rack before slicing.

Pancitos de Desayuno
ROYCE'S BREAKFAST BISCUITS

Serves 12

My husband Royce developed this recipe from his recollection of the Alabama breakfast biscuits his mother, Justina Louise Herd Murray, used to make. Serve for breakfast with butter and marmalade.

3   cups low protein flour
3   teaspoons baking powder
1   stick butter, unsalted
1   cup buttermilk

Preheat the oven to 425 degrees.

Blend the flour and baking powder well. Cut in the butter to obtain the consistency of coarse meal. Add the buttermilk and mix well, but do not overmix. Roll out the dough on a lightly floured surface to about $1/2$ inch thickness and cut 2-inch biscuits. Place biscuits on a baking sheet. Bake for 10 minutes.

Pancitos Ingleses
CHILEAN-STYLE SCONES

Serves 10

When I was a child Dr. Grace Johnson used to serve scones for tea in the afternoon. My mother learned the recipe from Dr. Johnson. There are many versions of these tea buns known as scones. In some of the Santiago's tearooms they serve scones at teatime together with other breads and cakes. You can serve them for breakfast with butter and marmalade. Leftovers can be saved and sliced, buttered, and toasted.

2	medium eggs
3	teaspoons confectioners sugar
6	tablespoons butter, unsalted
2	cups all purpose flour
2½	teaspoons baking powder
½	cup milk

Preheat the oven to 400 degrees.

Mix the eggs and sugar. Add the butter and mix well. Add one cup of flour, the baking powder, and half of the milk and mix well. Add the rest of the flour and milk and finish mixing. Pour the batter into buttered muffin molds. Bake for 12 minutes. Serve hot.

BOCADILLOS

HORS D'OEUVRES

Bocadillos in Chile have their origins in the famous *tapas* of Spain, although they never developed into the ritual they are in the motherland. They are bite-sized morsels or hors d'oeuvres served with drinks before lunch or at the cocktail hour. If you are in a bar or cocktail lounge you can ask for *algo para picar* ("something to pick on"), and the waiter will bring you the hors d'oeuvres of the day with your drinks.

Bocadillos are always served on a nice tray with toothpicks and cocktail napkins. The toothpicks can be the simple wooden ones or, in really elegant settings, they can be made of heirloom sterling silver elaborately decorated with semiprecious stones from the northern desert regions, such as royal blue lapis lazuli or emerald green malachite.

Bocadillos can be very simple dishes such as a bowl of pickled pearl onions or the delicious *Pasas del Huasco,* juicy plump raisins from the northern Huasco river valley. Or they can be elaborate seafood morsels such as *Canapés de Mariscos* (Shellfish Hors d'oeuvres, p. 33) or *Masitas de Erizos* (Sea Urchin Pastries, p. 34). Also common are dips such as *Palta Molida* (Avocado Dip, p. 35) or *Chancho en Piedra* (Chilean Salsa, p. 36).

When we were teenagers, my cousins Dory, Mary, and Julia Neale and I ate *Chancho en Piedra* during summer vacations at their grape vineyard in Maule, south of Santiago. During summer mornings we were allowed to walk, with Dory, the eldest, in charge, 4 kilometers over to the cold, crystalline Maule river to swim, or more likely, to be swept across the river by the fast-running currents of the snowmelt waters. Back home, sitting on the back porch, Mary would prepare *Chancho en Piedra* (Chilean Salsa) in a large *mortero* (stone mortar), and we would eat it with bread as a midday snack. After lunch everybody would have a siesta, napping the hot afternoon away.

In the evenings, out on the porch, after the sun went down, we could see the stars shining like diamonds in the clear Southern skies, and we could hear the gentle breeze playing among the grape leaves and the occasional call of an owl. And then, while nibbling on leftover *Chancho en Piedra* or other such *Bocadillos,* the older cousins would start telling scary stories to spook Julia and me. Like this one about the outlaw brothers Pincheira:

> *After the War of Independence finally ended in 1818, some 3,000 defeated Spanish soldiers were left to their own devices. As far as the Spanish Empire was concerned, there was no such thing as evacuating a vanquished army. So these heavily armed men headed south, turned into guerrillas, and behaved like bandits. The Pincheiras were the leaders of this army, which set up a secret camp and headquarters high in the Andes by the shores of Lake Epalufquén at the headwaters of the Ñuble river. From there they would ride down the mountain to raid the towns and villages in the Central Valley, including Maule. When the Pincheiras and their band showed up in town, terror spread. They would kill every man they saw, kidnap the young women, and steal all the valuables and food they could find. Then they would retreat to their lair, and the young women would never be seen again.*

It is said that the Pincheiras amassed a considerable treasure, which was buried and never retrieved. There are still people in the region between Maule and Los Angeles who look for that hidden cache. To this day, every time I prepare *Chancho en Piedra,* I fondly remember my cousins from Maule and the scary stories they used to tell.

Bocadillos

LITTLE MORSELS

Serves 8

Bocadillos are served in Chile before a dinner party or at a cocktail party with *Aperitivos*. The list of ingredients is flexible depending on availability. Serve on a nice tray with toothpicks and cocktail napkins.

½   **cup smoked mussels or oysters**
½   **cup stuffed green olives**
½   **cup black olives, pitted**
½   **cup rolled, stuffed anchovies**
½   **cup marinated artichokes, quartered**
½   **cup hearts of palm, sliced**
½   **cup pickled pearl onions**
½   **cup golden raisins**
½   **cup walnuts**

Most of the ingredients are sold in cans or jars already submerged in a marinade. Drain them well before using. Arrange ingredients in a large serving dish in small groups without mixing. Keep in refrigerator until ready to serve.

Canapés de Espárragos
HOT ASPARAGUS HORS D'OEUVRES

Serves 12

This recipe is from my Great-aunt Leonie's cookbook. These are elegant morsels and should be served with cocktails. Use a firm bread so the *canapés* don't become soggy or lose their shape. The ideal bread for these canapés is the French Pullman bread or *Pain de Mie,* but any sturdy sandwich loaf will do.

2   **tablespoons butter, unsalted**
4   **slices white bread**
½   **cup *Salsa Blanca* (White Sauce, p.211)**
½   **cup Parmesan cheese, grated**
¼   **cup milk**
12   **heads asparagus, blanched**
12   **strips red pimento**

Preheat the oven to 400 degrees.

Butter the bread, remove the crusts, and cut each slice into four triangles. Mix the *Salsa Blanca* and grated cheese. Add milk to adjust to a smooth but not runny consistency. Blanch the asparagus for 5 minutes in boiling salted water and then plunge into cold water to stop the cooking process. Place one head of asparagus over the bread triangle, cover with sauce and garnish with a strip of red pimento. Warm in the oven for 15 minutes. Serve hot.

Canapés de Palta
AVOCADO HORS D'OEUVRES

Serves 12

Great-aunt Leonie used to served hors d'oeuvres like these before lunch, when she entertained the extended family on weekends at their beach house in Concón. These are popular morsels in Chile. They should be prepared shortly before serving to avoid discoloration of the avocado. Use a firm bread such as French Pullman bread or *Pain de Mie* so that the canapés don't become soggy or lose their shape.

1   large ripe avocado

2   tablespoon *Mayonesa* (Mayonnaise, p. 205)

1   small lemon

1   teaspoon *Pasta de Ají* (Aji Paste, p. 207), optional

4   slices white bread

1   tablespoon small shrimp, cooked and peeled

1   tablespoon stuffed olives, sliced

1   tablespoon red pimento, sliced

1   tablespoon anchovies, soaked in milk and drained

Prepare an avocado purée by mixing mashed avocado with *Mayonesa,* lemon juice, and *Pasta de Ají.* Remove the bread crusts and cut each slice into four triangles. Cover the triangles with avocado purée and top with a garnish of shrimp, olives, pimento, or anchovies. Serve promptly.

Canapés de Mariscos
SHELLFISH HORS D'OEUVRES

Serves 12

This recipe is also from Great-aunt Leonie's cookbook. The kind of seafood used in this recipe depends upon availability. Other garnishes for these *canapés* include hard-boiled egg slices, cucumber slices, walnuts, tomato slices, and black olive slices. Use a firm bread such as French Pullman bread or *Pain de Mie* so that the canapés don't become soggy or lose their shape.

1   cup precooked king crab, crab, lobster, or shrimp (peeled)

½   cup *Mayonesa* (Mayonnaise, p.206)

4   slices white bread

½   cup sweet red pepper, julienned

Chop shellfish coarsely but small enough to be able to spread it. Mix chopped shellfish with *Mayonesa.* Remove the bread crusts and cut each slice into four triangles. Spread the mixture over triangles and garnish with red pepper.

Masitas de Erizos
SEA URCHIN PASTRIES

Serves 24

While sea urchins are sometimes considered an acquired taste, they are a delicacy in Chile. There are at least two subspecies of sea urchins: *erizos colorados* (red urchins) and *erizos negros* (black urchins); only the red ones are edible. Inside the round spiny shell of the urchin, there are five deep orange 2-inch strips that we call tongues. They are in fact the gonads; in Japanese sushi bars they are called roe or uni. These are what you eat. Sometimes inside the shell you find a small crablike mollusk that lives in symbiosis with the urchin; some people think this is the best part of the meal and eat it raw. For the sea urchins in this recipe you can substitute crab, clams, mussels, shrimp, crawfish, or chicken.

2½	cups all purpose flour (amount is approximate)
1	stick butter, unsalted
1	whole egg
1	cup *Salsa Blanca* (White Sauce, p. 211)
¼	cup milk
1	cup sea urchin tongues

1. Preheat the oven to 400 degrees.
2. Mix the flour, butter, ⅓ cup salted (to taste) water, and egg to form a thick dough, adding more flour if necessary. Roll the dough to ¼-inch thickness and cut 2-inch circles.
3. Cover small buttered pastry molds with dough circles to form small cups, prick the bottoms with a fork.
4. Bake for 10 minutes; the dough should be barely cooked. Let it cool down before filling.
5. Poach sea urchin tongues for 3 minutes in boiling water and cut into small cubes.
6. Mix *Salsa Blanca* with sea urchin. Add milk; the mixture should be smooth but not runny.
7. Fill the pastry cups with the mixture and warm in the oven for 15 minutes. Serve hot.

Palta Molida
AVOCADO DIP

Serves 4

This avocado dip is very popular in Chile. I have known this recipe for what seems like forever. *Palta* is the Chilean name for avocados. Chilean *paltas* have thin skins and are smaller than the California avocado. They are very buttery, and some are stringy. In this recipe you can substitute California avocados.

1   **large ripe avocado**
1   **small lemon**
   freshly ground black pepper, to taste
1   **tablespoon extra virgin olive oil**
   salt, to taste

Peel the avocado and, in a glass or ceramic container, mash with a fork. Quickly add the lemon juice to avoid browning (oxidation). Season with pepper, oil, and salt to taste. The result should be a little lumpy. Serve immediately with crackers.

Chancho en Piedra
CHILEAN SALSA

Serves 4

The word *chancho* in Chile usually refers to pork. There is no pork in this recipe, so I don't know how this sauce got its name, except of course, *piedra* refers to the stone mortar traditionally used in its preparation. This sauce can be eaten with bread as hors d'oeuvres. My husband thinks it is a dynamite snack. You can replace *ají* with any other green hot pepper.

1	large tomato, very ripe, peeled and chopped
3	cloves garlic, peeled and chopped
1	tablespoon fresh cilantro, chopped
1	small fresh *ají*, seeded and chopped
1	tablespoon extra virgin olive oil
	freshly ground black pepper, to taste
	salt, to taste
1	small lemon, juiced

Chop the tomato, garlic, cilantro, and *ají* in a food processor. Season with olive oil, black pepper, salt, and lemon juice. Store in a glass or ceramic container. Serve with a loaf of country style bread cut into rough chunks.

Paté de Ganso
GOOSE LIVER PATE

Serves 8

This pâté is also delicious when prepared with duck or chicken liver instead of goose liver. It is delightful as hors d'oeuvres and can also be served with a salad as a first course.

2 pounds goose liver
6 slices bacon
2 tablespoons unsalted butter
1 small onion, chopped
3 cloves garlic, chopped
1 tablespoon thyme leaves
¼ cup brandy
1 pinch black pepper, freshly ground
2 tablespoons Worcestershire sauce

Preheat the oven to 350 degrees.

Clean the livers to remove any fibrous material and chop. Sauté the bacon in 1 tablespoon of butter. Add the liver, onion, garlic, and thyme. Grind the liver mixture in a meat grinder or food processor. Season with the brandy, pepper, and Worcestershire sauce, mix well. For a smoother pâté, blend the mixture in a blender. Place the mixture in a buttered terrine or loaf baking dish. Bake 35 to 40 minutes. Store in the pan with a layer of goose fat on top (from a goose you recently roasted; see pp. 128–129). It keeps in the refrigerator for several days. Serve with toasted white bread cut in triangles.

Empanaditas Fritas
LITTLE FRIED TURNOVERS

Serves 12

This recipe is from the collection of my aunt Emma Bascuñán. *Empanadas* are of Spanish origin, but are now considered part of the classic Chilean *criolla* cuisine. *Empanaditas* are smaller than the more famous oven-baked *empanada.* Cheese is the traditional filling for *Empanaditas Fritas.* The most common soft cheese in Chile is *mantecoso,* but any soft cheese or mixture of cheeses can be used, including goat cheese or brie. Other common fillings for *Empanaditas Fritas* include precooked shellfish or chicken with *Salsa Blanca* (White Sauce, p. 211).

> 3 cups all-purpose flour
> 3 tablespoons shortening
> ½ cup milk
> salt, to taste
> 1 pound Monterey Jack cheese
> 1 cup vegetable oil
> confectioner's sugar (optional) to taste

1. Place the flour on a pastry board and make a hill with a hole in the middle.
2. Melt the shortening and pour it into the hole.
3. Combine the milk, ½ cup of water, and salt; warm the mixture up; and pour it into the hole.
4. With your hands, mix the flour with the liquid ingredients and knead it until smooth. (All this can also be done in an electric mixer.) Let the dough rest for about 20 minutes.
5. On a floured board roll the dough to a thickness of ⅛ inch. The dough is very elastic, and it may be a little hard to roll. Cut circles about 4 inches in diameter.
6. Put a small piece of cheese in the middle of each circle. Form the turnover and seal the edges with a little water. Use a fork to press down and produce a decorative edge. Place the turnovers on a piece of parchment paper until ready to cook.
7. Heat the oil in a frying pan and fry the turnovers until golden brown. Drain them on paper towels.
8. Sprinkle with sugar (optional) and serve hot. Leftovers can be reheated in the oven.

Galletas Picantes
SPICY CRACKERS

Serves 40

These hot spicy crackers come from Great-aunt Leonie's cookbook. The amount of flour depends on the type of flour and humidity, so add enough water to produce a dough that can be rolled and cut. A tasty variation is to sprinkle Parmesan cheese or pesto over the crackers before baking.

2 ½ cups all-purpose flour (approximately)
1 stick butter, unsalted
⅓ cup warm salted water (salt, to taste)
1 whole egg
  Pasta de Ají (Aji Paste, p. 207) to taste

Preheat the oven to 425 degrees.

Mix all the ingredients to make a dough; do not knead. Roll the dough about ¼ inch thick, cut circles about 2 inches in diameter. Bake the circles on a cookie sheet for about 15 minutes until golden. They keep well in an airtight container.

Serving Suggestion:

The crackers can be served warm or cold with a dip such as *Palta Molida* (Avocado Dip, p. 35).

Confites de Zanahoria
CARROT SWEETS

Serves 24

Occasionally, when you invite friends only for cocktails, you might choose to finish the party with something sweet. This recipe from my mother's cookbook is the ideal choice.

- 1 cup grated carrot
- 1 pound sugar
- 1 large orange, juice and grated peel
- ½ cup grated coconut

Simmer the carrot with the sugar and orange juice until it forms *almibar* (a thick syrup). Let it cool and add the orange peel. In your hands form small 1-inch balls with the mixture, and roll the balls in the grated coconut. Serve with toothpicks.

Papitas de Nueces
LITTLE WALNUT POTATOES

Serves 40

Like the preceding recipe, this is meant as a cocktail dessert. This recipe from Great-aunt Leonie's cookbook is just right for that purpose.

- 1 can sweetened condensed milk
- ½ pound ground walnuts
- ½ pound finely ground cookies
- 1 cup powdered chocolate or cocoa

Mix the condensed milk with the ground walnuts and cookies. Knead the mixture until homogeneous. In your hands, make small 1-inch to 1½-inch balls in the shape of a potato, add some dimples to resemble the potato eyes. Roll the balls in the chocolate and let them dry completely. Serve with toothpicks.

ENTRADAS

FIRST COURSE DISHES
AND APPETIZERS

The Chilean *Primer Plato* or *Entrada* is equivalent to the first course or appetizer in the United States. The word *Entrada* actually means entryway or front door and, therefore, this dish is the entrance to the meal to come. It is served on a salad plate and eaten with a salad fork and knife. *Entrada* usually consists of a small, cold or warm, salad or vegetable serving. Some favorites are *Salpicón* (Mixed Chicken or Mussel Salad, pp. 55 and 59), and *Espárragos* (Asparagus with Green Sauce, pp. 44-45). But to me, the most delicious *Entrada* is *Humitas* (Chilean Tamales, pp. 58-59).

Humitas is a traditional dish of the Chilean *criolla* cuisine. The ingredients and mode of cooking suggest an ancient origin. The name is derived from the Quechua word *huminta* which means corn leaves filled with corn paste. This dish, together with *Ceviche* (Scallops Marinated in Lemon Juice, pp. 47-48) and *Locro Falso* (Northern Vegetable Stew, p. 96), must be some remnant of the Inca occupation of northern and central Chile just before the Spanish conquest. The corn used in *Humitas* (and also in *Pastel de Choclo*, Corn and Beef

Casserole, pp. 84–85) is not the sweet corn we love in the United States for "corn-on-the-cob." It is instead a late-maturing, meaty, and creamy corn that grows in pear shaped husks, 8 to 9 inches long and 4 inches wide at the bottom. The husk leaves are quite wide, making it easier to form the *humita* pouches. There are about 19 different varieties of corn now cultivated in Chile, most of them imported from Peru in ancient times or from North America more recently. There are, however, at least two varieties, *choclero* and *cristalino Chileno*, that are native to Chile.

Because of its abundance in Chile, many *Entradas* naturally feature hot or cold seafood. Good examples are *Locos al Pil Pil* (Chilean Abalones with Green Sauce, p. 46), *Ceviche de Ostiones* (Scallops Marinated in Lemon Juice, pp. 47–48), *Machas al Horno* (Broiled Razor Clams, p. 51), *Pescado en Escabeche* (Pickled Fish in Lemon Marinade, p. 49), and *Palta Porvenir* (Avocado with King Crab, p. 53).

Escabeche is a Spanish dish of Moorish origin. It is common in Chile where it is prepared with virtually any fish or shellfish. *Escabeche* can also be prepared with chicken or small fowl such as *Codorníz Escabechada* (Pickled Quail Aspic, pp. 50–51). Other *pajaritos* (small birds) may be used, such as partridge (*perdíz*), squab or pigeon (*pichón*), turtledove (*tórtola*), and wild pigeon (*torcaza*). These succulent little birds are also prized in the Unites States and can sometimes be found in the food markets.

A very elegant *Entrada* is *Palta Porvenir* which features Patagonian king crab. This salad is served as a first course at the Cabo de Hornos Hotel in Punta Arenas. Punta Arenas is the southernmost city in the world, located on the Straits of Magellan at the tip of South America. Porvenir is a small town across the straits from Punta Arenas on the island of Tierra del Fuego, called "the land of fires" because that is all the ancient mariners could see of the island. The Straits of Magellan got its name from the Portuguese mariner Hernando de Magallanes who, sailing for the Crown of Spain, was the first European to reach Chilean territory in 1520. Magallanes left Spain in September 1519 with five weather-beaten sailing ships and 265 men, with the purpose of finding a route to the Far East by sailing west. The winter (July and August in the Southern Hemisphere) of 1520 found him in eastern Patagonia where he had to wait until the spring to continue his journey. By November 1, he entered the infamous strait. It took him 38 long days to navigate to the other side where he met and named the Pacific Ocean. He called it pacific because of the very rare calm waters he encountered that day; ironically, those southern waters are usually an area of enormous waves and ferocious winds.

Magallanes continued his difficult and painful trip west with his crew plagued by illness, famine, and mutiny. He reached the Philippine islands where he died fighting the natives. His second in command, Juan Sebastián del Cano, carried on the westward voyage and arrived back in the port of Sevilla, Spain, three years later with only one ship and seventeen Spaniards. They were the first men to circumnavigate the globe; those were truly heroic and difficult days of first travels and discovery. It is hard to imagine now what it was like to spend years at sea without maps, radio, fresh food, or modern conveniences!

More than three centuries later, in 1831, another exceptional traveler came through that notorious strait at the end of the world. It was the young Charles Darwin, traveling as naturalist on board the *HMS Beagle* with captain Robert FitzRoy at the helm. The Beagle also sailed through the Straits of Magellan on a trip around the world. It is said that during this trip Darwin gained a whole new understanding of the living species and their origin. Decades later he wrote the remarkable and earth-shaking *Origin of the Species*. In the Chilean Patagonia, these famous travelers are remembered and honored today by several geographical landmarks: Darwin Mountain Range, Beagle Channel, FitzRoy Island, and of course the unforgettable *Estrecho de Magallanes*.

Alcachofas
ARTICHOKES WITH LEMON HERB DRESSING

Serves 6

Artichokes were imported from Spain in colonial times and are very popular in Chile. Therefore there are many recipes for artichokes, including soup (*Sopa de Verduras,* p. 67), omelet (*Tortilla de Verduras,* p. 57), casserole (*Pastel,* p. 87), or stuffed, but this recipe, my mother's way of serving artichokes, is my favorite. This dish is served as a cold first course.

6	**large artichokes**
½	**medium lemon**
6	**tablespoons *Aliño para Ensaladas*** **(Lemon Herb Dressing, p. 203)**

Remove lower artichoke leaves and cut off the stem (save it for a soup). Place artichokes standing up in a pot of boiling water and add the lemon half, this helps keep the artichokes green. Simmer the artichokes for 30 minutes in enough water to almost cover them. Then remove the artichokes from the water and allow them to drain and cool to room temperature.

To serve, place the whole artichoke, leaves and all, on a salad plate. In a separate small bowl, put about 2 tablespoon of *Aliño de Ensaladas* and place a small bowl of water near the plate to rinse your fingers.

Espárragos
ASPARAGUS WITH GREEN SAUCE

Serves 6

Like artichokes, asparagus can be prepared in soup, omelet, soufflé, and so on, but this is my favorite way to have asparagus. (For others, look up *Tortilla de Verduras* (Vegetable Omelet, p. 57) or *Sopa de Verduras* (Vegetable Soup, p. 67). In this recipe *Pebre* (Green Sauce) can be replaced with *Mayonesa* (Mayonnaise, p. 206), or *Aliño para Ensaladas* (Lemon Herb Dressing, p. 203).

36 stalks fresh asparagus
12 tablespoons *Pebre* (Green Sauce, p. 204)

Peel the tough, white ends of the asparagus stalks. Slice them to about the same size; I prefer them 6 to 7 inches long. Cook them in boiling water for about 5 to 10 minutes depending on the size of the stalk. Do not overcook; they should be tender but firm. Remove the delicious beauties to a bowl with iced water to stop the cooking process and maintain the bright green color. To serve, place six cooled (but not chilled) asparagus on each plate and spoon some *Pebre* over their middles.

Tomates Rellenos con Choclo
CORN-STUFFED TOMATOES

Serves 4

Tomatoes are native to the New World. In pre-Columbian times, a wild type of cherry tomato was common in Chile; the modern large tomato is a recent import. During the summer in Chile, tomatoes are plentiful, large, juicy, and very flavorful, like home-grown tomatoes. There are many ingredients for stuffing these fresh tomatoes, including mussels, chicken, peas, avocados, and potatoes.

4   large ripe tomatoes
1½ cup corn kernels, precooked
½   cup chopped ham
½   cup onion, peeled, chopped, and washed in hot water
4   tablespoons *Mayonesa* (Mayonnaise, p. 205)
2   cups lettuce, shredded

Cut off the top of the tomatoes and remove the inner pulp with a spoon; remove and discard the seeds and chop the pulp. Mix the tomato pulp with the corn, ham, onions, and 2 tablespoons *Mayonesa*. Fill the hollowed out tomatoes with the mixture and top with a dollop of *Mayonesa*. Serve cold on a bed of shredded lettuce.

Locos al Pil Pil
CHILEAN ABALONES WITH GREEN SAUCE

Serves 6

The *Loco* is sometimes called abalone because it resembles the Californian abalone. But they are actually a different species, *C. Concholepas. Locos* have been harvested for food since prehistoric times, and 12,000-year-old mounds of *loco* shells have been found along the coast of Chile. Before 1986, *locos* were plentiful in Chile and this salad was commonly served. Canned *locos* are sometimes available but they are not nearly as good as the fresh ones. In 1983, my husband Royce and I had this salad for a memorable lunch in a riverboat restaurant on the Calle-Calle river in Valdivia. Each plate had six large (4 inches long) whole *locos* on it, and we were able to make a meal out of it. I am sorry that *locos* are not yet readily available in the United States, but for this recipe you can substitute California abalone (if you can afford it), shrimp, mussels, or scallops.

- 6   **large fresh *locos* or precooked canned *locos***
- 1   **cup *Pebre* (Green Sauce, see p. 204)**
- 3   **cups lettuce, finely shredded**

To prepare fresh *locos* first remove the shell and clean them. Then beat them with a meat tenderizer (These steps are usually performed by the fishmonger). Another recommended tenderizing treatment is to place the *locos* (without shells) in a burlap bag with either ashes or wood dust and beat the bag against the floor until tender. Although this sounds like a rather harsh treatment, it is absolutely necessary. Once the *locos* are tender, it is easy to remove the small hard nail attached to the side of the animal. Boil the *locos* (use an enameled pot and wooden or plastic utensils) in 2 quarts of unsalted water with half a cup of oil and a floating cork (this is supposed to help tenderize them) for at least 2 hours or until tender (45 minutes in a pressure cooker). Serve cold, two *locos* per person, on a bed of lettuce with a spoonful of *Pebre* on top.

Ceviche de Ostiones
SCALLOPS MARINATED IN LEMON JUICE

Serves 8

This dish is common in the northern region of Chile and in Peru, but not in Spain. Its origin is probably Inca or earlier, but the marinating juices must have originally been something other than lemon and orange, since these were unknown in the New World before the arrival of the Spaniards. Perhaps native acidic fruits such as pineapple, papaya, *naranjilla,* or *pepino* were used. *Ceviche* is made with all kinds of raw fish and shellfish such as salmon, tuna, trout, sole, swordfish, shrimp, crab, mussels, and oysters. The type of vegetable used depends on availability; this particular mix is my own choice. Scallops (*ostiones*) are common in Chile and I think they adapt wonderfully to this recipe. They are usually served with the bright red roe on, which makes them especially tasty. Those who are squeamish about raw seafood should not be afraid of this recipe. The citrus juices will completely cook the seafood. If the seafood is fresh, the dish is not fishy in taste. Serve alone as a first course or as a main course with a side dish.

1   pound bay scallops
2   cups lemon juice
1   cup orange juice
1   cup onion, finely julienned
½   cup green onions, finely chopped
½   cup carrots, julienned
1   cup sweet red pepper, julienned
1   cup sweet green pepper, julienned
3   cloves garlic, finely minced
1   tablespoon *Pasta de Ají* (Aji Paste, p. 207)
1   cup plum tomatoes, peeled, diced, and seeded
    freshly ground black pepper, to taste
½   cup fresh cilantro, finely chopped

In a glass or ceramic container, marinate scallops in 1½ cups of lemon juice for 2 hours in the refrigerator. Make sure the scallops are totally submerged in the lemon juice. After 2 to 3 hours discard lemon juice, wash scallops, pat them dry, and put them into a clean glass or ceramic container. Cover with the remaining lemon and orange juices, add the rest of the ingredients, mix, garnish with cilantro, and serve cold. This will keep in the refrigerator for up to 24 hours.

Pescado a la Vinagreta
FISH IN VINEGAR SAUCE

Serves 6

This recipe is from my aunt Ema Neale Silva de Welt, who always made simple and inexpensive food look elegant and sophisticated. In Chile the most common and inexpensive white fish is hake. This recipe would often be prepared with hake (*merluza* or *pescada*), but any fish with white meat can be used. Serve alone as a first course or as a main course with a side dish.

2	pounds white fish fillets
	freshly ground black pepper, to taste
1	large lemon
1	cup *Caldillo* (Fish Stock, p. 65) or water
½	cup white wine
1	cup *Mayonesa* (Mayonnaise, p. 205)
1	tablespoon *Mostaza* (Mustard Sauce, p. 208)
1	large pickled cucumber, diced
2	tablespoons fresh, flat leaf parsley, chopped
1	teaspoon white wine vinegar
1	small onion, peeled and finely chopped

Season the fish with pepper and lemon juice. In a nonreactive pan poach the fish in the *Caldillo* and wine over low heat for about 15 minutes. Remove the fish from the liquid and allow to cool. Mix *Mayonesa* with *Mostaza,* cucumber, parsley, vinegar, and pepper. Wash the onion in hot water and add to the *Mayonesa* mixture. Serve the fish with a tablespoon of *Mayonesa* on top of each portion.

Pescado en Escabeche
PICKLED FISH IN LEMON MARINADE

Serves 6

Escabeche is a Spanish dish of Moorish origin and is prepared with virtually any fish or shellfish. This recipe is from my mother's cookbook; she prefers to use a rather expensive fish such as *corvina* (Chilean sea bass). The pickling procedure is designed to preserve food, including vegetables, poultry, and seafood, in an acidic medium, usually white wine vinegar, or a mixture of white wine and lemon and/or orange juice. Serve the fish alone as a first course or as a main course with a side dish.

½ cup flour
6 fillets tuna, bass, swordfish, or salmon
3 tablespoons olive oil
2 large carrots, julienned
1 large onion, peeled and julienned
6 cloves garlic, peeled and finely chopped
1 large sweet red pepper, julienned
1 large sweet green pepper, julienned
  freshly ground black pepper, to taste
1 pinch fresh, flat-leaf parsley, chopped
1 bay leaf
1 cup white wine
½ cup lemon juice

Lightly flour the fish fillets and sauté in oil over low heat for 3 minutes per side; do not brown. Remove fish and sauté the carrots, onions, garlic, and red and green peppers in the same pan; again, do not brown. Add black pepper, parsley, and bay leaf. Place half the vegetables in a glass or earthenware pan, place the fish on top, and cover with the rest of the vegetables. Add wine and lemon juice, cover and marinate in the refrigerator for 24 hours. Serve cold.

Codorníz Escabechada
PICKLED QUAIL ASPIC

Serves 8

Codorníz is the Spanish quail. The wild quail in Chile is called *queltegue,* its Mapuche name. This recipe can be made with any small bird, including partridge (*perdíz*), squab or pigeon (*pichón*), turtledove (*tórtola*), wild pigeon (*torcaza*), and Cornish hen. Wild birds are tough and bitter. After plucking they must be thoroughly washed in cold water and marinated in white wine and lemon juice overnight before cooking.

8	fresh quails or Cornish hens, plucked and cleaned
½	cup white wine
½	cup white vinegar
¼	cup olive oil
2	large carrots, julienned
2	medium onions, julienned
1	large sweet green pepper, julienned
10	whole black peppercorns
2	bay leaves
½	sprig fresh rosemary
½	sprig fresh thyme
1	orange leaf
	salt, to taste
1	envelope unflavored gelatin
	lettuce leaves as needed

1. Remove the birds' backbones and cut the birds in half. Remove the ribs and any other small bones except the thigh and wing bones. Save all bones and giblets.
2. Wrap cheesecloth around the birds and tie them with string to help them keep their shape while cooking.
3. Put the birds in an enameled or stainless steel casserole with bones, giblets, wine, vinegar, and oil. Add the carrots, onions, and green pepper. Make a cheesecloth bag with the peppercorns, bay, rosemary, thyme, and orange tree leaf (if available), and add it to the pot.
4. Add ½ cup of water and simmer for about ½ hour, or until tender. Check the juices and add salt if necessary.

5. Remove the cheesecloth and strings from the birds. Place them, skin side down, in a glass or ceramic shallow dish, arrange the onions, carrots, and peppers around them. Strain the pan juices and reserve.
6. Dissolve the gelatin in the reserved hot juice (this creates an aspic) and pour it over the birds and vegetables.
7. Refrigerate overnight. Before serving unmold onto a bed of lettuce on a serving dish and allow the dish to come to room temperature.

Machas al Horno
BROILED RAZOR CLAMS

Serves 6

Machas (*Mesodesma donacium*) are a type of razor clam from the Pacific coast of South America. They were harvested in prehistoric times along the coast of Chile and archaeologists have found their shells in large mounds where the native Chileans used to live. The shell resembles an elongated clam, and the meat is pink. This recipe, from my aunt Emma Bascuñán, is very popular and can be found in most seafood restaurants in Chile. You can substitute regular clams, oysters, mussels, or scallops for the razor clams.

24   whole *machas,* or razor clams
½   cup butter, unsalted
    freshly ground black pepper, to taste
1   pinch fresh cilantro, finely chopped
½   cup white wine
½   cup bread crumbs, grated
½   cup Parmesan cheese, grated

Clean the clams and save the shells. Put one *macha* in each shell, add a little butter, pepper, cilantro, and wine, and cover with a mixture of bread crumbs and Parmesan cheese. Broil for 6 to 7 minutes. Serve hot.

Empanadas Chilenas
CHILEAN MEAT TURNOVERS

Serves 10

This is another recipe from the collection of my aunt Emma Bascuñán. *Empanadas* are known in Spain and other Latin American countries where they are made with many different fillings, including cheese, seafood, and vegetables. But in Chile the traditional stuffing is *Pino,* a juicy beef and onion filling. *Pequenes,* the poor people's version of *empanadas*, are *empanadas* filled with a spicy onion filling and no meat. My husband thinks of *empanadas* as the Chilean hamburger because they are available almost everywhere and you can eat them on the go. In the village of El Arrayán, on the way to the ski resorts of Farellones and La Parva, there are some country style restaurants that bake some of the best *Empanadas Chilenas* I have ever tasted. Serve *empanadas* as a first course or as a main dish with a salad.

2   cups *Pino* (Beef and Onion Filling, p. 150)
5   cups bread flour, approximately
1   cup vegetable shortening
2   large egg yolks
1   tablespoon white vinegar
1   teaspoon salt
1¼ cup water, approximately
3   large hard-boiled eggs, peeled and cut in wedges
1   small egg white

1. Prepare the *Pino* filling a day in advance.
2. Preheat the oven to 400 degrees.
3. Heap the flour on a pastry table, make a depression in the center, and add the shortening, egg yolks, and vinegar. Mix well using your fingers.
4. Dissolve the salt in the water. Sprinkle some water over flour mixture and rub the dough between your hands until it is smooth and fairly stiff.
5. Gather the dough in a ball and knead it until it is no longer sticky, adding water and flour as needed (these three steps can be done in an electric mixer).
6. Allow the dough to rest for 30 minutes. Then roll the dough to about ⅛ inch thick or thinner. The dough will be stiff, elastic, and difficult to roll at first.
7. Cut circles about 9 inches in diameter. Place about 2 tablespoons of *Pino* in the center of each pastry circle, making sure there is at least one olive in each *empanada,* and add an egg wedge.

8. Dip your fingers in the filling juices and run them around the pastry's edge. Fold the dough to make a semicircular turnover, and press around the filling, removing the trapped air and sealing the turnover; use a fork to make a decorative edge.
9. Paint the top with egg white. Bake 20 to 30 minutes or until golden brown. Serve hot.

Palta Porvenir
AVOCADO WITH KING CRAB

Serves 2

Centolla (Patagonian king crab), the southern version of Alaska king crab, is abundant in the Pacific Ocean near the coast of Patagonia and Tierra del Fuego. *Centollas* and Alaska king crabs are usually sold already cooked so you may not need to bother with the cooking, but they are best when freshly cooked.

½ whole *centolla* or Alaska king crab
1 large ripe avocado
1 medium lemon
2 tablespoons *Mayonesa* (Mayonnaise, p. 205)
1 bunch lettuce, finely shredded

Boil *centolla* alive, the same way you cook a lobster. When cool, cut the crab in half and save one half for another dish. Remove the leg meat from the shell, including the meat next to the legs, making sure to save the large claws whole for garnish. Peel the avocado, cut it in half, and sprinkle with lemon juice to prevent browning. Season the *centolla* meat with some of the *Mayonesa*. Put an avocado half on each serving plate on a bed of lettuce. Pile the *centolla* meat over the avocado halves, top with *Mayonesa,* and garnish with *centolla* claws.

Torta Pascualina
SPINACH TORTE

Serves 10

The original name of this recipe may refer to Christmas, which in Spanish is called *Pascua*. Another possibility is that it was named after someone named Pascual, in any event it is delicious and quite filling. This recipe is from my mother's cookbook. In Chile the cheese used in most cooking is *mantecoso,* a strong-flavored soft cheese. I have substituted Monterey Jack. You can also substitute a readymade tomato sauce for the *Salsa de Tomates.* This can be served as a hot first course or as a vegetarian main course.

1	pound spinach or Swiss chard
2	cups french bread, cubed
1	cup milk
1	medium onion, peeled and finely chopped
3	cloves garlic, peeled and finely chopped
1	tablespoon olive oil
1	tablespoon butter, unsalted
	freshly ground black pepper, to taste
	nutmeg, freshly ground to taste
2	large beaten eggs
½	pound Monterey Jack cheese, grated
4	cups all-purpose flour
¼	cup corn oil
1	large whole egg
¼	cup olive oil
1	cup *Salsa de Tomates* (Tomato Sauce, pp. 212–213)

1. Preheat oven to 375 degrees.
2. Blanch the spinach in boiling water for 2 minutes. Drain the spinach thoroughly and finely mince it.
3. Soak the bread in the milk and then purée the mixture.
4. Sauté the onion and garlic in the olive oil and butter.
5. Remove from the stove and add the spinach, bread mixture, black pepper, and nutmeg; mix well.
6. Add the beaten eggs and the cheese; set aside.

7. Mix the flour, corn oil, whole egg, and enough salted water to form a firm dough. Lightly knead the dough until it becomes easy to roll.
8. Divide the dough into five parts and roll circles about 9 inches in diameter.
9. To assemble the torte, place one layer of the dough in the bottom of a buttered, 9-inch mold. Brush some olive oil over the dough. Follow with some of the spinach mixture. Add another dough layer and continue to alternate dough and spinach, ending with a dough layer coated with oil.
10. Bake about 45 minutes. Unmold, cut in wedges, and serve hot with *Salsa de Tomates* on top.

Salpicón de Pollo
MIXED CHICKEN SALAD

Serves 6

The word *Salpicón* derives from the verb *salpicar,* meaning to sprinkle or spatter, which, in this context, implies a mixture sprinkled with this and that. *Salpicón* is prepare with a medley of cooked meats or seafood and various optional vegetables including tomatoes, red and green peppers, fresh *ají,* summer squash, zucchini, eggplant, onions, and so on. Leftovers are perfect for *Salpicón.* When pasta is included, short pasta, such as penne, bow ties, or shells, is best; spaghetti or other long noodles are not appropriate. *Salpicón* is served cold as a first course.

> 1   cup leftover cooked chicken, diced
> 1   cup leftover pasta
> ½   cup carrots, julienned and blanched
> ¼   cup capers
> ½   cup black olives
> 1½ cups green onions, sliced
> ½   cup *Aliño para Ensaladas* (Lemon Herb Dressing, p. 203)
> 1   tablespoon *Ají* or other fresh hot pepper, finely chopped

In a salad bowl (avoid metal bowls) mix together all the ingredients and allow them to marinate for 30 minutes before serving cool as a first course.

Tortilla de Papas
POTATO OMELET

Serves 6

Potatoes are native to Chile and grow high in the northern Andes and in the southern regions and Patagonia. Like many Chilean dishes, the *Tortilla de Papas* is a common Spanish dish. It can be served cold as a first course, or cut into small bite-sized portions as an hors d'oeuvre, or hot in larger portions as a main course.

8   **medium potatoes, peeled and thinly sliced**
6   **tablespoons olive oil**
1   **medium onion, peeled and sliced**
1   **medium red bell pepper, sliced**
3   **cloves garlic, peeled and chopped**
1   **link chorizo, diced**
4   **large eggs, separated**
1   **pinch cream of tartar**

1. Fry the potatoes in 2 tablespoons of oil and drain them over absorbent paper.
2. Sauté the onion, bell pepper, garlic, and chorizo.
3. Beat the egg whites with cream of tartar to form soft peaks. Beat the egg yolks and fold into the egg whites; fold in all the other ingredients, trying not to deflate the whites.
4. Heat 2 tablespoons of oil in a large omelet pan. Pour the egg mixture into the pan and cook until the lower part is brown.
5. Invert the omelet with the help of a large dish (see *Tortilla de Papas,* p. 53, for more detailed instructions).
6. Heat another 2 tablespoons of oil in the pan and slide the omelet back in, uncooked side down. Cook until the other side is brown. Serve immediately or allow to cool and serve cold.

Tortilla de Verduras
VEGETABLE OMELET

Serves 6

This recipe was adapted from my mother's cookbook, she uses it as a way to recycle leftover vegetables. In Chile, as in Spain, *tortilla* means "omelet." The Spanish type of omelet is cooked on both sides by flipping it over in the pan. It is not stirred or folded as in the French style. Other types of *tortillas* include fillings such as seafood, chorizo, chicken, and so on, but the technique for preparing is the same as described here. Many precooked vegetables can be used for *tortillas,* including peas, corn, julienned or grated carrots, chopped spinach, chopped Swiss chard, cut asparagus, cut artichoke hearts, sliced onions, sliced or julienned zucchini, and combinations of these vegetables. This dish is the kind that invites the cook to be inventive; you can select the filling you like best. Serve as a hot first course or as a side dish.

- 1 small onion, peeled and sliced
- ½ cup mushrooms, sliced
- 5 tablespoons olive oil
- 1 cup green beans, precooked
- 4 large eggs, separated
- 1 pinch cream of tartar

1. Sauté the onion and mushrooms in 2 tablespoons of oil, add the beans, and set aside.
2. Beat the egg whites with cream of tartar to form soft peaks. Beat the egg yolks and fold in. Fold in all the other ingredients; try not to deflate the eggs.
3. Heat the remaining oil in an omelet pan. Pour in the egg mixture, and cook until one side is golden brown.
4. To turn the omelet use a dish a little larger than the frying pan. Remove the pan from the heat, hold the dish upside down over the pan with one hand, hold the pan with the other hand, and flip the omelet over onto the dish. (Make sure you don't burn yourself with the hot dish or pan juices.)
5. Slide the omelet back into the pan with the golden brown side up. Shake it into place and slowly cook other side until golden brown. Serve hot.

Humitas
CHILEAN TAMALES

Serves 10

My mother taught me how to prepare this recipe in every detail. Historians cannot agree on whether this recipe was copied from the Mexican tamale or was developed independently in ancient Peru. *Humitas* are common in central Chile, where Royce and I have savored them at the Temuco Social Club. You may use yellow corn in this recipe, but you must adjust the thickness of the mixture to a creamy consistency by adding milk if it's too thick or cornmeal if it's too thin. Serve as a first course or as a main course with *Tomates a la Chilena* (Chilean Tomato and Onion Salad, p. 161).

> **12** **ears fresh corn**
> **1** **large onion, peeled and finely chopped**
> **1** **tablespoon corn oil**
> **1** **tablespoon *Ají de Color* (Chilean sweet paprika)**
> **or Spanish paprika**
> **freshly ground black pepper, to taste**
> **1** **pinch fresh basil, chopped**
> **1** **tablespoon *Pasta de Ají* (Aji Paste, p. 207, optional)**
> **⅓** **cup milk or cream (optional)**
> **salt, to taste**

1. The corn should have large, wide, good-looking leaves. Peel the corn and wash it. Select the best leaves and save them. If the leaves are stiff, blanch them.
2. Remove the kernels from the cobs and grind them in the food processor. (Traditionally the corn kernels are grated by hand; the only difference is that the food processor leaves more skin in the mixture.)
3. Sauté the onion in the oil, add the paprika, black pepper, and basil. Add the *Pasta de Ají* or other hot sauce if you like.
4. Mix all the ingredients; if the mixture is too thick (it should be a thick creamy consistency), add a little milk or cream and add salt to taste.
5. To assemble, place two corn leaves together, overlapping the wide ends and leaving the tips facing out.

6. Put 2 tablespoons of the corn mixture in the middle of the leaves. Fold the sides to the middle, overlapping them in the center by about 2 inches. Fold one end over, stand the *humita* on the folded end, and tap it down to remove air bubbles. Fold the other end over. Fasten with string made of torn corn leaves.

7. Cook the *humitas* in a large pot of boiling water for 25 minutes. The *humitas* are cooked when the leaves have turned completely yellow. Serve hot.

Salpicón de Choros
MIXED MUSSEL SALAD

Serves 6

Choros (*Mytilus chorus*) are Chilean mussels; there are several types including a very small one (about 1 inch long) called *choritos*. The standard size *choro* is similar to the North American type. A very large one (up to 12 inches long) is called *choro zapato* and is frequently found in the south of Chile. Smoked seafood is typically prepared in the south of Chile; the technique of smoking for preserving seafood dates back to precolonial times. *Salpicón* is a common salad in Chile and there are many variations. Mussels can be replaced by diced leftover meat, chicken, or crabmeat. The vegetables depend on seasonal availability and may include spinach, artichokes, asparagus, or beans.

    1   cup smoked mussels
    2   cups romaine lettuce, shredded
    1   large carrot, julienned and blanched
    2   large tomatoes, peeled and diced
    2   cups corn kernels, precooked
    1   large ripe avocado, diced (optional)
    ½   cup *Aliño para Ensaladas* (Lemon Herb Dressing, p. 203)
    3   medium hard-boiled eggs, peeled and sliced

Mix vegetables and mussels in a large bowl, add the *Aliño* and let the salad rest for a few minutes to let the flavors mix. Serve in salad bowls with a garnish of egg slices.

SOPAS

SOUPS

In this chapter you will find three basic stocks: *Consomé de Ave* (Chicken Stock, p. 64), *Caldillo* (Fish Stock, p. 65) and *Caldo* (Beef Stock, p. 66). Although these stocks are well known and can be found in most general cookbooks, I have included them here because they are essential for the preparation of many of the soups in this chapter and because they are my own unique versions of the classics. Of course the stocks can be replaced by unsalted canned stocks, but they really are not the same.

 Consomé de Ave is the basis for vegetable soups such as *Sopa de Verduras* (Vegetable Soup, p. 67) and *Crema Quillotana* (Avocado Soup, p. 69). My mother also uses this stock for *Consomé de Ave* (see p. 64), which she considers a remedy for all ailments.

 Caldillo is the generic name for all fish soups and for the fish stock. The *caldillos* include some of the most fabulous Chilean soups; my favorite is *Caldillo Marinero* (Sailor's Fish Soup, pp. 73–74). This dish is served in every "hole-in-the-wall" bistro along the Chilean coastline, and every one of these places has its own version depending on seafood availability and location. The one presented here is my own recipe.

Caldo is the basic brown beef stock used in the classic *criolla* cuisine dishes *Ajiaco* (Beef and Potato Soup, pp.74–75), *Cazuela de Vaca* (Beef and Vegetable Soup, pp. 76–77), and *Valdiviano* (Jerky Soup, pp. 79–80). The principal ingredients for *Valdiviano* are *charqui* (beef jerky), stale bread, onions, and pumpkin, all foodstuffs that can be stored for a long time, so it is ideal for feeding your family on a cold winter night or a hungry garrison in times of siege. The name *Valdiviano* refers to the southern port of Valdivia. Founded in 1552 as a military fort in the heart of the Araucanía, and named in honor of the conquistador Don Pedro de Valdivia, the town suffered constant attacks and sieges from the Mapuches, a fierce southern native tribe. In 1539, the forty-year-old Don Pedro was a distinguished captain in the Spanish army in Peru when he decided to sell all his considerable assets to finance an expedition south. Scholars will tell you that there were "compelling military and geo-political reasons" for the conquest of Chile, but life is sometimes more basic and simple than that. This is my interpretation of the birth of the romantic city of Santiago, my home town.

Don Pedro left Cuzco, Peru in January 1540, accompanied by a dozen adventuresome Spanish men and the twenty-nine-year-old, strong and courageous widow, Doña Inez de Suarez. Don Pedro and Doña Inez were in love, but he had a wife and children in Spain, so marching south to the end of the world allowed them to start a new life together and, at least for a while, live away from those who condemned their forbidden love. It took Don Pedro and his rag-tag expedition a year to cross the fearsome Atacama desert. In 1541 they arrived at the shores of the Mapocho river which flows from the nearby Andes, and on February 12, they founded the capital of Chile, Santiago de la Nueva Extremadura. Santiago was named in honor of Saint James, patron saint of the Spanish army, and Don Pedro's native province of Extremadura, Spain. Coincidentally, this also means "the new end of the world." Don Pedro wrote back to Carlos V, King of Spain that, although the local Mapuche tribes were not at all welcoming, the Mapocho river valley is paradise:

> *There is no better land on this earth to live and multiply. I say this*
> *because life here is easy, pleasant and most healthy. This land has only*
> *four mild winter months when it rains one or two days with the new*

moon. The rest of the days are warm enough that you don't need a fire. And the summer is so mild with such delicious breezes that a man can walk under the sun all day long without discomfort. This land is abundant in pastures and garden fields for all kinds of animals and crops. There is plenty of fine woods for houses and fire and very rich minerals. It is so prosperous with abundant waters and streams that wherever seeds are sown they flourish such that it seems God created this land for his own delight.

In spite of constant battles against the Mapuches, Don Pedro and Doña Inez lived happily together in the village of Santiago until 1549, when the Inquisition caught up with them and ended their illicit love affair. To make her an honest woman, Doña Inez was forced to marry one of Don Pedro's lieutenants. Meanwhile Don Pedro, in a suicidal military campaign, marched further south where in 1553, he died in battle near the Fort of Tucapel. The Mapuche tribes fought the Spaniards for three hundred years and were never conquered in battle. Yet, they were finally subdued by a combination of European diseases, *aguardiente* (hard liquor), and the relentless tenacity of the Spaniards to acquire new lands. The war in Arauco was more costly for Spain than the entire conquest of the rest of the New World.

Consomé de Ave
CHICKEN STOCK

Serves 8

I use this stock as a base for soups and sauces. It is also the basis of the medication my mother prepared to cure all ailments; her panacea consisted of a bowl of chicken stock served over a whole raw egg, which she called *Caldito de Ave* (Little Chicken Soup). To prepare, you break a raw egg into a soup bowl, pour the boiling chicken stock over it, and stir. This cooks the egg white, but not the yolk.

1	whole chicken, cut into pieces
2	tablespoons vegetable oil
1	large onion, peeled and chopped
2	large carrots, chopped
1	cup celery, chopped
6	cloves garlic, whole and unpeeled
1	tablespoon *Aliño* (Mixed Dried Herbs, p. 205)
2	bay leaves
6	whole black peppercorns

In a stock pot brown the chicken pieces in oil. Add the vegetables and sauté. Add the garlic, *Aliño,* bay leaves, peppercorns, and about 8 cups of water. Bring to a boil and simmer for 3 hours. Remove the chicken pieces and save them for another recipe, such as *Salpicón de Pollo* (Mixed Chicken Salad, p.55). Strain and discard the solids, and refrigerate or freeze the stock without removing the fat. The fat will form a sealing layer on top of the stock. Remove the fat before using the stock.

Caldillo
FISH STOCK

Serves 8

Caldillo is the base stock for all fish soups and sauces. It is prepared with any available fish parts and shrimp, crab, and lobster shells. It can also be served alone as a light soup with some garnishes such as chopped parsley and a lemon slice.

1   pound seafood parts (heads, bones, tails, and shells)
1   large onion, peeled and chopped
4   stalks celery, chopped
2   medium carrots, chopped
6   whole black peppercorns
1   bay leaf
1   pinch *Aliño* (Mixed Dried Herbs, p. 205)
1   medium lemon, halved
4   cups white wine

In a large stock pot, combine the ingredients and simmer for 1 hour. The volume of cold water to be added (about 4 cups) depends on the amount of fish bones you have; as a rule, add enough water to cover the bones generously. Cool and strain the stock; save the stock and discard everything else. The stock will keep frozen for several weeks.

Caldo

BEEF STOCK

Serves 8

This is a light brown stock, so it is more suitable as the base for hearty beef soups and sauces.

1	pound beef bones
4	tablespoons vegetable oil
1	cup onions, peeled and chopped
6	cloves garlic, unpeeled and whole
1	cup carrots, chopped
1	cup celery, chopped
1	cup plum tomatoes, chopped
1	tablespoon *Aliño* (Mixed Dried Herbs, p. 205)
12	whole black peppercorns
2	bay leaves

Preheat the oven to 450 degrees.

In a roasting pan brown the bones for 20 minutes. In a stock pot with 2 tablespoon of oil, brown the vegetables. Add the bones, approximately 8 cups of water, *Aliño*, peppercorns, and bay leaves and bring to a slow simmer. Deglaze the roasting pan (dissolve the caramel formed around the pan with water), and add the juices to the pot. Simmer for at least 6 hours. Strain the stock and discard the vegetables and bones. Store the stock in the refrigerator or freezer without removing the fat. Remove the fat before using the stock.

Sopa de Verduras
VEGETABLE SOUP

Serves 6

This recipe was adapted from my Great-aunt Julia's cookbook. Other vegetables that can be used in this recipe include spinach, Swiss chard, carrots, asparagus, artichokes, roasted red peppers, corn, squash, peas, and beans. Other combinations of vegetables may also be used, but vegetables such as asparagus and artichokes are better as garnish.

1   **large onion, peeled and finely chopped**
3   **cloves garlic, peeled and chopped**
2   **tablespoons olive oil**
3   **cups precooked spinach or other vegetable**
3   **cups *Consomé de Ave* (Chicken Stock, p. 64)**
½   **cup bread, cubed**
2   **tablespoons fresh parsley or cilantro, chopped**

Sauté the onion and garlic in oil for about 5 minutes. If using a fresh, raw vegetable, such as diced red sweet peppers, add it to the onion/garlic mixture and sauté until soft. The vegetables can also be cooked in the *Consomé* to add more flavor to the soup. Add the precooked vegetables and sauté for 10 minutes. Reserve some of the vegetables to be added as garnish at the end. Add the *Consomé* and bread and simmer for 20 minutes. Purée in the food processor or blender, return to the saucepan, and bring to a boil. Return the reserved vegetables to the soup and serve hot with herbs on top. Garnish with parsley or cilantro.

Crema de Tomates
CREAM OF TOMATO SOUP

Serves 6

I adapted this recipe from one in my mother's cookbook. Tomatoes originated in the Andean regions and several varieties had colonized most of the New World in pre-Columbian times. In Chile, a small cherry tomato was common in ancient times. Modern large tomatoes were introduced to Chile by the Spaniards. Because plum tomatoes are not common in Chile, this soup is usually prepared with salad tomatoes or canned tomatoes, but I prefer the plum tomatoes.

6	**large plum tomatoes**
1	**medium onion, peeled and finely chopped**
2	**tablespoons olive oil**
2	**tablespoons flour**
2	**cups *Consomé de Ave* (Chicken Stock, p. 64)**
	salt, to taste
	freshly ground black pepper, to taste
1	**large hard-boiled egg, grated**
½	**cup fresh basil, chopped**

Blanch the tomatoes in boiling water for 15 seconds, remove them to a bowl filled with cold water. Peel the tomatoes and purée them in the blender. In a large pan, sauté the onion in oil, add the flour and stir until cooked. Add the *Consomé* and the tomato purée stirring with a whisk to dissolve any lumps. Simmer for 30 minutes, and add salt and pepper to taste. Serve the soup hot, garnished with the egg and basil. [To hard boil eggs, pierce the raw egg at the round end (the air bag end) with a pin and cook in boiling water for 7 minutes.]

Crema Quillotana
AVOCADO SOUP

Serves 6

I have eaten this fabulous, rich soup at the Pehue Inn in the wild Torres del Paine National Park in Chilean Patagonia. The name refers to Quillota, a town north of Santiago that is famous for its *paltas* (avocado), *chirimoya* (custard apple), and *lúcuma* groves. The market and street fair in Quillota offer these fruits at their best: enormous *chirimoyas,* ripe green and black *paltas,* and the largest *lúcumas* I have ever seen.

1   **medium onion, peeled and finely chopped**
3   **tablespoons olive oil**
2   **tablespoons flour**
4   **cups *Consomé de Ave* (Chicken Stock, p. 64)**
2   **large avocados**
1   **teaspoon lemon juice**
     salt, to taste
1   **pinch fresh cilantro, chopped**

Sauté the onion in oil, add the flour, and stir to cook the flour. Add the *Consomé.* (For this soup you can include some of the chicken fat in the stock, but this is optional.) In a glass or ceramic container, peel and purée the avocados and immediately add the lemon juice to avoid oxidation and browning. At the last minute add the avocado purée to the soup and stir well; do not boil. (Boiling causes avocados to turn dark and lose their taste.) Add salt to taste and serve hot, garnished with cilantro.

Gazpacho
COLD TOMATO SOUP

Serves 8

Gazpacho is a traditional Andalusian cold soup. Usually a combination of tomatoes, cucumbers, bread, garlic, onions, and peppers, there are many variations of this soup. White *gazpachos* from Andalusía are made without tomatoes, and include bread, garlic, almonds, grapes, lemon, orange, and eggs. The white *gazpachos* are called *Ajo Blanco, Porra,* and *Cachorrera.* In Morocco, the cold tomato soup is first cooked and then chilled. It is more spicy and has no bread. This version is my own.

1	medium onion, peeled and finely diced
6	cups tomato juice
3	cloves garlic, peeled and puréed
1	teaspoon *Pasta de Ají* (Aji Paste, optional, see p. 207)
4	tablespoons extra virgin olive oil
3	tablespoons sherry vinegar
3	tablespoons dry sherry
1	medium lemon, juiced
2	stalks celery, peeled, stringed, and finely diced
2	large green peppers, diced
3	large plum tomatoes, peeled, seeded, and diced
	salt, to taste
	freshly ground black pepper, to taste
1	pinch fresh cilantro, chopped (other herbs optional)

Wash the onion in hot water to remove its sharpness. Pour the tomato juice into a glass or ceramic container. Add the onions, garlic, *Pasta de Ají,* oil, vinegar, sherry, and lemon juice and stir. Store in the refrigerator until ready to serve. Add all the other ingredients just before serving. Garnish with cilantro.

Caldillo de Congrio
CONGER EEL SOUP

Serves 6

My Great-aunt Julia always cooked for the family right up until she died at age 99. Simple and delicious, *Caldillo de Congrio* is one of the most ancient and popular fish soups in Chile and one that Great-aunt Julia prepared the best. For the pre-Columbian Chileans, fish soups and stews were a common meal because of the abundance of seafood. Conger eel is highly appreciated, not too expensive, and available year-round. It is more of a meaty fish than an eel. Since it is not readily available outside Chile, you can substitute other fish, but adjust the cooking time so that the fish is not over-cooked.

4   **medium onions, peeled and julienned**
¼   **cup olive oil**
4   **medium plum tomatoes, peeled, seeded, and sliced**
    freshly ground black pepper, to taste
1   **whole red conger eel (approximately 2 pounds)**
½   **cup white wine**
4   **cups *Caldillo* (Fish Stock, p. 65)**
6   **slices lemon**

In a soup pan, sauté the onion in oil. Add the tomatoes and pepper and slowly cook for 10 minutes. Remove the conger skin and cut into 2-inch steaks. Place the conger steaks over the vegetables, add the wine and *Caldillo,* and slowly simmer for 20 minutes or until the conger is tender. Serve in soup bowls with a lemon slice as garnish.

Variation:
Replace the conger eel steaks with salmon fillets. Cook the salmon with the skin on for only 10 minutes. After the fish is cooked, remove the skin before serving.

Caldillo de Erizos
SEA URCHIN SOUP

Serves 6

I modified this recipe from one in my mother's cookbook. In Chile, sea urchins are a delicacy, often eaten raw *al Pil Pil,* that is with *Pebre* (Green Sauce, p. 204) as seasoning. The edible part of the urchin is inside the spiny shell, where there are five bright orange, 2- to 3-inch "tongues" (actually the gonads). The tongues have a mild seafood flavor, but they are an acquired taste.

6   medium fresh sea urchins
1   large onion, peeled and julienned
2   tablespoons olive oil
2   tablespoons *Ají de Color* (Chilean sweet paprika)
    or Spanish paprika
6   cups *Caldillo* (Fish Stock, p. 65)
6   small potatoes, cut in halves
1   large egg, beaten
2   tablespoons flat-leaf parsley, finely chopped
6   wedges lemon

Clean and precook the sea urchin tongues for 3 minutes in boiling water. Sauté the onion in oil and add the paprika. Add the *Caldillo* and simmer for 20 minutes. In a separate saucepan cook the peeled potatoes for 20 minutes. Add the potatoes and the beaten egg to the *Caldillo.* The egg will cook and the soup will show white and yellow streaks, not a homogeneous blend or French-style "liaison." Serve the *Caldillo* hot in soup plates. Add 5 or 6 precooked sea urchin tongues and top with parsley and a lemon wedge.

Variation:
If you substitute other shellfish for the sea urchins, just cook it in the *caldillo* for 3 minutes. Then remove and save it to add to the soup plate at the end. The rest of the recipe is the same.

Caldillo Marinero
SAILOR'S FISH SOUP

Serves 6

This is my own adaptation of this quintessential Chilean soup, which can be found in any seaside restaurant, elegant or modest, up and down the Chilean coast. The ingredients vary with the seasons, location, and availability; but any seafood is acceptable. Serve as a second course or as a light main course.

2	medium onions, peeled and julienned
2	tablespoons olive oil
6	cloves garlic, peeled and chopped
6	medium plum tomatoes, peeled, seeded, and cubed
	freshly ground black pepper, to taste
1	tablespoon *Ají de Color* (Chilean sweet paprika) or Spanish paprika
1	teaspoon *Pasta de Ají* (Aji Paste, p. 207, optional)
6	cups *Caldillo* (Fish Stock, p. 65)
6	small potatoes, peeled and halved
6	pieces salmon filets, or any firm fish
12	medium shrimp
12	medium mussels, shelled and cleaned
12	medium oysters, shelled and cleaned
	fresh, flat-leaf parsley, chopped, to taste
6	wedges lemon

1. Sauté the onions in the oil. Add the garlic, tomatoes, pepper, paprika, and *Pasta de Ají* and sauté until the onion is soft and transparent.
2. Add the *Caldillo* and bring to a boil. Add the potatoes.
3. Poach the fish in the broth for about 10 minutes and remove to a warm serving dish or tureen (remove the fish skin if necessary).
4. Cook the shrimp in the broth for 3 minutes. Remove the shrimp, peel and discard the shells, and place the shrimp in the serving dish.
5. Cook the mussels in the broth for 2 minutes, and then remove them to the serving dish.
6. Cook the oysters in the broth for 1 minute.

7. Pour the soup and the oysters into the serving dish and serve immediately garnished with parsley and lemon wedges.

Variations:

Use scallops and cook them like the shrimp. Use clams and cook them like the mussels. Use haddock, cod, or hake and cook them like the salmon.

Ajiaco
BEEF AND POTATO SOUP

Serves 8

Ajiaco is traditional hearty soup from the Chilean *criolla* cuisine and one from my mother's cookbook. The rather unusual name suggests that *ají* may once have been a principal ingredient in this soup but at some later time was abandoned. *Ajiaco* can be a meal by itself, or it can be served as a second course in a small soup bowl.

2 **pounds eye of round beef, lean**
3 **tablespoons olive oil**
2 **medium onions, sliced**
1 **tablespoon *Ají de Color* (Chilean sweet paprika) or Spanish paprika**
1 **tablespoon dry thyme, crushed or ground**
1 **tablespoon dry oregano, crushed or ground freshly ground black pepper, to taste**
8 **cups *Caldo* (Beef Stock, see p. 66)**
1 **whole fresh or dried *ají* (optional)**
1 **pound potatoes, peeled**
1 **medium *Sevillana* (tart) orange, juiced salt, to taste**
1 **pinch fresh parsley, chopped**
2 **large hard-boiled eggs, cut into wedges**

1. Preheat the oven to 375 degrees.
2. Rub the beef with oil and bake for 30 minutes. Cut the meat into strips, return it to its juices and set aside.

3. Sauté the onions with paprika, thyme, oregano, and pepper until transparent.
4. Add the *Caldo* to the onions and bring to a boil, add the *ají*. Add the meat with its juices to the soup and simmer for 30 minutes.
5. Cut the potatoes, in lengthwise wedges or the shape of country-style french fries, and add to the soup, simmer for 15 minutes.
6. Add the orange juice, check for salt, and let it rest, off the heat, for 10 minutes. (*Sevillana* oranges can be replaced by half a Valencia orange and half a lemon.)
7. Serve in soup bowls garnished with parsley and eggs. (To hard boil eggs, pierce the round end of the raw eggs (the air bag end) with a needle and cook in boiling water for 7 minutes.)

Sopa de Sémola
SEMOLINA SOUP

Serves 6

I once visited my aunt Emma Bascuñán for lunch, though I had indigestion. She insisted that I stay and served me this soup, which is prepared for sick people. She sprinkled chopped parsley in my bowl and grated Parmesan cheese in hers. It is quite delicious, and I definitely felt better afterward. Several historical accounts mention that in the early years of the conquest of Chile, when food was scarce, people would eat a *Sopa de Maiz* (Maize Soup); such a soup was probably very similar to this one.

6 cups *Consomé de Ave* (Chicken Stock, p. 64)
6 tablespoons semolina or very fine cornmeal
 salt, to taste
6 pinches parsley, finely chopped

Bring the *Consomé* to a boil. Slowly add the semolina, stirring constantly. Simmer the mixture for 10 minutes, add salt if necessary. Serve hot with the parsley on top. Or garnish with Parmesan cheese.

Cazuela de Vaca
BEEF AND VEGETABLE SOUP

Serves 6

I found this recipe in Great-aunt Leonie's cookbook, but this classic is found in every Chilean cookbook. *Cazuela* is a hearty dish of Spanish origin also known as *Puchero* or *Cocido.* It takes its name from the type of clay pot, *cazuela,* in which it used to be prepared. This version is a typical example of the Chilean *criolla* cuisine and it was popular during the colonial era as it is mentioned in the literature of the time. The ingredients include Old World foods such as beef or chicken, onions, and carrots, as well as New World staples such as potatoes, pumpkin, and corn. *Cazuela* can also be prepared with a whole hen, or a turkey hen cut into 6 to 8 pieces, in which case it is called *Cazuela de Ave* or *Cazuela de Pava.* Serve as a second course or as a main course.

1 ½	pounds beef cut into 6 pieces, include some with bones
2	tablespoons olive oil
1	medium grated carrot
2	medium carrots cut into 2-inch pieces
3	cloves garlic, peeled and chopped
1	large onion, peeled and chopped
1	medium sweet green pepper, chopped
6	cups *Caldo* (Beef Stock, p. 66) or cold water
	freshly ground black pepper, to taste
1	pinch *Ají de Color* (Chilean sweet paprika)
	or Spanish paprika
6	small potatoes, peeled
6	pieces pumpkin, peeled
2	whole corn ears, each cut into 3 pieces
½	cup converted rice
1	cup sliced green beans
	salt, to taste
1	tablespoon fresh cilantro or flat-leaf parsley, finely chopped
1	pinch *Pasta de Ají* (Aji Paste, optional, see p. 207)

In a large saucepan, brown the meat in the oil. Add the carrot, garlic, onion, and green pepper, and sauté for a few minutes. Add the *Caldo* or cold water, black pepper, and paprika; cover and cook for about 1 hour until the meat is tender. Add the potatoes, pumpkin, corn, and rice and cook another 20 minutes. Add the green beans and cook for another 5 minutes; add salt to taste. Serve hot in a large soup dish garnished with cilantro. *Pasta de Ají* is optional and can be added at the table.

Crema de Ajo y Almendras
GARLIC ALMOND SOUP

Serves 6

This recipe was inspired by the traditional Andalusian *Ajo Blanco,* which is served cold. I serve this soup hot, garnished with almond slivers.

4	slices crustless white bread, diced
2	cups milk
8	ounces almonds, peeled
1	cup garlic cloves, peeled and chopped
3	cups *Consomé de Ave* (Chicken Stock, p. 64)
3	tablespoons extra virgin olive oil
1	medium lemon, juiced and zest grated
	freshly ground black pepper, to taste
1	tablespoon *Pasta de Ají* (Aji Paste, p. 207)
	salt, to taste
1	pinch fresh cilantro, finely chopped
2	tablespoons almond slivers

Soak the bread in 1 cup of milk. Simmer the almonds in the other cup of milk for 30 minutes. Simmer the garlic in 1 cup of *Consomé* for 1 hour. Purée the bread mixture, the almonds in milk, and the garlic in *Consomé.* In a nonreactive soup pot, mix the purées and add the oil, lemon juice, lemon zest, black pepper, *Pasta de Ají,* and the rest of the *Consomé* and milk. Bring to a boil, check for needed salt, and garnish with the cilantro and almond slivers; serve hot.

Sopa de Albóndigas
MEATBALL SOUP

Serves 6

This recipe is from my Great-aunt Julia's cookbook and, as always, she made me feel that this simple soup was something special. This type of soup is common in Spain as well as in Chile. These meatballs can also be fried and served as the main course called *Fricandelas* (Spicy Fried Meatballs, p. 147).

1	small onion, peeled and finely chopped
3	tablespoons fresh, flat-leaf parsley or cilantro, chopped
4	tablespoons olive oil
1	pound lean ground beef
2	tablespoons flour
4	tablespoons bread crumbs
3	large eggs, beaten
½	cup rice
3	cloves garlic, chopped
1	medium sweet green pepper, julienned
2	medium carrots, julienned
1	tablespoon *Ají de Color* (Chilean sweet paprika) or Spanish paprika
1	tablespoon *Aliño* (Mixed Dried Herbs, p. 205)
1	bay leaf
6	cups *Caldo* (Beef Stock, p. 66), boiling
1	cup tomato juice
6	small potatoes, peeled and halved
	salt, to taste
	freshly ground black pepper, to taste

Sauté the onion and parsley in 1 tablespoon oil. In a bowl combine the onions, beef, flour, bread crumbs, and eggs; mix well to a soft paste. Sauté the rice in 3 tablespoons oil with the garlic, pepper, carrots, paprika, *Aliño,* and bay leaf. Add the boiling *Caldo* and the tomato juice and bring back to a boil. Add the potatoes and simmer for 15 minutes. Form the round meat balls, about 1½ inches in diameter, and cook them in the boiling broth for about 15 minutes. Just before serving, check for needed salt and pepper, and serve hot.

Valdiviano
JERKY SOUP

Serves 8

Valdiviano is a deliciously hearty soup of the Chilean *criolla* cuisine and has a legend associated with it. In the 1770s, the colonial mayor of Santiago, Don Luis Manuel Zañartu, used chained convicts and prisoners of the Arauco war to build the Calicanto, the first stone bridge over the Mapocho river. The working circumstances were brutal because the chained men had to labor submerged up to the waist in the icy cold Andean waters of the river from dawn to dusk. Legend has it that Zañartu was charged with inhuman treatment of the prisoners, not because of the cruelty of the work, but because of the awful state of the *Valdiviano* that was fed to the convicts once a day. Zañartu actually lost his job. The bridge was eventually finished in 1782.

Sevillana oranges, which are very tart, can be replaced by half a lemon and half a Valencia orange. Beef jerky can be replaced by an inexpensive fresh beef cut, such as eye of round. Serve as a second course or main course dish.

1	cup white bread with crusts trimmed, cubed
1	cup milk
1	cup pumpkin
1	tablespoon olive oil
2	tablespoons *Ají de Color* (Chilean sweet paprika) or Spanish paprika
4	medium onions, peeled and sliced
½	pound beef jerky, roasted and chopped
1	pinch dried oregano, crushed freshly ground black pepper, to taste
1	pinch cumin powder
4	cups *Caldo* (Beef Stock, p. 66)
8	large eggs
2	whole Seville oranges (*Sevillanas*), juiced
1	pinch fresh, flat-leaf parsley, chopped

1. Preheat the oven to 450 degrees
2. Soak the bread in the milk.
3. Roast the pumpkin for 20 minutes.

4. Heat the oil and paprika in a frying pan. Sauté the onion and, when golden, add the beef jerky. Add the oregano, black pepper, and cumin.

5. Transfer the mixture to a stock pot, add the stock and boil for 30 minutes.

6. Purée the pumpkin, bread, and milk together; add to the soup.

7. Boil the eggs in their shells for one minute to precook the whites. Break the eggs into individual serving soup dishes, being sure to include the cooked part of the white next to the shell.

8. Add the orange juice to the soup, bring to a boil, and pour over the eggs to finish cooking them.

9. Sprinkle with parsley and serve hot.

VERDURAS Y LEGUMBRES

VEGETABLES AND
LEGUMES

This section is divided into two parts: baked vegetable casseroles and vegetable stews and legumes. Some of the recipes are actually vegetarian, such as *Porotos Granados* (Summer Bean Stew, p. 97), *Pastel de Zapallitos Italianos* (Zucchini Casserole, p. 87), and *Pimentones Rellenos* (Stuffed Bell Peppers, p. 93). Others contain some meat, chicken, or seafood, such as *Pastel de Choclo* (Corn and Beef Casserole, pp. 84–85), *Arroz a la Valenciana* (Rice Valencia Style, pp. 92–93), *Carbonada* (Beef and Vegetable Stew, p. 102), and *Charquicán* (Beef and New World Vegetable Stew, pp. 103–104), but the main ingredient is still the vegetable. The meat is included primarily as a flavoring.

Squashes, beans, potatoes, and corn figure prominently in this chapter because they are at the core of Chilean *criolla* cuisine. This is, of course, no accident; it shows the subtle influence of pre-Columbian cooking on today's Chilean cuisine. I say subtle because in many cases the vegetables do not name the dish, but if you look carefully, you invariably find that they define the ingredients.

There are many recipes for squashes, and pumpkins in my family's cookbooks. I have included a few of my favorites. Squashes and pumpkins are very abundant in Chile both in summer and in winter. All squashes and pumpkins (*Cucurbita* species) are indigenous to the New World. They have been cultivated for about 6,000 years and were a staple in the diet of pre-Columbian inhabitants of Chile.

The *zapallo* (*Cucurbita maxima,* winter squash) originated in northern Chile and is cultivated in hot climates as well as cold; it grows as far south as the climate permits agriculture to be practiced. It is an essential ingredient in many classic Chilean *criolla* cuisine dishes including *Cazuela de Vaca* (Beef and Vegetable Soup, pp. 76–77), *Charquicán* (Beef and New World Vegetable Stew, pp. 103–104), and *Mote con Zapallo* (Hominy with Pumpkin, p. 176). *Zapallo* is a very large pumpkin, weighing 20 to 40 kilograms., with thick, heavy, dark green skin and bright orange flesh. It can be stored for months at room temperature. Varieties of Chilean *zapallo* that have become popular in the United States include Acorn, Banana, Boston Marrow, Buttercup, Golden Delicious, and Hubbard. When you go to the market in Chile to buy *zapallo,* the grocer has a big saw handy to cut you a piece of the *zapallo.* No knife would do the job, and you certainly don't want to carry the whole thing home!

I have also included many recipes for bean stews, soups, and salads. In this chapter you will find three classic stews featuring fresh, ripe beans, *Porotos Granados* (Summer Bean Stew, p. 97), *Porotos con Masamorra* (Beans and Corn Stew, p. 98), and *Porotos de Invierno* (Beans in Winter, p. 99). Beans (*Phaseolus vulgaris*) have been cultivated in the New World for more than 7,000 years and were a staple in the diet of the pre-Columbian Chileans. The beans in Chile are of the Lima type, and many varieties are sold in the Chilean markets, including *porotos granados,* which are used fresh, and *porotos pallares,* which are dried. Beans contain about 20 percent protein and 64 percent carbohydrates. When combined with corn as in *Porotos con Masamorra,* the dish contains a complete set of amino acids, the building blocks of proteins which are essential for rebuilding our muscles and vital organs. This fact had not escaped the nutritionist at my boarding school. Without exception, she served us beans at least once a week. And yet I still love beans!

Locro Falso (Northern Vegetable Stew, p. 96) and *Papas a la Huancaina* (Potatoes in Spicy Sauce, p. 95) are two recipes that are popular in the northern cities of Arica and Iquique. These dishes are also popular in southern Peru, especially in the city of Arequipa. This is not surprising since Arica and Iquique were in Peruvian territory before the War of the Pacific. During Spanish colonial times the borders between the colonies were never well defined, and later this triggered border conflicts. Between 1879 and 1884, Chile waged war against Peru and Bolivia to secure its northern borders. The war started in the Pacific; the Peruvian ironclad ship *Huascar* rammed its bow against the weaker Chilean frigate *Esmeralda,* which sank in the bay of Iquique. From the sinking ship, the Chilean captain Don Arturo Prat, in a heroic act, ordered his men to board the *Huascar,* and with sword in hand, jumped over shouting the famous words *"al abordaje muchachos!"* (to board, lads!). Every surviving sailor on board followed him and they all died fighting on the deck of the *Huascar.* This courageous deed inspired the Chilean soldiers, who then fought a ferocious Atacama desert campaign that took them to the outskirts of Lima. In that war Chile won the northern provinces of Tarapacá from Peru and Antofagasta from Bolivia.

Pastel de Choclo
CORN AND BEEF CASSEROLE

Serves 8

Pastel de Choclo is one of the most classic examples of Chilean *criolla* cuisine, combining a native product like corn with European meat. The word *choclo* is the Mapuche name for corn. The type of corn used for this recipe is not the long, narrow corn-on-the-cob type, but a short, wide, yellow corn called *choclero* or *cristalino Chileno* that yields a creamier paste when grated. In this recipe you can use the common yellow corn and adjust the consistency with cream or cornmeal. Both this *pastel* and the next recipe have a rather unusual topping of sugar, which caramelizes in the oven. This is very important for the authenticity of these dishes. Furthermore, both *pasteles* use *Pino* (Beef and Onion Filling) as a filling, which gives them the same taste as the *Empanadas Chilenas* (Chilean Meat turnovers, pp. 52–53) and *Papas Rellenas* (Potatoes Stuffed with Beef and Onion, p. 179). This is a variation on a recipe from Rosario Guerrero, Chilean cook to the late Mrs. Felicia Montealegre de Bernstein (Leonard Bernstein's wife). Ms. Guerrero's recipes were published in the *New York Times.* My mother has a similar recipe in her cookbook.

2	cups *Pino* (p.150)
2	tablespoons olive oil
8	tablespoons butter, unsalted
1	whole chicken, cut into pieces
16	ears fresh yellow corn, grated
3	large eggs
¼	cup milk
	salt, to taste

1   pinch cream of tartar

**3   whole hard-boiled eggs, peeled and cut into wedges
       salt, to taste**

⅓   cup confectioners sugar

1. Prepare *Pino* the day before.
2. The following day preheat the oven to 400 degrees.
3. Heat the oil and 2 tablespoons of butter, add the chicken, and brown it on both sides.
4. In a separate pan, slowly cook the grated corn with 6 tablespoons of butter, stirring constantly until the mixture boils and thickens (about 5 minutes after boiling).
5. Remove from the stove, and mix the egg yolks with the milk, and stir in. Add more milk if the mixture is too thick. Add salt to taste.
6. Beat the egg whites with the cream of tartar, to form stiff peaks and fold them into the corn mixture. Set aside.
7. Spread the *Pino* in an oiled baking dish. Arrange the hard-boiled eggs and the chicken over the *Pino*. Cover all of it with the corn mixture. Sprinkle the corn mixture with the confectioners sugar.
8. Bake until the top is golden brown, about 25 minutes. Serve hot.

Variation:

Frozen corn kernels (not canned corn) can be substituted for the fresh corn. To prepare, grind 8 cups of corn kernels in a food processor and then pass them through a vegetable strainer to remove most of the skins.

Pastel de Papas
POTATO AND BEEF CASSEROLE

Serves 8

My mother used to prepare this dish, mainly in the winter, instead of *Pastel de Choclo*, when fresh corn was not available. This is another example of Chilean *criolla* cuisine. In this recipe, the native product, potatoes, is combined with beef, which is of European origin, to produce a very tasty casserole.

2 cups *Pino* (Beef and Onion Filling, p. 150)
10 medium yellow potatoes, peeled and cut into quarters
½ cup cream (approximately)
2 large eggs, separated
1 pinch cream of tartar
salt, to taste
freshly ground black pepper, to taste
4 whole hard-boiled eggs, peeled and cut into wedges
1 tablespoon olive oil
⅓ cup confectioners sugar

1. Prepare the *Pino* a day ahead.
2. The next day, preheat the oven to 400 degrees.
3. Put the potatoes in enough cold water to cover them and simmer for 20 minutes or until tender. Drain and purée the potatoes, add the cream and egg yolks. Add more cream if the purée is too stiff (this depends on the type of potato used).
4. Beat the egg whites with the cream of tartar, to form stiff peaks and fold them into the potato mixture. Add salt and pepper to taste.
5. Spread the *Pino* in an oiled baking dish.
6. Arrange the hard-boiled egg wedges over the *Pino*.
7. Cover the casserole with the potato mixture. Sprinkle the top with sugar.
8. Bake about 25 minutes, until golden brown. Serve hot.

Pastel de Zapallitos Italianos
ZUCCHINI CASSEROLE

Serves 8

Zucchini in Chile is known as "little Italian squash" probably because it was popularized by the Italian immigrants early in this century. This *pastel* is quite different from the preceding ones; it has no *Pino* and no sugar topping. Serve it as a vegetarian main course, as a side dish, or as a hot first course. Other vegetables, such as artichokes, carrots, cabbage, and spinach can also be used in this recipe.

1	cup white bread, cubed
1	cup milk
6	medium zucchini or summer squash
1	cup *Caldo* (Beef Stock, p. 66) or water
1	medium onion, peeled and finely chopped
3	cloves garlic, peeled and chopped
3	tablespoons olive oil
2	medium eggs, beaten
1	cup Parmesan cheese, grated
	freshly ground black pepper, to taste
	salt, to taste
½	cup bread crumbs, grated

Preheat the oven to 375 degrees.

Soak the bread in milk. Cut the zucchini into 1-inch cubes and blanch them in the boiling *Caldo* or water for about 5 minutes. Remove the zucchini, reduce the liquid to about ½ cup, and add it to the bread. Sauté the onion and garlic in oil. Mix in the bread and zucchini mixture, the eggs, and ½ cup of the cheese. Add salt and pepper to taste. Spread in a buttered baking dish, sprinkle with the remaining cheese mixed with the bread crumbs, and bake for 30 minutes until golden brown on top. Serve hot.

Zapallitos Italianos Rellenos
STUFFED ZUCCHINI

Serves 8

This recipe can be prepared with zucchini, summer squash, or eggplant. This recipe is a variation on recipes I found in my mother's cookbook and also in Mariana Bravo's cookbook. My modification includes the use of soy sauce and Worcestershire sauce instead of salt, and for extra flavor. Optional ingredients mentioned in my mother's recipe include chopped shrimp and/or chopped ham; this recipe is a vegetarian main course.

8	medium zucchini or summer squash
1	large onion, peeled and finely chopped
3	cloves garlic, peeled and finely chopped
3	tablespoons olive oil
1	cup mushrooms, finely chopped
16	tablespoons bread crumbs
1	tablespoon soy sauce
1	tablespoon Worcestershire sauce
1	pinch *Aliño* (Mixed Dried Herbs, pp. 206–207)
1	tablespoon mustard
½	cup Parmesan cheese, grated
½	cup bread crumbs, grated

1. Preheat the oven to 400 degrees.
2. Cut the zucchini in half, lengthwise, and blanch them in boiling water for 3 minutes (or blanch in the microwave oven in a covered container; time will depend on the type of oven used). Allow them to cool.
3. To prepare the stuffing remove the center part of the zucchini where the seeds are and purée the pulp in the food processor or blender. Save the zucchini shells for stuffing.
4. To prepare the stuffing, sauté the onions and garlic in oil until transparent. Add the mushrooms and sauté them. Add the zucchini pulp, bread crumbs, soy sauce, Worcestershire sauce, *Aliño,* and mustard and mix well.
5. Place the zucchini shells in a baking pan and spoon the stuffing into the shells. Sprinkle the tops with the cheese mixed with bread crumbs.
6. Bake for 30 minutes until golden brown on top. Serve hot.

Variation:

If you want to include either shrimp or ham, replace the 1 cup of mushrooms with ½ cup of mushrooms and ½ cup of chopped shrimp or ham.

Berengenas al Horno
BAKED EGGPLANT

Serves 8

Although eggplants are of the same botanical family as potatoes, tomatoes, and peppers (*Solanum*), they are not native to the New World. Eggplants originated in India and were introduced into Spain and Europe by the Moors in the Middle Ages. From there they traveled to Chile, and now there are many recipes for eggplant in Chilean cookbooks. This is a variation on one of my mother's recipes. Eggplants are very popular in Chile during the summer. Hybrid eggplants are long, narrow, and very tender, so they do not need the salting pretreatment that large and mature eggplants require. This recipe uses a Chilean soft fresh cheese called *quesillo* and a more mature, very flavorful cheese called *mantecoso*. In this recipe, I have substituted ricotta and Monterey Jack, which are more readily available in the United States.

8	medium hybrid eggplants
4	tablespoons olive oil
2	cups *Salsa de Tomates* (Tomato Sauce, pp. 212–213) or *Salsa de Carne* (Meat-Based Sauce, p. 214)
1	cup ricotta cheese
1	cup Monterey Jack cheese, shredded
½	cup Parmesan cheese, grated
½	cup bread crumbs, grated

Preheat broiler to 450 degrees.

Peel the eggplants (if eggplants are young and tender they don't need to be peeled) and cut them into ½-inch slices. Coat the slices with oil. Place the oiled slices on a baking sheet and broil for 15 minutes, turning once. Arrange the eggplant slices in one layer in an oiled baking dish. Cover the slices with half of the *Salsa de Tomates* followed by a layer of ricotta and Monterey Jack cheese. Make another layer of the remaining eggplant slices, cover with the remaining *Salsa de Tomates,* and finish with a mixed layer of Parmesan cheese and bread crumbs. Bake for 35 minutes and serve hot.

Berengenas Rellenas
STUFFED EGGPLANT

Serves 8

I have modified this recipe of my mother's by replacing *machas* (razor clams) with a shrimp stuffing. You could use other seafood, chicken, or a vegetarian stuffing such as corn.

4	medium eggplants
1	medium onion, peeled and finely chopped
1	cup bread, diced
½	cup *Consomé de Ave* (Chicken Stock, p. 64) or water
3	cloves garlic, peeled and finely chopped
4	tablespoons olive oil
1	pinch dry or fresh thyme
1	leaf dry or fresh bay
1	pound cooked shrimp, shelled
	freshly ground black pepper, to taste
½	cup red pepper roasted, and chopped
1	small lemon, juiced
	salt, to taste
3	medium eggs, lightly beaten
1	pinch fresh, flat-leaf parsley, finely chopped
½	cup Parmesan cheese, grated
½	cup bread crumbs

1. Preheat the oven to 350 degrees.
2. Cut the eggplants in half and bake them for 15 minutes; remove them from the oven and allow to cool. (You can also cook the eggplants in the microwave oven.) Increase oven temperature to 375 degrees.
3. With a spoon, remove the center pulp and seeds of the eggplant; purée the pulp and seeds in food processor. Save the eggplant shell for stuffing. Soak the bread in the stock or water.
4. To prepare the stuffing sauté the onion and garlic in oil until transparent. Add the eggplant pulp, thyme, bay leaf, shrimp, black pepper, red pepper, and lemon juice. Mix well and cook about 5 minutes; taste and add salt if necessary.
5. Remove from the heat, add the eggs, soaked bread, and parsley.

6. Place the eggplant shells in an oiled baking dish. Stuff them with the prepared mixture and sprinkle with the Parmesan cheese mixed with bread crumbs.
7. Bake for 15 to 20 minutes, until golden brown on top.

Variation:
If you prefer a vegetarian recipe substitute 1 cup of chopped and sautéed mushrooms for the shrimp.

Budín de Zapallitos Italianos
LAYERED ZUCCHINI PIE

Serves 8

This recipe of my Great-aunt Julia's is similar to *Berengenas al Horno* (Baked Eggplant, p. 89), except that in this recipe the vegetable is prefried instead of prebroiled. The zucchini can be replaced by summer squash or eggplant. This recipe is a vegetarian main course.

2 cups *Betún de Cervesa* (Beer Batter, p. 214)
4 medium zucchini, cut in ¼-inch slices
½ cup frying oil
1 tablespoon olive oil
2 cups *Salsa de Tomates* (Tomato Sauce, pp. 212–213)
½ cup Parmesan cheese, grated
½ cup bread crumbs, grated

Preheat the oven to 425 degrees.

Prepare the *Betún de Cervesa,* coat the zucchini with the batter, and fry until golden in the frying oil. Remove the slices and drain them on paper towels. In an oiled baking dish, arrange a layer of the fried zucchini, cover them with *Salsa de Tomates,* and then repeat the process, finishing with a topping of Parmesan cheese mixed with bread crumbs. Bake for about 15 minutes until the cheese melts. Serve hot.

Arroz a la Valenciana
RICE VALENCIA STYLE

Serves 8

Rice was first cultivated in the Far East. It was introduced to Europe, probably in the eighth century A.D. by the Moors, and cultivated in the marshes around Valencia. This recipe is similar to paella Valenciana, the Spanish dish from Valencia. My grandfather, Agusto Bascuñán Aldunate, who was known as a "grand gourmand," prepared this rice casserole with conger eel and Chilean abalones. My version uses converted long grain rice instead of the traditional Valenciano short grain, and shrimp and mussels instead of my grandfather's more exotic seafood.

12	large shrimp, peeled and deveined
1	medium lemon
1	pound Spanish chorizo, sliced
4	tablespoons olive oil
1	pound boneless, skinless, chicken breast
1	large onion, peeled and chopped
1	large sweet green pepper, chopped
1	large sweet red pepper, roasted and chopped
1	large garlic head, peeled and chopped
2	cups converted rice
6	medium plum tomatoes, peeled and chopped
	black pepper, freshly ground, to taste
3½	cups *Consomé de Ave* (Chicken Stock, p. 64)
½	cup dry sherry
1	pinch Spanish saffron
1½	cup fresh or frozen peas
12	large mussels
1	pinch fresh, flat-leaf parsley, chopped

1. Preheat the oven to 350 degrees.
2. In a glass or ceramic container, marinate the shrimp in lemon juice for at least 1 hour in the refrigerator.
3. Sauté the chorizo in oil in a paella pan (a round, shallow, covered pan). Remove the chorizo, set aside, and keep warm.
4. Cut the chicken into 8 pieces and sauté them in the same pan; remove and keep warm.

5. Sauté the onion, green pepper, red pepper, and garlic in the same pan until transparent. Add the rice and brown lightly. Add the tomatoes and black pepper.
6. Bring the *Consomé* to a boil with the sherry and the saffron; add the boiling stock to the rice.
7. Add the chorizo and chicken to the pan; stir once and do not stir thereafter.
8. Bake uncovered for 15 minutes.
9. Sprinkle the peas over the top, add the shrimp and the mussels (hinge down) in a decorative arrangement. Cover, and bake for another 10 minutes.
10. Garnish with parsley and serve hot.

Pimentones Rellenos
STUFFED BELL PEPPERS

Serves 6

This is a common way of stuffing vegetables. The peppers can be replaced by tomatoes, squash, zucchini, onions, cabbage, eggplant, beets, and so on. The cheese can be replaced by beef, pork, chicken, or lamb, which would make the dish more like a Middle Eastern recipe. This recipe is for a vegetarian main course.

12 large green or red bell peppers
3 cups *Arroz Graneado* (Pilaf, p. 183), cold
1 cup Parmesan cheese, grated
½ cup *Consomé de Ave* (Chicken Stock, p. 64) or water
4 cups *Salsa de Tomates* (Tomato Sauce, pp. 212–213), warm

Preheat the oven to 375 degrees.

Cut the top off each pepper and remove the seeds. Mix the cold *Arroz Graneado* with ½ cup of the cheese. Stuff the peppers with the rice mixture. Sprinkle the rest of the cheese on top of the peppers. In a Dutch oven, arrange the stuffed peppers and carefully pour the *Consomé* or water into the bottom of the pan. Cover and bake for about 45 minutes. Serve hot with warm *Salsa de Tomates* on top.

Tallarines Bontú
NOODLES AND CHICKEN IN WHITE SAUCE

Serves 6

This recipe of my aunt Emma Bascuñán, like several others of her repertoire, may have been inherited from my grandfather. Although in Chile pasta is common and very popular, I have included only a few pasta recipes in this book because most pasta recipes have been recently imported from Italy and thus have not had time to evolve into something uniquely Chilean. In Chile, the cheese used would be *mantecoso,* but this is not readily available in the United States, so I have substituted mozzarella, which has a milder flavor.

2	tablespoons butter, unsalted
1	cup mushrooms, chopped
2	tablespoons flour
2½	cups milk
½	cup whipping cream
1	whole chicken breast, cooked
	freshly ground black pepper, to taste
1	pinch nutmeg, freshly grated
½	package spaghetti or fetuccini
2	tablespoons olive oil
1	cup mozzarella cheese, grated
1	tablespoon Parmesan cheese, grated

1. Preheat the oven to 375 degrees.
2. Melt the butter in a saucepan and sauté the mushrooms for about 5 minutes.
3. Add the flour and cook for approximately 2 minutes. Add the milk and cream and stir to homogenize; slowly bring to a boil.
4. Add the chicken, pepper, and nutmeg.
5. Cook the noodles *al dente* following the package instructions; drain them; transfer to a bowl, and coat them with oil.
6. In a buttered baking dish, arrange layers of noodles, chicken mixture, and the mozzarella, finishing with the Parmesan cheese.
7. Bake for about 30 minutes.

Papas a la Huancaina
POTATOES IN SPICY SAUCE

Serves 4

This potato dish originates from northern Chile; it is especially prevalent in the port of Arica, near the Peruvian border. This dish is also popular in southern Peru, especially in the city of Arequipa. Be aware that the *Pasta de Ají* or hot red pepper sauce is essential (not an option) to this preparation.

2   **medium onions, julienned**
2   **medium lemons, juiced**
8   **large potatoes**
½   **pound feta cheese**
½   **cup *Mayonesa* (Mayonnaise, p. 205)**
1   **tablespoon *Pasta de Ají* (Aji Paste, p. 207)**
    milk or cream as needed

Marinate the onions in the lemon juice for 2 hours. Cook the potatoes in their skins in simmering water for 30 to 40 minutes or until tender; this depends upon the size of the potatoes. In the blender process the feta cheese, *Mayonesa,* and *Pasta de Ají* until smooth. Remove the onions from the lemon juice and add the juice to the cheese sauce. If the sauce is too thick you can thin it with milk. Peel the potatoes, serve two hot potatoes per plate topped with the room temperature sauce.

Locro Falso
NORTHERN VEGETABLE STEW

Serves 4

Locro is a stew popular in Bolivia, Peru, Ecuador, and Argentina. It is likely that *locro* was a dish of the ancient Aimará in the area in of the former Inca empire territory. Its ingredients and mode of preparation are consistent with ancient pre-Columbian cuisine. In Chile this dish is called *falso* (false) presumably because the real thing is prepared up north in Peru and Bolivia.

2	pounds potatoes peeled
1	cup green beans, cut into 1 ½-inch pieces
2	large carrots, peeled and cubed
1	small fresh *ají* or other hot pepper, seeded and chopped
1	small sweet red pepper, cubed
2	medium onions, finely chopped
3	cloves garlic, finely chopped
1	tablespoon *Ají de Color* or Spanish paprika
1	pinch oregano
½	cup vegetable oil
2	cups corn kernels
2	cups pumpkin, cubed
6	medium tomatoes, peeled and cubed

Simmer the potatoes, green beans, carrots, *ají,* and sweet red pepper for 15 minutes in just enough water to cover the potatoes. In the meantime sauté the onions and garlic with the paprika and oregano in the oil. After 15 minutes of simmering, add the onion mixture, corn, and pumpkin to the potatoes and continue simmering for another 10 minutes. Add the tomatoes and cook for another 5 minutes; the finished product should be a thick stew. Serve hot.

Porotos Granados
SUMMER BEAN STEW

Serves 8

Porotos Granados is the most celebrated summer stew of the Chilean *criolla* cuisine. The mode of cooking, stewing, and the principal ingredients in this recipe (beans, corn, tomatoes, pumpkin, and *ají*) are all products of the New World suggesting pre-Columbian origin. This recipe is an adaptation of my mother's recipe. Fresh beans may be hard to find in the United States, so dried, medium-size, white beans may substitute, though the flavor is not as authentic.

4   cups fresh ripe pod beans
1   cup pumpkin or squash, diced
1   whole fresh green *ají*
1   medium onion, peeled and chopped
1   tablespoon *Ají de Color* or Spanish paprika
3   tablespoons olive oil
4   whole plum tomatoes, peeled seeded, and diced
    freshly ground black pepper, to taste
1   tablespoon fresh basil, chopped
2   ears fresh yellow corn, cut in 1 ½-inch slices
    salt, to taste

Shell the beans and place them in a large saucepan with enough water to cover. Add the pumpkin and *ají* and simmer for about 30 minutes. In the meantime, sauté the onion and paprika in the olive oil. Add the onion mixture, tomatoes, pepper, basil, and corn to the beans; simmer for another 15 minutes. Before serving taste and add salt if necessary. Serve hot.

Porotos con Masamorra
BEANS AND CORN STEW

Serves 4

Adriana Nuñez, my mother's faithful cook prepared this dish for me during one of my recent summer visits to Santiago. While visiting, I took the opportunity to spend time in her kitchen and look over her shoulder while she worked and I wrote down this recipe. In recent years, my mother has opted for meals with fewer spices, which has created conflict with her cook, who is still very fond of garlic, *aji*, and spices. The ingredients in this recipe are mainly of New World origin, and the mode of preparation suggests a pre-Columbian origin. I indicate fresh white beans in the ingredients, but any fresh ripe shell bean will do.

1	pound fresh white beans, shelled
1	cup pumpkin, diced
2	earsfresh corn, grated
1	bay leaf
1	large onion, peeled and finely chopped
3	cloves garlic, peeled and finely chopped
1	teaspoon *Ají de Color* or Spanish paprika
2	tablespoons olive oil
	salt, to taste
	black pepper, freshly ground, to taste
1	tablespoon fresh basil, chopped

Boil the beans, pumpkin, corn, and bay leaf in enough water to cover them, for 30 minutes or until tender. Sauté the onion, garlic, and paprika in the oil. Add the onion mixture to the beans and simmer over low heat for another 15 minutes. Add salt and pepper to taste. The consistency should be that of a thick stew. Garnish with basil and serve hot.

Porotos de Invierno
BEANS IN WINTER

Serves 8

There was a time in Santiago when fresh vegetables such as beans, corn, tomatoes, and peppers were available only in the summer. So dishes like this one, which uses dried beans and canned tomatoes, were the next best thing to *Porotos Granados* (Summer Bean Stew). This stew tastes wonderful on a cold winter day.

1	cup dried white beans
2	cups *Consomé de Ave* or *Caldo* (Chicken or Beef Stock, pp. 64, 66)
1	can stewed canned tomatoes (8 ounces)
1	can green or red sweet peppers
1	bay leaf
1	pinch *Aliño* (Mixed Dried Herbs, pp. 206–207)
1	tablespoon freshly ground black pepper
1	pound lean pork shoulder or loin, cubed
2	tablespoons olive oil
1	medium onion, peeled and diced
1	medium carrot, grated
1	stalk celery, diced
3	cloves garlic, peeled and chopped
1	tablespoon *Ají de Color* or Spanish paprika
1	tablespoon *Pasta de Ají* (Aji Paste, p. 207)
½	teaspoon ground cumin
⅓	cup sherry

Soak the beans in 4 cups of water overnight. The next day, discard the water and simmer the beans in the stock with the tomatoes, peppers, bay leaf, *Aliño,* and black pepper for about 2 hours. In the meantime, in a frying pan, brown the pork in the oil and add it to the beans. In the same pan, sauté the onion, carrot, celery, and garlic until soft; add the paprika, *Pasta de Ají,* and cumin and mix well. Add this mixture to the beans. Deglaze the sauté pan with the sherry and add it to the beans. Serve hot. This stew tastes even better the next day!

Garbanzos con Longaniza
CHICK PEAS WITH FRESH SAUSAGE

Serves 6

My mother frequently prepared this dish using *tocino* (bacon) or *salchicha* (hot dog) instead of *longaniza* (summer sausage). *Garbanzos* were a frequent dish in my boarding school menu, and a memory from childhood. The addition of soy sauce is my own contribution to this recipe. Garbanzos originated in the Middle East, where they have been in cultivation for about 7,000 years. The recipe is of Spanish origin, but now is part of the Chilean *criolla* cuisine.

1	pound dried chick peas
1	bay leaf
2	whole smoked sausage, sliced
2	tablespoons olive oil
1	large onion, peeled and chopped
1	large carrot, grated
1	teaspoon *Ají de Color* or Spanish paprika
	black pepper, freshly ground, to taste
4	cloves garlic, peeled and chopped
¼	cup port
1	tablespoon soy sauce
1	pinch *Pasta de Ají* (Aji Paste, optional, see p. 207)

Soak the chick peas in 4 cups of cold water overnight, the next day discard the water. Simmer the chick peas with the bay leaf in 2 quarts of water for 2 hours or until tender. In the meantime, sauté the sausage in the oil, add the onion, carrot, paprika, black pepper, and garlic. When the chick peas are ready, add the sausage mixture to them. Deglaze the sauté pan with port and add it to the chick peas. Add soy sauce and *Pasta de Ají* (optional) and simmer another 30 minutes. Serve hot.

Lentejas con Chorizo
LENTILS WITH HARD SAUSAGE

Serves 4

While in boarding school in Santiago, I was served lentils at least once a week. I have modified the original recipe from Great-aunt Leonie's cookbook and added soy sauce for a little oriental touch. Lentils originated in the Middle East and have been in cultivation for about 9,000 years. This recipe is of Spanish origin but is now considered a classic example of Chilean *criolla* cuisine.

12	ounces dried lentils
2	quarts water
1	tablespoon *Ají de Color* or Spanish paprika
1	teaspoon cumin powder
	black pepper, freshly ground, to taste
1	tablespoon dried oregano, crushed
1	bay leaf
½	pound chorizo, sliced
2	tablespoons olive oil
1	large onion, peeled and chopped
1	large carrot, grated
2	stalks celery, chopped
4	cloves garlic, peeled and chopped
1	tablespoon tomato paste
1	tablespoon soy sauce
¼	cup port
2	tablespoons Parmesan cheese, grated

Make sure the lentils are clean and free of small stones. In a large saucepan cover the lentils with water and bring to a boil. Add the paprika, cumin, pepper, oregano, and bay leaf and simmer for 2 hours. Sauté the chorizo in the oil, add the onion, carrot, celery, and garlic and sauté until transparent. During the last hour of cooking add the tomato paste, soy sauce, and the chorizo mixture. Deglaze the sauté pan with port and add it to the lentils. The resulting stew should be moist but not runny. Serve with grated Parmesan cheese on top.

Carbonada
BEEF AND VEGETABLE STEW

Serves 8

Another recipe from my mother's cookbook, *Carbonada* is one of the traditional recipes of Chilean *criolla* cuisine. It combines Old World ingredients such as beef, rice, onions, and carrots with New World foods such as potatoes, beans, peppers, and pumpkin. The name of this dish suggests that, at one time, it was prepared over coals (*carbón*), probably during colonial times, or perhaps even earlier.

1	pound lean eye of round, diced
1	tablespoon *Ají de Color* or Spanish paprika
2	tablespoons olive oil
1	teaspoon *Pasta de Ají* (Aji Paste, optional, see p. 207)
2	cups potatoes, peeled and diced
1	cup carrots, peeled and diced
1	cup pumpkin, peeled and diced
8	cups *Caldo* (Beef Stock, p. 66)
1	teaspoon *Aliño* (Mixed Dried Herbs, pp. 206–207) in a cheesecloth bag
1	tablespoon converted rice
½	cup green beans, sliced
1	cup fresh or frozen peas
1	tablespoon fresh, flat-leaf parsley, chopped
	salt, to taste
	black pepper, freshly ground, to taste
1	large egg yolk

In a soup pan, sauté the beef and paprika in the oil. Add the *Pasta de Ají*, potatoes, carrots, and pumpkin and sauté for another 5 minutes. Bring the *Caldo* to a boil and add the *Aliño* bag. Add the *Caldo* to the beef mixture, stir, cover, and simmer for 30 minutes. Add the rice and continue to simmer for 15 minutes. Add the green beans and peas and simmer for another 5 minutes. Remove from the heat; remove the *Aliño* bag and add the parsley. Add salt and pepper to taste. Mix the beaten egg yolk in a teaspoon of the hot stock and stir into the stew. Serve immediately.

Charquicán
BEEF AND NEW WORLD VEGETABLE STEW

Serves 6

Charquicán is a typical recipe of the Chilean *criolla* cuisine. As is usually the case, it combines Old World ingredients such as beef, onions, garlic, and peas with New World foods such as potatoes, corn, and beans. The name of this dish suggests that it was originally prepared with *charqui* (this word derives from the Quechua word *cusharqui* which means dried meat and is the origin of the English word *jerky*). In pre-Columbian times, jerky was made of *guanaco* (Andean camelid) or *huemúl* (Andean deer); today beef is more commonly used. A popular and inexpensive variation to this recipe is *Charquicán de Cochayuyo* (seaweed stew) which replaces the meat with the less expensive seaweed. *Cochayuyo* grows all along the Chilean coast, it grows in long green strands that can reach up to 100 meters. When harvested it is folded into bundles and allowed to dry in the sun where it turns brown and very hard.

2 pounds lean round beef rump or other inexpensive beef cut
1⅓ cup *Caldo* (Beef Stock, p. 66)
1 teaspoon *Ají de Color* or Spanish paprika
1 medium onion, peeled and chopped
3 cloves garlic, peeled and chopped
1 cup pumpkin, diced
3 medium potatoes, diced
1 pinch *Aliño* (Mixed Dried Herbs, pp. 206–207)
1 pinch cumin
black pepper, freshly ground, to taste
2 tablespoons olive oil
1 package fresh or frozen green beans (10 ounces)
1 package fresh frozen corn kernels (10 ounces)
salt, to taste
1 pinch fresh, flat-leaf parsley, chopped

Cut the beef into strips and simmer in ⅓ cup *Caldo* for 1 hour. Shred the beef and save the juices. Sauté the shredded beef with the paprika, onion, garlic, pumpkin, potatoes, *Aliño,* cumin, and pepper in the oil. After about 10 minutes, add the rest of the *Caldo* and the saved juices; simmer for 15 minutes. Add the frozen vegetables, check for salt, and cook for 5 minutes. Serve topped with parsley.

Variation:

To prepare *Charquican de Cochayuyo,* replace the meat with about 1 pound of dry *cochayuyo*. To cook *cochayuyo* you must soak it overnight in water and vinegar and then boil it in water and vinegar for about 1 hour until tender. Then cut it into 1-inch cubes, sauté and continue with the rest of the recipe.

Arroz con Hígado de Ave
RICE WITH CHICKEN LIVERS

Serves 4

In Chile, rice is prepared with many different flavorings, including meats, seafood, and vegetables. It may be served as a main course, as in this recipe, or just as a side dish as in *Arroz Graneado* (p. 183). The most common type of rice used in Chile is the *Valenciano* short grain rice, but I have become accustomed to long grain rice and I prefer to use it in all my rice dishes now.

 1   **pound chicken livers, chopped**
 2   **tablespoons olive oil**
 1   **medium onion, peeled and chopped**
 1   **cup converted rice**
 2   **cups *Consomé de Ave* (Chicken Stock, p. 64)**
 1   **large carrot, grated**
     black pepper, freshly ground, to taste
     salt, to taste

Sauté the chicken livers in the oil until just barely brown, do not overcook. Add the onion and rice and sauté until translucent. Bring the *Consomé* to a boil and add it; also add the carrot and black pepper. Simmer for 20 minutes. Check for salt and serve hot.

PESCADOS Y MARISCOS

FISH AND
SHELLFISH

Seafood occupies center stage in Chilean cuisine. Legendary stars such as *Locos al Pil Pil* (Chilean Abalones with Green Sauce, p. 46) for a first course, *Caldillo Marinero* (Sailor's Fish Soup, pp. 73–74) as second course, or *Chupe de Mariscos* (Shellfish, Bread, and Cheese Casserole, pp. 110–111) for a main course easily upstage any vegetable, beef, or poultry recipe on the menu. In the following chapter you will notice that these luminaries are, like all our Chilean *criolla* cuisine, the successful marriage of ancient recipes of Spain with local Chilean ingredients.

Chupe de Mariscos is the ultimate test of a consummate Chilean chef. The main ingredients of *Chupe* are seafood, milk, bread, and cheese. Traditionally, *Chupe* is prepared and served in individual earthenware *pailas,* which are small, shallow terra cotta casseroles, about 6 inches in diameter and 1 to 2 inches deep. *Pailas* and other traditional Chilean pottery are handmade in the town of Pomaire and sold throughout Chile.

Pomaire is a beautiful village southwest of Santiago in a fertile agricultural valley, surrounded by the Mallarauco hills. Here, in 1541, the native Chilean Mapuche tribes congregated to prepare the first assault against Santiago, which had been founded only six months earlier. Mallarauco is a word of the Mapuche language originating from the Mapuche words *malla,* a wild potato, and *raghco,* which means clay water. The name Pomaire, on the other hand, is a word derived from Quechua, the language of the Incas. Thus, it is believed that this ancient village was originally populated by indigenous peoples from the north.

In Pomaire, many ancient traditions and customs have been faithfully preserved and are clearly expressed in the unique and well-known styles of pottery made there of which there are three basic types: miniatures, decorative, and utilitarian or practical. The miniatures are small figures and sculptures of great beauty depicting animals, birds, and religious objects. Decorative pottery is larger in size and includes decorated jars, vases, and sculptures. Utilitarian pottery is the most popular and includes *ollas* (cooking pots), *pailas* (casseroles), *maceteros* (planters), and *tinajas* (large jars). Pomaire is also known for its traditional *criolla* cuisine, especially its delicious *mantecoso* cheese. Over the years I have collected Pomaire pottery to use in my kitchen and display around my house. The soft, friendly shapes remind me of home, keep me in touch with my roots, and warm my heart.

The predominance of seafood in Chilean cuisine is a direct result of the abundance of fish and shellfish along the 3,000-mile Chilean coast. The long and fertile coastline is bathed by the cold, nutrient-rich Humboldt current, which creates an ideal marine environment for the large variety of fish and shellfish that thrive in the Chilean territorial waters. Some of the fish familiar to the Chilean coastline, rivers, and lakes are *albacora* (albacore tuna), *salmón* (pacific salmon), *pejerreyes* (pacific whiting), *truchas* (rainbow trout), *róbalo* (pacific haddock), *bacalao* (pacific cod), and *merluza* (hake). The numerous shellfish include *ostiones* (scallops), *choritos* (small mussels), *choros zapato* (large mussels), *centollas* (patagonian king crab), *ostras* (oysters), *erizos* (sea urchins), *jaibas* (crabs), *camarones* (shrimp), *langostinos* (crawfish), and *langosta* (*Palinurus fronialis*, pacific lobster) from the island of Juan Fernandez.

Some marine species found in Chilean waters are unique to the Chilean coast, for example, *machas* (razor clamlike shellfish), *congrio* (conger eel), *corvina* (a Chilean basslike fish), and *locos* (Chilean abalones). It is a pity that *locos* are not currently available in North America because nothing can replace their fabulous flavor, texture, and aroma. *Loco* is a white/gray, bowl-shaped shellfish about the size of your hand. It is not at all related to the Californian abalone, although the latter is a tasty substitute in my *locos* recipe. *Locos* is actually the species *Concholepas concholepas,* a carnivorous marine snail that lives on rocks just below the surface and down to about 90 feet. Harvesting *locos* has been tightly restricted since 1986, due to excessive harvesting for large scale export, primarily to the Far East, that depleted the natural beds. Therefore, one has to search hard, and sweet-talk the local fishmonger, to find *locos* in Chilean markets and restaurants.

In the Chilean winter of August 1995, I accompanied my mother to the fish market in Santiago in search of *locos.* To our delight, we found large fresh *locos* for sale, at what my mother thought were astronomical prices. I did not argue with the fishmonger; I was willing to pay any price for this rare delicacy, which I had not tasted fresh for several years. In Chile it is customary for the fishmonger to soften the *locos,* which can be tough and rubbery if not prepared properly. Softening the *locos* requires that they be pounded repeatedly and in just the right way. So my mother said to the fishmonger: "I have special guests from abroad coming to lunch today, so please, remember to soften the *locos* until very tender," to which the man very courteously and with a straight face replied, "Don't you worry, miss, I will be thinking of my mother-in-law while I pound them."

Fortunately, my husband holds his mother-in-law in deep affection.

Albacora con Salsa de Palta
ALBACORE WITH AVOCADO SAUCE

Serves 4

Albacore tuna is very abundant on the Chilean coast; sometimes fishermen catch enormous specimens that weigh over 1,000 pounds. You can substitute yellowfin tuna or swordfish in this recipe. There are many ways to prepare this wonderful fish, but grilling is my favorite.

1	cup *Salsa de Palta* (Avocado Sauce, p. 212)
4	1-inch thick center-cut albacore steaks
4	cloves garlic, finely chopped
	black pepper, freshly ground, to taste
4	tablespoons olive oil
	salt, to taste
4	teaspoons fresh cilantro, finely chopped

1. Prepare the *Salsa de Palta.*
2. Rub the albacore steaks with the garlic, pepper, and olive oil.
3. Grill the steaks over hot coals or under the broiler about 3 to 4 minutes per side; do not overcook.
4. Add salt to taste. Serve hot topped with *Salsa de Palta* and garnished with cilantro.

Serving Suggestions:
Ensalada de Arroz (Rice and Avocado Salad, p. 168) or *Ensalada de Porotos* (Bean Salad with Lemon Herb Dressing, p. 164) are delightful side dishes to complete this entrée.

Budín de Salmón
SALMON SOUFFLÉ WITH AVOCADO SAUCE

Serves 4

This is a specialty of my aunt Emma Bascuñán and may have originated from my grandfather's recipes because he had an appreciation for French cooking. It can be prepared with other fish such as tuna, or with less expensive fish such as hake or cod.

2   cups crustless white bread, cut into cubes
¾   cup milk
1   cup cooked salmon, skinned, boned, and cubed
3   medium eggs, separated
2   tablespoons *Salsa Blanca* (White Sauce, p. 211)
1   pinch nutmeg, grated
1   cup *Salsa de Palta* (Avocado Sauce, p. 212)

Preheat the oven to 350 degrees.

Soak the bread in the milk. Blend the salmon and bread mixture in the food processor. Add the egg yolks, *Salsa Blanca,* and nutmeg; mix well. Beat the egg whites to form stiff peaks and fold into the salmon mixture. Butter a 4-cup loaf mold, put wax paper or parchment paper in the bottom and butter the paper. Pour the mixture into the mold and bake in a bain-marie for about 40 minutes. Check periodically with a knife to see if it is dry and set. When ready, remove from the mold, slice, and garnish with *Salsa de Palta.* Serve hot.

Serving Suggestions:
A simple salad such as *Porotitos Verdes* (Green Bean Salad with Lemon Herb Dressing, p. 162) is enough to complement this elegant soufflé.

Chupe de Mariscos
SHELLFISH, BREAD, AND CHEESE CASSEROLE

Serves 8

Chupe is a classic dish of the Chilean *criolla* cuisine. In Chile, *Chupe* is an oven-prepared casserole dish that always includes seafood or meat, bread soaked in milk or cream, cheese, Chilean paprika (*ají de color*), and *Pasta de Ají*. This recipe was adapted from that of the Chilean chef Ms. Rosario Guerrero, the long-time cook of the late Mrs. Felicia Montealegre de Bernstein (Leonard Bernstein's wife). Similar recipes are found in my mother's and Great-aunt Julia's cookbooks. When locos (Chilean abalones) were abundant in Chile, before 1986, *Chupe de Locos* was a common seafood casserole. An inexpensive and locally popular version of this casserole uses *cochayuyo* (seaweed) instead of seafood.

12	ounces crustless white bread
2	cups milk
½	tablespoon *Ají de Color* or Spanish paprika
1	teaspoon *Pasta de Ají* (Aji Paste, p. 207)
	black pepper, freshly ground, to taste
½	cup olive oil
1	bay leaf
1	medium onion, peeled and chopped
1	stalk celery, chopped
1	teaspoon dried oregano, crushed
1	pound fresh bay scallops
2	cups *Caldillo* (Fish Stock, p. 65) or water
1	pound fresh medium shrimp
½	pound precooked crab meat
1	pound mozzarella cheese, grated
1	tablespoon unsalted butter
	salt, to taste
2	large hard-boiled eggs, peeled and cut into wedges
½	cup Parmesan cheese, grated

1. Preheat the oven to 400 degrees.
2. Cut the bread into small pieces and soak in the milk for about 1 hour.
3. To the bread mixture add the paprika, *Pasta de Ají,* pepper, and oil; mix well and set aside.

4. Tie the bay leaf, onion, celery, and oregano in a cheesecloth bag.
5. Boil the scallops in the *Caldillo* with the cheesecloth bag for 1 minute. Remove the scallops and set aside.
6. In the same water boil the shrimp for 2 minutes. Remove and set aside.
7. Add 1 cup of the fish stock to the bread mixture.
8. Peel the shrimp and add all the seafood and mozzarella cheese to the bread mixture.
9. Check for salt and then pour the mixture into a buttered baking dish.
10. Distribute the egg wedges evenly over the mixture and gently push them down into the mixture to cover, being careful not to crumble them. Sprinkle with Parmesan cheese.
11. Bake about 30 minutes or until golden brown. Serve hot.

Congrio Frito
FRIED CONGER EEL

Serves 2

Congrio is a scaleless, fishlike eel, with a thick body and eellike tail. It is found in deep (down to 300 meters), cold ocean waters, and is usually sold in sizes between 18 and 30 inches long. There are at least two subspecies of *congrio*: *congrio colorado* (red conger) and *congrio negro* (black conger). Both have white, tasty, delicious, tender flesh, but my mother prefers the red conger. In Chile this is a national favorite, best eaten at a seaside restaurant. This recipe also works well with grouper fillets.

2   1½-inch steaks conger eel
1   medium lemon
    salt, to taste
1   cup *Betún para Frituras* (Frying Batter, p. 215)
1   cup frying oil

In a glass or ceramic container, marinate the fish in lemon juice with salt for 30 minutes. Prepare the batter. Heat the oil in a frying pan. Dip the fish steaks into the batter and place in the hot oil. Cook 5 to 7 minutes or until golden brown on both sides. Serve hot.

Serving Suggestions:
This recipe is usually accompanied by fried potatoes and *Tomates a la Chilena* (Chilean Tomato and Onion Salad, p. 161).

Corvina al Horno
BAKED CHILEAN BASS

Serves 6

This recipe was derived from one in my mother's cookbook. My aunt Emma Bascuñán served this entrée the first time my husband Royce was invited to dinner at her home. *Corvina* is a fish from deep, cold ocean waters. The meat is wonderful, very white and tender, with a mild fish taste. It has been compared to the Atlantic bass. You can substitute any white fish.

1	whole *corvina* or bass
1	pinch dried oregano, crushed
1	pinch fresh, flat-leaf parsley, chopped
3	cloves garlic, peeled and chopped
2	tablespoons butter, unsalted
	black pepper, freshly ground, to taste
1	large white onion, peeled and sliced
2	glasses white wine
1	medium lemon
	salt, to taste

Preheat the oven to 375 degrees.

Cut the fish into convenient serving portions (4 to 6 ounces). Rub the herbs, garlic, and butter over the fish; sprinkle with black pepper. Put the fish in a glass or ceramic baking dish, cover with the onion, and add the wine, lemon juice, and more pepper. Bake for 30 minutes. Add salt to taste, and serve hot with the baking juices.

Serving Suggestions:

This dish may be complemented with *Papitas Duquesa* (Little Fried Potato Balls, p. 181) and *Tomates al Horno* (Baked Stuffed Tomatoes, p. 169).

Croquetas de Jaibas
SPICY CRAB CAKES

Serves 2

Croquetas are made in Chile with precooked fish, shellfish, chicken, leftover beef, spinach, artichokes, and other vegetables. The aji paste and the Chilean paprika impart their unique flavor to these cakes and you will find them quite different from the more common North American version.

½	**pound crab meat, precooked**
½	**small white onion, peeled, finely chopped, and sautéed**
1	**large egg, beaten**
½	**small lemon, juiced**
	black pepper, freshly ground, to taste
1	**pinch *Ají de Color* or Spanish paprika**
	***Pasta de Ají* (Aji Paste, p. 207) to taste**
½	**cup flour**
1	**tablespoon unsalted butter, melted**
1½	**cupsfine bread crumbs**
½	**cup corn oil**
2	**tablespoons *Mayonesa* (Mayonnaise, p. 205)**

In a glass or ceramic container, mix the crab meat with the onion, egg, lemon juice, pepper, paprika, *Pasta de Ají*, flour (add through a sieve to prevent lumps), and butter; mix well. Form cakes about 2 inches in diameter and refrigerate for at least 1 hour. Be sure to place them on individual wax paper squares so that they don't stick and they will be easier to handle. Coat the cakes with bread crumbs and fry in hot oil until golden brown on both sides. Serve hot with a dollop of *Mayonesa* on top.

Serving Suggestions:

I like to serve the cakes with a fresh salad such as *Apio con Palta* (Avocado and Celery Salad, p. 165.

Medallones de Salmón

SALMON MEDALLIONS WITH ORANGE AND TOMATO SAUCE

Serves 2

I developed this recipe from a Cordon Bleu recipe with advice from my aunt Emma Bascuñán. Pacific salmon has become common in Chile now that this wonderful fish is being raised commercially in the cold, pristine waters of the southern Chilean lakes. Chile is now the second largest exporter of salmon. *Sevillana* orange can be replaced by ½ lemon and ½ Valencia orange.

2   **salmon steaks**
1   **medium *Sevillana* (tart) orange**
1   **tablespoon olive oil**
2   **tablespoons unsalted butter, softened**
1   **tablespoon tomato purée**
    black pepper, freshly ground, to taste
1   **pinch fresh cilantro, chopped**
2   **slices orange**

Remove the skin and bones from the salmon steaks. Each salmon steak now consists of two pieces. Arrange the two pieces head-to-tail to form the medallion, and secure them with toothpicks. Extract the juice of the orange. Marinate the medallions in the orange juice for 1 hour or more, using a glass or ceramic container. Sauté the medallions in oil, turning to brown both sides, pour the marinade juices into the pan, and continue to cook until the fish is tender. Mix the softened butter with the tomato purée, black pepper, and cilantro. Place a spoonful of the butter mixture over each medallion and garnish with an orange slice. Serve hot.

Serving Suggestions:
Purée de Papas (Mashed Buttermilk Potatoes, p. 180) and *Tomaticán* (Tomato and Corn Stew, p. 170) go well with the salmon medallions.

Pejerreyes Fritos
FRIED WHITINGLIKE FISH

Serves 2

Pejerreyes are small fish, 8 to 10 inches long, from Chile's cold ocean waters. They are akin to the Norwegian whiting and are sometimes called smelt. They thrive along the coast of Chile where the Humboldt current runs. One New Year's eve, my husband Royce and I dined on these scrumptious fishes on the end-of-the-world island of Tierra del Fuego. They were served broiled with butter, rather than fried, garnished simply with boiled potatoes and lemon, and accompanied by a chilled Chilean Riesling.

2   whole *pejerreyes* or trout
1   cup *Betún para Frituras* (Frying Batter, p. 215)
½   cup frying oil
1   small lemon

This fish should be treated the same way as small trout; remove the interiors and gills but leave on the head and tail. You can cook the fish either open (butterfly style) or folded in the shape of the fish (this will affect the cooking time). Prepare the batter. Heat the oil in a frying pan. Dip the fish in the batter and place it in the hot oil. Brown the fish on both sides; total cooking time should be 10 minutes per inch of thickness. Serve hot with half a lemon per plate.

Serving Suggestion:
Pejerreyes are usually served with something like *Papas con Mayonesa* (Potato Salad, p. 167).

Langosta
LOBSTER WITH WINE AND CREAM SAUCE

Serves 4

Lobster in Chile is the most luxurious and expensive meal you can offer to your guests. It comes to the mainland from the Chilean islands of Juan Fernandez. These lobsters are larger than the ones from New England and have a distinctive textured shell. In the Juan Fernandez islands the locals prepare lobster in a celebrated *Cazuela* (Meat and Vegetable Soup, pp. 76–77) called *Perol*. Back on the mainland, I asked my mother how she would prepare a lobster. She consulted with her sister Emma and this recipe is what they gave me.

1	bottle dry white wine
4	medium onions, peeled and coarsely chopped
4	small carrots, peeled and coarsely chopped
1	bay leaf
1	pinch flat-leaf parsley, chopped
1	large live lobster
3	tablespoons unsalted butter
1	tablespoon olive oil
1	teaspoon *Ají de Color* or Spanish paprika
1	medium onion, finely chopped
1	medium carrot, grated
	freshly ground white pepper to taste
	salt, to taste
¼	cup cream

1. Mix half the wine with 2 cups of hot water.
2. To the liquid add the coarsely chopped onions, carrots, bay leaf, and parsley and bring to a boil.
3. Add the live lobster to the boiling liquid and simmer for 12 minutes.
4. Remove the lobster from the stock and let it cool for a bit until you can safely handle it. Save the stock for a *Caldillo* (Fish Stock, p. 65).
5. Remove the legs, tail, and claws and discard the shell.
6. Cut the tail and leg meat into bite-sized pieces and leave the claws whole.
7. In a sauté pan melt the butter with the oil, add the finely chopped onion, the grated carrot, paprika, and salt and pepper to taste.

8. Sauté the vegetables until transparent and then add the lobster and the remaining wine.
9. Cook uncovered for about 10 minutes.
10. Add the cream and stir. Serve the lobster hot with the sauce on top and arrange the claws in a decorative way.

Serving Suggestion:
Accompany this lavish meal with something simple like *Arroz Graneado* (Pilaf, p. 183).

Salmón con Alcaparras
SALMON WITH CAPERS

Serves 4

My husband Royce and I had fresh-caught salmon prepared in this manner in the El Paraiso restaurant by Lake Rupanco in the South of Chile. This recipe also works well with flounder and trout, but the capers are essential. Similar recipes of fish and capers are common in Andalusía, Spain.

4   **slices salmon filets**
1   **cup white wine**
½   **cup lemon juice**
2   **tablespoons olive oil**
    black pepper, freshly ground, to taste
½   **cup capers**

In a glass or ceramic container, marinate the salmon in the wine and lemon juice for at least 1 hour. Remove the salmon and boil the marinade to reduce by half. Sauté the salmon in the olive oil until both sides are lightly brown, sprinkle on the pepper. Pour the reduced marinade over the salmon, cover and cook at low heat for 8 to 10 minutes. During the last minute of cooking add the capers. Serve immediately.

Serving Suggestions:
This fabulous entrée can be complemented with *Arroz Amoldado* (Molded Rice, p. 184) and *Zapallitos Saltados* (Sautéed Zucchini, p. 171).

Curanto en Olla or *Pulmay*
MAPUCHE SEAFOOD CASSEROLE

Serves 8

Curanto is a meal similar to the New England clambake and the Hawaiian luau. A pit lined with hot rocks is layered with seafood, potatoes, beans, and a whole suckling pig. This is covered with very large (up to 4 feet in diameter) *nalca* leaves, a plant that grows wild in the southern regions and is a relative of the rhubarb. *Curanto* is still prepared for special occasions and celebrations on the southern islands of Chiloé and Tenglo. This recipe is a kitchen adaptation of *curanto* (*en olla* means in a stew pot), which is also known by its Mapuche name *Pulmay.* The traditional seafood ingredients include *picorocos* (extra large sea barnacles), mussels, clams, and fish fillets. Other ingredients are smoked pork, chicken, potatoes, and *Milcao* (p. 194). I have adapted the ingredients to North American tastes.

1	bottle dry white wine
1	head garlic with skin, cut in half
1	pound mussels, cleaned, in their shells
1	pound clams, cleaned, in their shells
1	whole chicken, cut into 8 pieces
	freshly ground black pepper, to taste
1	pound chorizo (Spanish sausage), cut into 8 pieces
8	small smoked pork chops
8	medium potatoes, washed, with skins
1	pound haddock fillets, or any firm white fish
1	pound shrimp, cleaned, with shells
2	medium Savoy cabbages
	chopped fresh parsley as needed

1. Into a very large stew pot pour half of the wine and add the garlic. Turn on the heat, and when the wine starts simmering add the rest of the ingredients as follows:
2. On one side, at the bottom, place the mussels and clams. On the other side put the chicken pieces, skin side down, and sprinkle with the black pepper.
3. Next add the chorizo and pork chops in one layer.
4. Then add the potatoes in one layer.

5. Last add the fish fillets and the shrimp in one layer.
6. Pour in the rest of the wine and cover all the ingredients with several layers of cabbage leaves.
7. Cover the pot tightly and simmer 90 minutes to 2 hours.
8. Serve the seafood, pork, chicken, and potatoes on a platter and serve the juices separately in soup cups sprinkled with chopped parsley.

AVES

POULTRY

There was a time in Chile when chicken was rare and expensive and reserved for Sunday family dinners. Often country people maintained a small chicken coop in the backyard from which they collected daily eggs and the occasional bird. Today chicken is abundant; many successful poultry farms supply the markets with fresh eggs and birds. Now we can indulge our taste for chicken frequently.

The chicken recipes in this chapter are typical of the variety of dishes that Chilean cooks have developed or adapted for their menus. For example, *Escabeche* (Pickled Hen, Pickled Quail Aspic, pp. 50–51, 123) comes to us from Moorish Spain, Andalusía, Algiers, and Morocco and is now common throughout the Hispanic world. *Pollo al Vino Tinto* (Chicken in Red Wine, p. 124) is similar to the Andalusian dish *Pollo Flamenco,* which uses white wine instead of red.

Turkey was also rare at one time and was reserved for parties and holidays when one had the challenge of feeding a large crowd. My recipe for *Pavo Asado* (Roasted Holiday Turkey with Walnut Sauce, pp. 134–135) comes from that tradition. But today, turkey, like chicken, is readily available and inexpensive. We can afford to use it less formally and more often.

Geese, ducks, quail, and other small birds remain rare in Chilean markets and are not readily available. In the countryside, however, you can see abundant *ganso* (wild goose), *pato* (duck), *perdíz* (partridge), *queltegue* (lapwing), *pichón* (squab or pigeon), *tórtola* (turtledove), and *torcaza* (wild pigeon). Country cooks, who usually have a game hunter in the family, have developed or adapted several recipes for wild birds. I have included a few of the more popular ones, such as *Perdices a lo Duque* (Partridge à la Duke with Mushroom Sauce, pp. 132–133), *Pato con Naranjas* (Duck with Oranges, pp. 130–131), and *Ganso Asado* (Roasted Goose with Spicy Mushroom and Cranberry Sauce, pp. 128–129).

The wild ducks and geese of Chile are migratory birds. Other birds that travel the Chilean skies include the *flamenco chileno* (*Phoenicopterus chilensis,* flamingo), which nests in Tarapacá and spends summers in Patagonia, and the *cisne de cuello negro* (*Cygnus melancoryphus,* black-necked swan), which winters in Coquimbo and flies to Patagonia in the summer.

Tarapacá is the northern-most region of Chile, where it shares borders with Peru and Bolivia. In this region there are several *salares,* ancient lakes that dried up and left salty, mineral-rich residues. High up in the Andes, a few of those lakes have been able to survive without drying. They are home to the flamingo and other water birds who nest in islands of floating reeds. At 15,000 feet, one such place is the deep, cobalt-blue Lago Chungara in the Lauca National Park. (Lauca is also home to the graceful, elusive, and rare *vicuña,* a small camelid with a precious silky wool coat.)

Lake Chungara is surrounded by and reflects the mighty volcanoes Parinacota and Pomerape. The area is used for religious rituals by the Aimará peoples of the high Andean plateau. The twin volcanoes are considered sacred and represent the Aimará deity Mallcu, creator and protector of all living creatures. They are part of the territory of Chile's ultimate wild, indomitable flyer, the *cóndor Chileno* (*Vultur griphus*). This most impressive of creatures, with its wing span of about ten feet, is the world's largest flying bird. It can soar silently and effortlessly far above the highest peaks of the Andes from Tarapacá to Tierra del Fuego. I have seen them quietly gliding in the cloudless Patagonian sky, and they are most inspiring. In 1834, this bird was incorporated into the national emblem to symbolize freedom and the unconquerable spirit of the Chilean people.

Gallina en Escabeche
PICKLED HEN

Serves 4

This recipe is from my Great-aunt Julia. *Escabeche* is a recipe that can be prepared with other fowl, white fish, or salmon. *Escabeche* is an excellent way to preserve food that might otherwise spoil in hot weather; the acidity of the vinegar or lemon juice prevents airborne bacteria from spoiling the food. Remember to use an enameled or stainless steel pan when cooking with vinegar.

1	whole hen
3	tablespoons flour
3	tablespoons olive oil
1	large onion, peeled and julienned
2	large carrots, julienned
4	cloves garlic, peeled and minced
	black pepper, freshly ground, to taste
2	bay leaves
½	cup white wine
½	cup *Vinagre Aromático* (Flavored Vinegar, p. 202)
1	cup frozen peas
	salt, to taste

Cut the hen into four portions (2 breast halves and 2 legs with thigh) and coat them with flour; save the rest of the bird for *Consomé* (Chicken Stock, p. 64). In a sauté pan heat the oil and brown the chicken parts on both sides. Remove the chicken and sauté the onion, carrots, and garlic until transparent and soft. Add the black pepper and bay leaves and put the chicken back on top. Add the wine and vinegar and cook, covered, over low heat for 40 minutes. Add the peas and cook for another 5 minutes; add salt to taste. Serve hot or cold.

Serving Suggestion:
Serve as a main course with *Arroz Graneado* (Pilaf, p. 183).

Pollo al Vino Tinto
CHICKEN IN RED WINE

Serves 6

My mother used to prepare this dish, but she never wrote down the recipe. So I have developed this recipe from what I remember the dish tasted and looked like.

3	**whole chicken breasts (or 2 half breasts)**
3	**tablespoons olive oil**
1	**large onion, peeled and chopped**
1	**large green pepper, chopped**
1	**cup carrot, sliced**
1	**cup mushrooms, cut into quarters**
1	**head garlic, peeled and chopped**
6	**large plum tomatoes, peeled and chopped**
1	**pinch *Aliño* (Mixed Dried Herbs, pp. 206–207)**
	black pepper, freshly ground, to taste
3	**bay leaves**
3	**cups red wine**
	salt, to taste

Separate the chicken breasts into six half breast portions and remove the skin and fat. In a saucepan heat the oil and brown the chicken. Add the onion, green pepper, carrot, mushrooms, and garlic and sauté until soft. Add the tomatoes, *Aliño*, black pepper, and bay leaves and sauté for another 10 minutes. Add the wine and simmer for 40 minutes uncovered. Remove the chicken and keep it warm. Reduce the sauce by half and return the chicken to the sauce. Add salt if necessary and serve hot.

Serving Suggestion:
Serve with *Fideos con Salsa de Nueces* (Noodles with Walnut Sauce, p. 185) and *Guiso de Acelgas* (Swiss Chard Stew, p. 172).

Pollo con Mostaza y Crema
CHICKEN WITH MUSTARD AND CREAM

Serves 6

The old Southern American saying "The way to a man's heart is through his stomach" is universal. This is one of my husband's favorite dishes. Beef or pork tenderloin can be substituted for chicken. In Chile this dish would be prepared with regular cream because sour cream is not common.

1	pound boneless, skinless chicken breast
2	tablespoons olive oil
1	pinch *Aliño* (Mixed Dried Herbs, pp. 206–207)
	black pepper, freshly ground, to taste
1	medium onion, peeled and chopped
1	cup mushrooms, sliced
1	medium sweet green pepper, chopped
1	medium sweet red pepper, chopped
3	cloves garlic, peeled and chopped
1	tablespoon *Mostaza* (Mustard Sauce, p. 208)
	or Dijon mustard
1	cup sour cream
½	cup Parmesan cheese, grated

Cut the chicken into 1-inch cubes. In a saucepan heat the oil and brown the chicken. Add the *Aliño*, black pepper, onions, mushrooms, and peppers and sauté them for a few minutes. Cover and let the chicken cook for 10 minutes. Add the garlic, *Mostaza*, and sour cream and heat through but do not boil. Add Parmesan cheese on the serving plate.

Serving Suggestion:
Serve with *Humitas en Olla* (Tamales in Stewpot, p. 175) or simply over noodles.

Pollo con Salsa de Nueces
CHICKEN IN WALNUT SAUCE

Serves 6

I adapted this recipe from one in my Great-aunt Julia's cookbook by replacing the cream with buttermilk, something I learned to do in the southern United States. This recipe is ideally suited to leftover chicken.

½   cup dry sherry
½   small orange, juiced
½   small lemon, juiced
½   cup buttermilk
½   cup walnuts, finely chopped
    black pepper, freshly ground, to taste
1   pinch *Aliño* (Mixed Dried Herbs, pp. 206–207)
    salt, to taste
1   bunch green onions, chopped
3   tablespoons olive oil
1   medium whole chicken, cooked, boned, skinned, and shredded

In a nonreactive saucepan over low heat, reduce the sherry, orange juice, lemon juice, and buttermilk to about half. Add the walnuts, pepper, and *Aliño;* check for salt and add if necessary. In a separate pan, sauté the onions in the oil, add the chicken and warm through. Pour walnut sauce over the chicken and mix. Serve hot.

Serving Suggestion:
Serve with *Arroz Graneado* (Pilaf, p. 183) and *Zapallitos Saltados* (Sautéed Zucchini, p. 171).

Pollo con Tocino
CHICKEN WITH BACON SAUCE

Serves 8

This is my adaptation of a traditional French recipe for chicken stew since the style of preparation is also typical of Chilean home-cooked stews.

8   **medium chicken breasts, skinned and halved**
2   **cups red wine**
4   **slices bacon, julienned**
2   **tablespoons olive oil**
1   **medium onion, peeled and sliced**
3   **stalks celery, sliced**
4   **medium carrots, sliced**
1   **cup mushrooms, sliced**
1   **head garlic, peeled and chopped**
1   **tablespoon *Aliño* (Mixed Dried Herbs, pp. 206–207)**
3   **bay leaves**
    black pepper, freshly ground, to taste
1   **tablespoon soy sauce**
1   **tablespoon apple jelly**

Marinate the chicken in the wine for 1 hour in the refrigerator. Sauté the bacon in the oil. Once the bacon has rendered its fat, sauté the chicken in the same pan. Add the onions, celery, carrots, mushrooms, and garlic and sauté them until soft. Add the wine from marinade, the *Aliño,* bay leaves, pepper, soy sauce, and jelly. Simmer for about 1 hour and serve hot.

Serving Suggestion:
Serve with *Mote con Zapallo* (Hominy with Pumpkin, p. 176) and *Guiso de Berengenas y Tomate* (Eggplant and Tomato Stew, p. 174).

Ganso Asado

ROASTED GOOSE WITH SPICY MUSHROOM AND CRANBERRY SAUCE

Serves 6

This recipe can be made with either goose, duck, or pheasant (pheasant is rare and expensive in Chile, and not native to the region; the few that are raised were originally imported from Asia). Chilean dried mushrooms are found in specialty delicatessen stores in the United States, but if you cannot find them, you can use other dried mushrooms such as Portobello or shiitake.

1	large goose, plucked and cleaned
1	cup white wine vinegar
2	tablespoons *Aliño* (Mixed Dried Herbs, pp. 206–207)
1	cup Chilean dried mushrooms, chopped
3	tablespoons olive oil
1	large onion, peeled and chopped
3	medium red apples, cubed with skin
1	stalk celery, chopped
1	tablespoon *Pasta de Ají* (Aji Paste, p. 207)
	black pepper, freshly ground, to taste
1	large lemon, juiced
½	cup dry sherry
1	cup goose stock (recipe follows)
½	cup cranberry or blackberry sauce

To prepare the goose:

1. Clean the bird and save the goose liver for a *pâté* (see p. 37) and the giblets and neck for the stock. Remove the excess fat from the bird's cavity.
2. In a glass or ceramic container, marinate the goose overnight in the vinegar, 1 tablespoon of *Aliño*, and enough water to cover the bird.
3. Next day, discard the marinating liquid. Preheat the oven to 350 degrees.
4. Remove the uropigium (*rabadilla,* the tail, sometimes called the pope's or parson's nose) where the bird's oil gland is located; this gland is bitter and inedible.
5. Soak the mushrooms in warm water.
6. In a saucepan heat the oil and sauté the onion, apples, and celery stalk. After a few minutes add 1 tablespoon of *Aliño,* the *Pasta de Ají,* and pepper.

7. Drain the mushrooms and save the mushroom juice for the stock; be sure to discard the sand that usually accumulates at the bottom of the soaking bowl.
8. Add the drained mushrooms to the apple mixture, mix well, and remove from the stove.
9. Rub the bird, inside and out, with the lemon juice. Stuff the bird's cavity with the apple mixture.
10. Truss and tie the legs together so that the stuffing stays in place. Prick the bird's skin on the sides so that the fat can drain out as it cooks.
11. Bake the bird for about 2 ½ hours. After 1 hour remove and discard the accumulated fat from the baking pan.
12. When ready, remove the bird from oven and let it rest for 15 minutes before carving. Remove the stuffing from the bird; the stuffing should be served hot as a side dish.
13. Discard any fat and deglaze the roasting pan with sherry and 1 cup of goose stock.
14. Make a sauce by blending the roasting juices with the rest of the stock and add the cranberry sauce, mix well.
15. Serve the goose pieces hot, covered with the sauce, and the stuffing on the side.

Serving Suggestion:
Serve with *Arroz Amoldado* (Molded Rice, see p. 184).

Serve with *Arroz Amoldado* (Molded Rice, see p. 184).

2	tablespoons vegetable oil
1	large onion, peeled and chopped
1	large carrot, chopped
1	stalk celery, chopped
1	bay leaf
6	whole black peppercorns
1	whole red dried *ají* (hot pepper)
1	tablespoon *Aliño* (Mixed Dried Herbs, pp. 206–207)

Goose Stock:
1. Heat the oil in a pan.
2. Chop the neck and giblets and brown them in the hot oil.
3. Add 2 cups of water and the onion, carrot, celery, bay leaf, peppercorns, whole *ají, Aliño,* and reserved mushroom juice.
4. Simmer the stock for about 1 hour.
5. Strain the stock and discard the meat and vegetables. Reduce the stock by half.

Pato con Naranjas
DUCK WITH ORANGES

Serves 4

Duck and orange combinations are found in many French recipes, but this one is probably of Spanish origin because it is very old in Chile, and French influence in Chilean cuisine is rather recent. Furthermore, as Penelope Casas, author of *The Foods and Wines of Spain,* points out, the ingredients are of Andalusian origin. Oranges, together with other citrus fruits, were introduced to Europe by the Moors, probably in the eighth century A.D. Citrus fruits are now a major crop in the northern valleys of Chile.

1	**5 to 6 pound duck, plucked and cleaned**
1	**cup white wine vinegar**
1	**tablespoon *Aliño* (Mixed Dried Herbs, pp. 206–207)**
2	**medium onions**
2	**large carrots**
1	**stalk celery, diced**
3	**cloves garlic**
2	**large *Valencia* oranges**
6	**whole peppercorns**
1	**bay leaf**
1	**cup white wine**
1	**teaspoon honey**
4	**whole cloves**
	black pepper, freshly ground, to taste
	salt, to taste

1. Preheat the oven to 450 degrees.
2. Carve the duck to separate the breast and legs; save the rest of the bird for the stock. Save the duck liver for a *pâté* (see p. 37).
3. Remove most of the fat and save it for the stock. Discard the uropigium (*ravadilla* or tail, sometimes called the pope's or parson's nose) where the bird's oil gland is located; this gland is bitter tasting.
4. In a glass or ceramic container, prepare the marinade with the vinegar and *Aliño*. Marinate the duck breasts and legs overnight; add enough water to the marinade to cover bird.

5. Prepare the stock by first browning the bones and extra duck parts in the oven for 30 minutes.
6. Coarsely chop 1 onion, 1 carrot, the celery and garlic, and 1 orange.
7. Transfer the browned bones to a stock pot and add the chopped vegetables, peppercorns, bay leaf, and enough water to cover.
8. Simmer for about 2 hours.
9. Strain the stock and discard all bones and vegetables. Separate the fat from the stock and reduce the stock by about half; save the rendered fat.
10. Add salt to taste.
11. The next day, prick the duck's skin with a knife to allow the fat to drain while cooking.
12. In a saucepan heat and melt the duck fat you saved from the stock, and brown the duck pieces.
13. Remove the breasts; keep them warm.
14. Remove and discard all excess fat.
15. Finely chop 1 onion, and grate 1 carrot; add to the pan and sauté until soft.
16. Peel, julienne, and blanch the orange rind; save the orange juice.
17. Add the reduced stock, the wine, honey, cloves, pepper, and orange juice. Simmer over low heat for about ½ hour.
18. Add the reserved breasts and warm up for about 10 minutes. Serve hot with strained juices and julienned orange rind on top.

Serving Suggestion:

Serve with *Arroz Graneado* (Pilaf, p. 183).

Perdices a lo Duque
PARTRIDGE À LA DUKE WITH MUSHROOM SAUCE

Serves 4

This recipe was adapted from one of my Great-aunt Julia's recipes. I don't know the origin of this preparation, *a lo Duque* or Duke's Style. During colonial times, some nobility titles were granted to Chileans by the crown of Spain, but all titles of nobility were abolished in Chile after independence in 1810. Other small birds (*pajaritos*) may be prepared with this recipe, such as quail (*codorníz*), pigeon (*pichón*), turtledove (*tórtola*), wild pigeon (*torcaza*), and Cornish hen. The wild birds are tough and bitter, and they must be thoroughly washed in cold water and marinated in white wine and lemon juice overnight. For store-bought birds 1 hour of marinating should be enough. Portobello mushrooms may be substituted for Chilean dried mushrooms.

4	large fresh partridges or Cornish hens, plucked and cleaned
2	cups dry white wine
1	cup Chilean dried mushrooms, chopped
4	slices bacon
3	tablespoons olive oil
1	small onion, peeled and finely chopped
3	cloves garlic, chopped
1	bay leaf
	black pepper, freshly ground, to taste
4	whole cloves
1	tablespoon unsalted butter
1	cup fresh mushrooms, quartered
2	tablespoons sifted flour
	salt, to taste
1	pinch fresh, flat-leaf parsley, chopped

1. Marinate the wild birds in wine overnight or the Cornish hens for 1 hour.
2. Soak the dried mushrooms in warm water for about 1 hour. Then separate the mushrooms from the juices, save both the mushrooms and the juices, and discard any sand that appears at the bottom of the soaking bowl.
3. Remove the birds from marinade, and save the marinade.
4. Wrap the bacon slices around the birds and secure them with toothpicks.

5. In a saucepan heat the oil and brown the birds on all sides.
6. While browning the birds, add the onion, garlic, bay leaf, pepper, and cloves.
7. After browning, add the soaked mushrooms and reserved juice and marinating wine. Cover and simmer over low heat for about ½ hour, or until tender.
8. In a separate saucepan melt the butter and sauté the fresh mushrooms.
9. Remove the birds to a warm serving plate.
10. Strain the juices, discard the vegetables, and thicken the sauce with the flour. Add salt if necessary.
11. Add the sautéed fresh mushrooms to the sauce.
12. Serve the birds hot with the sauce and parsley on top.

Serving Suggestion:

Serve with *Arroz Graneado* (Pilaf, p. 183) and *Guiso de Acelgas* (Swiss Chard Stew, p. 172).

Pavo Asado

ROASTED HOLIDAY TURKEY WITH WALNUT SAUCE

Serves 10

Pavo Asado is served on special occasions and holidays in Chile. Years ago, when turkey was expensive and rare, this dish was reserved for Christmas Eve midnight dinner and New Year's Eve celebrations. Luisa Letelier, my father's long-term secretary and friend, prepared this wonderful walnut sauce to accompany the New Year's Eve turkey dinner. In the United States this recipe seems appropriate for Thanksgiving dinner. My step-daughter Marian loves this dish and now she serves it with her own Thanksgiving dinners.

1	whole turkey (about 10 to 12 pounds)
1	small lemon
4	cups *Relleno para Aves* (Poultry Stuffing with Apples, Walnuts, and Mushrooms, p. 136)
1	pound sliced bacon
2	tablespoons vegetable oil
1	small onion, chopped
1	small carrot, chopped
1	stalk celery, chopped
1	clove garlic, chopped
6	whole peppercorns
1	tablespoon *Aliño* (Mixed Dried Herbs, pp. 206–207)
½	cup dry sherry or brandy
1	cup walnuts, finely chopped

To prepare the turkey:

1. Preheat the oven to 325 degrees.
2. Clean the bird inside and out. Remove the neck, heart, liver, and other parts that often come from the butcher stuffed in the cavity; you will need this for the stock.
3. Rub the inside of the bird with lemon juice.
4. Position the bird in the center of a large baking pan and fill the front and back cavities with *Relleno para Aves*. Tie the legs to hold the cavity closed.
5. Cover the outside of the bird, especially the breasts, with the bacon slices to prevent burning and to baste the bird during baking.

6. Bake for about 4 hours for a 12 pound bird. Check for doneness by sticking a knife in the breast; if the juices are clear and not pink, the bird is ready. Do not overcook or the bird will be dry.

7. While the bird is roasting, prepare the sauce as follows:
Sauté the reserved giblets in the oil, add the onion, carrot, celery, garlic, peppercorns, and *Aliño*. Add about 3 cups of cold water and simmer for about 3 hours. Strain the stock and discard meats and vegetables. Reduce the stock by half and save.

8. When the bird is ready, remove it from the oven and let it rest for a few minutes before carving. Discard the bacon.

9. Remove the bird juices from baking pan and add them to the stock; skim off the fat.

10. Deglaze the baking pan with the sherry or brandy, and add to sauce.

11. Add the minced walnuts to the sauce and bring it to a boil.

12. Serve the sauce hot over turkey slices.

Serving Suggestion:

Serve with *Papitas Asadas* (Roasted Potatoes, p. 178) and *Tomates al Horno* (Baked Stuffed Tomatoes, p. 169).

Relleno Para Aves
POULTRY STUFFING WITH APPLES,
WALNUTS, AND MUSHROOMS

There are numerous variations on this recipe that use some kind of bread crumbs, fruits, nuts, herbs, and aromatics. I developed this recipe from one in the *Cordon Bleu Cookery Course* book. You can use this recipe to stuff chicken, turkey, quail, Cornish hen, and so on. This recipe can be prepared the previous day and kept in the refrigerator overnight. You can substitute other dried mushrooms for the Chilean mushrooms.

1	cup Chilean dried mushrooms, chopped
½	cup brandy
2	tablespoons olive oil
3	slices bacon, chopped
2	cups onion, peeled and chopped
2	cups celery, chopped
2	cups apple, peeled and chopped
3	cloves garlic, peeled and minced
1	cup walnuts, coarsely chopped
1	tablespoon *Aliño* (Mixed Dried Herbs, pp. 206–207)
1	bay leaf
	black pepper, freshly ground, to taste
3	cups croutons (or stale cornmeal bread, diced)
	salt, to taste

Soak the mushrooms in the brandy. In a sauté pan heat the olive oil and sauté the bacon. Add the onion, celery, apple, and garlic. Strain the mushrooms; and discard the sandy residue that accumulates at the bottom of the soaking bowl. Add the mushrooms and the strained juices to the sauté pan. Cook for a few minutes until the vegetables are soft. Add the walnuts, *Aliño,* bay leaf, black pepper, and croutons. Mix well, and check for needed salt. The birds can be stuffed with cold or warm mixture, but cook the bird immediately after stuffing.

Pollo a la Parrilla
GRILLED BARBECUED CHICKEN

Serves 8

I developed this recipe inspired by the traditional style of barbecued chicken common in the southern United States and by my Chilean grilling style. In my house, my husband does all the outdoor cooking; he is the expert. For more healthy eating, I remove the skin of the chicken breasts, but this recipe works just as well with the skin on and with other chicken parts such as legs and thighs.

> **8   half skinless chicken breasts**
> **3   cups *Adobo para Parrillada* (Barbecue Sauce, pp. 210–211)**

Remove any extra fat from the chicken breasts. Place them inside a large plastic bag, pour in the *Adobo* marinade, close the bag, and marinate for about 2 hours in the refrigerator. Grill the chicken over charcoal, basting with the remaining marinade. It should take about 15 minutes depending on the temperature of the coals. For added flavor, add wet hickory chips to the coals. Cook the rest of the marinade in an enameled or stainless steel saucepan for 5 minutes and serve it over the chicken.

Serving Suggestion:
Serve with a *Papas con Mayonesa* (Potato Salad, p. 167) and *Apio con Palta* (Avocado and Celery Salad, p. 165).

CARNES

MEATS

Today the preferred meats in Chile are beef, pork, and lamb, so most of my recipes feature these meats. These foodstuffs were all introduced by the conquistadors in colonial times and recipes such as *Carne Mechada* (Roast Beef Flavored with Vegetables, pp. 142–143), *Riñones al Jerez* (Kidneys in Sherry Sauce, p. 151) and *Chanchito Lechón* (Pork Baked in Milk, p. 154) are undoubtedly of European ancestry.

Before the colonization, the principal meats available to the original people of Chile were *guanaco* (Andean camelid), *huemúl* (Andean deer), *cuy* (*viscacha,* small Andean rodent), and *coipo* (*nutria,* South American beaver). Recipes such as *Anticuchos* (Meat Grilled on Skewers, p. 158), *Charquicán* (Beef and New World Vegetable Stew, pp. 103–104), and *Estofado* (Beef or Rabbit Stew with Vegetables and Port Sauce, p. 145) are adaptable to these native meats. The first two probably are of pre-Columbian origin.

Guanacos are one of four Andean camelid species; the others are the small wild *vicuñas* and the domesticated *alpacas* and *llamas.* The *alpacas* are raised for their exceptional silky wool. *Llamas* are very strong and enduring, and they are raised both as pack animals and for their meat and milk. *Llamas* are now becoming popular in the United States; they are employed as pack animals for hikers in the Appalachian and Rocky Mountains. They are also truly excellent sheepherders; *llamas* are instinctively protective of herds and do not need to be trained as do dogs. They eat the same feed as sheep, and they live up to 20 years, much longer than dogs who, under working conditions, live only about 3 to 4 years.

Another native species, the *huemúl* is a graceful deer that lives in the forested areas of Southern Chile, is about 4 feet tall, and weighs about 200 pounds. This unusual and beautiful animal was incorporated into the Chilean national emblem in 1834 to symbolize its combination of grace and strength. Once plentiful, today it is rare, almost extinct, due to overhunting and habitat loss to European herds.

Starting in the 16th century, cattle, pigs, and sheep were very successfully introduced in Chile. Sheep thrive in the mountainous areas and in the southern grasslands. Pigs and cattle have made the central valleys their home. Cattle have done well in Chile, but nothing compared to the enormous herds on the other side of the Andes, in the Argentinean pampas. That does not mean that we haven't had our share of cattle rustlers.

Legend has it that there was one José Miguel Neira, born to a peasant, part Mapuche, family in the year 1775 near the village of Cumpeo in the Chilean province of Maule. As a child, José Miguel was forced to work, dawn to dusk, as a shepherd on a local hacienda. When he was a teenager, he rebelled against his miserable fate and decided to live free of subjugation. He fled the hacienda and ended up with the sinister and feared band of Paulino Salas, alias *El Cenizo*. Neira learned the ways of the outlaw, riding wild horses, skillfully handling his *corvo* (the dreaded curved knife of the bandit) and his saber. The band assaulted travelers and stole cattle and valuables all along the central valley from Rancagua to Chillán. By the time Neira was in his mid-twenties he was admired and feared by the rest of the band, a smart, strong, fearless, and natural leader. Thus began the Chilean legend of Neira, the Bandit.

By 1810, when the War of Independence began, Neira had become acquainted with Manuel Rodriguez, the patriot and national hero, and was persuaded to join the patriotic cause. Rodriguez was a lawyer from Santiago who became an urban guerrilla to fight against the royal Spanish army during the War of Independence. In 1814, the revolutionaries were cornered by the royalists in Rancagua, including the commander-in-chief of the revolutionary army, General Don Bernardo O'Higgins. The survivors were forced to retreat to the other side of the Andes to recover and rearm. After the Rancagua disaster, repression and terror forced many patriots to flee, but Rodriguez and Neira stayed the course. Neira was appointed colonel in the revolutionary army and given orders to harass and terrorize the royalist countryside. Rodriguez did the same in Santiago, and between them they had the entire royalist army in "a quiver," running around in circles but never catching them.

By 1817 O'Higgins and his army returned to finally defeat the royalist army in the famous battle of Maipú. As always happens after war, soldiers must return to civilian life, so Neira and his band returned to the bandit life. The new independent government, however, was eager and determined to reestablish law and order. So it passed that José Miguel Neira, bandit and outlaw to some, guerrilla, patriot, and hero to others, met his death in front of a firing squad in the city of Talca in 1817.

The popular leader, Rodriguez, lived long enough to see his beloved Chile independent and free of foreign domination but was assassinated by unknown villains in 1818. The national hero, Don Bernardo O'Higgins, illegitimate son of the Irish Viceroy of Peru, Don Ambrosio O'Higgins and the Chilean lady Doña Isabel Riquelme, went on to become the first president of Chile with the official title of *Director Supremo*. Every city, town, and village in Chile has at least one O'Higgins street, square, or statue honoring, with genuine affection, the Founding Father of the Republic of Chile.

Carne Mechada
ROAST BEEF FLAVORED WITH VEGETABLES

Serves 6 to 8

I learned this recipe from my mother. The name *carne mechada* refers to the ancient technique of introducing flavorings in the form of a wick (*mecha* in Spanish) or a match. Lard was often applied to meat in this form; strands of lard were pushed into the meat to season and moisten it. In this recipe, vegetables are used instead of lard.

1	whole lean eye of round
1	large carrot
4	green onions
10	cloves garlic, peeled
½	cup olive oil
1	tablespoon *Pasta de Ají* (Aji Paste, p. 207)
	black pepper, freshly ground, to taste
½	cup port
	salt, to taste

1. Preheat the oven to 450 degrees.
2. Following the meat grain, make long, deep holes in the meat; make the holes on the cross-section side of the meat. Use a knife to make the holes and enlarge them with some other utensil (or your fingers) so that you can insert the vegetables.
3. Prepare the vegetables: cut the carrots into long pencil-like pieces and cut the green onions in half if they are too thick.
4. Insert the vegetables deep into the holes in the meat.
5. Coat the meat with a mixture of oil and *Pasta de Ají*, sprinkle with pepper.
6. Put the meat in a roasting pan and roast for 7 minutes. Reduce the oven temperature to 325 degrees and cook for another 45 minutes.
7. Remove the meat from the oven and allow the roast to rest in a separate, warm plate while you deglaze the roasting pan.
8. Pour the port into the hot pan and dissolve the caramelized juice residues over medium heat on the stovetop. Reduce the juices until the alcohol has evaporated and the juices have thickened.
9. Use the deglazing juices as a sauce over the roast slices.

Tomates a la Chilena (Chilean Tomato and Onion Salad, p. 161) and *Papitas Asadas* (Roasted Potatoes, p. 178) are a good accompaniment for this roast.

Asado Jugoso
MARINATED JUICY ROAST BEEF

Serves 12

This is my mother's recipe for the perfect roast beef; pink and juicy in the center, crusty and caramelized on the outside. The marinade is my own addition and is optional; my mother just sprinkles coarsely ground black pepper over the roast and nothing else.

1   **whole eye of round**
1   **cup *Adobo para Asado* (Roast Marinade, p. 209)**

Remove the silver skin and fat from the roast. Spread the marinade over the roast and place it in a large plastic bag; close the bag and stir the marinade around. Marinate the beef for at least 2 hours, preferably overnight. Preheat the oven to 500 degrees. Place the meat in a roasting pan and roast for 7 minutes. Lower the heat to 325 degrees and continue roasting for 30 to 40 minutes, depending on the thickness of the roast. Remove the meat from the oven and allow it to rest for 10 minutes before slicing. In the meantime, simmer the remaining marinade to reduce by half and serve it over the roast slices.

Serving suggestion:
Serve with a salad such as *Apio con Palta* (Avocado and Celery Salad, p. 165), *Arroz Graneado* (Pilaf, p. 183), or *Papitas Duquesa* (Little Fried Potato Balls, p. 181).

Carne a la Cacerola
BRAISED BEEF IN RED WINE SAUCE

Serves 6

This recipe is a modified version of a recipe from Great-aunt Leonie's collection. It is a classic example of the Chilean *criolla* cuisine with its origins in Spain. I have added soy sauce to the recipe, although this ingredient is not typically Chilean. Living abroad has taught me to appreciate soy sauce as a lovely flavor enhancer. This recipe is applicable to other types of meat such as rabbit and hare, venison, and other game (but remember to marinate the wild game at least overnight or longer).

2	pounds round beef chuck or other inexpensive cut
2	cups red wine
½	cup red wine vinegar
1	tablespoon soy sauce
2	tablespoons *Ají de Color* or Spanish paprika
1	tablespoon cumin powder
	black pepper, freshly ground, to taste
2	tablespoons olive oil
1	large onion, peeled and cubed
2	medium carrots, sliced
1	medium bell pepper, cubed
3	cloves garlic, peeled and chopped
1	bay leaf
¼	cup *Caldo* (Beef Stock, p. 66)
6	medium potatoes, peeled and quartered
1	package frozen peas (10 ounces)

Remove the fat from the beef. In a glass or ceramic pan, marinate the beef with the wine, vinegar, soy sauce, paprika, cumin, and pepper for at least 3 hours in the refrigerator. In an enameled, Teflon-coated, or stainless steel pan, brown the beef in the oil. Add the onion, carrots, bell pepper, garlic, and bay leaf. Add the *Caldo* and the marinade and simmer for 1 hour or until the meat is tender. Add the potatoes and simmer for another 30 minutes. Add the frozen peas and simmer another 5 minutes. Add salt to taste and serve hot.

Estofado
BEEF OR RABBIT STEW WITH VEGETABLES AND PORT SAUCE

Serves 6

This recipe is a modification of my mother's *Estofado*; hers does not include mushrooms or soy sauce. Most of the traditional *Estofado* recipes use rabbit instead of beef, but unless you have a hunter in the family, rabbit or hare may be hard to find, so I have replaced it with beef. This stew is reminiscent of Spanish and Provençal beef or rabbit stews. They also include some kind of meat cooked for a long time in stock with vegetables and herbs.

2	pounds rump roast or other inexpensive lean cut, cubed
3	tablespoons olive oil
1	large onion, peeled and chopped
1	large carrot, sliced
1	large red sweet pepper, sliced
6	large mushrooms, sliced
3	cloves garlic, peeled and chopped
6	whole black peppercorns
1	pinch *Aliño* (Mixed Dried Herbs, pp. 206–207)
1	bay leaf
½	cup port
1	tablespoon soy sauce
½	cup *Caldo* (Beef Stock, p. 66)
12	medium fresh or canned plum tomatoes, peeled
1	package fresh or frozen peas or green beans (10 ounces)

Preheat the oven to 325 degrees.

In a large, heavy casserole with a lid, heat the oil and brown the beef. Add the onion, carrot, red pepper, mushrooms, garlic, peppercorns, *Aliño*, and bay leaf, and sauté for about 5 minutes. Add the port, soy sauce, *Caldo*, and tomatoes and cover the casserole. Braise in the oven for about 1½ hours. Add the peas or beans and cook for another 5 minutes. Serve the beef hot with the vegetables and juices.

Serving suggestion:
Serve as main course with *Papitas Duquesa* (Little Fried Potato Balls, p. 181) and *Tomaticán* (Tomato and Corn Stew, p. 170).

Bistec a lo Pobre

CHILEAN STYLE BEEFSTEAK

Serves 2

Bistec a lo Pobre is a steak, onions, eggs, and French fries dish. It literally means "Poor people's Steak." However, the name is ironic since this dish is a rather lavish meal. Although it is popular in Chilean bistros and informal restaurants, it is not necessarily cheap, and the label may simply be satirical, in the vein of the common Chilean humor.

5 ½	tablespoons olive oil
1	large onion, peeled and julienned
	salt, to taste
	black pepper, freshly ground, to taste
2	large potatoes
½	cup frying vegetable oil
2	10 ounce New York strip steaks, about 1 inch thick
2	cloves garlic, peeled and minced
4	whole eggs
1	pinch fresh, flat-leaf parsley, chopped

1. In a frying pan heat 3 tablespoons of oil and slowly sauté the onions, stirring occasionally, until they caramelize; this can take a good 30 minutes.
2. Add salt and pepper to taste, remove the onions to a dish and keep them warm.
3. Peel the potatoes and keep them submerged in a bowl of water to avoid oxidation.
4. Just before frying, slice the potatoes French fry style, dry them carefully, and fry them in at least 1 inch of frying oil until golden; do not crowd them.
5. Remove the potatoes and drain over paper towels; add salt to taste and keep them warm.
6. Rub the steaks with the minced garlic and fry them in a very hot oiled pan or griddle. Brown one side first until juice droplets start to appear on top, then turn the meat and fry it for just 1 more minute.
7. Add salt and pepper to taste and keep the steaks warm.
8. Fry the eggs, sunny side up, in the same pan or griddle as the steaks and add salt and pepper to taste.
9. Arrange the food on the serving plate like this: the steak in the middle with the eggs on top, the fried potatoes on one side and the onions on the other.
10. Garnish with parsley.

Fricandelas
FRIED MEATBALLS

Serves 4

Fricandelas are a very popular Chilean home cooking tradition. They are known in Spain as *fricadelas,* and there are many variations in the ingredients. Meatballs, of course, are known the world over, and each culture has its own variations. This version is from my aunt Emma Bascuñán.

1	pound ground chuck
1	small onion, finely chopped
1	medium egg
2	cloves garlic, peeled and finely minced
¼	cup flat-leaf parsley, finely chopped
1	pinch oregano
1	pinch black pepper, freshly grated
1	tablespoon *Pasta de Ají* (Aji Paste, p. 207)
	salt, to taste
½	cup vegetable oil

In a mixing bowl, combine all the ingredients except the oil. Mix well and form into golf-sized balls. In a frying pan, heat the oil so that when you put in the meatballs it "sings" back at you. Carefully place the meatballs around the frying pan and brown them on all sides. After they are done, place the *fricandelas* on paper towels for a few minutes to drain the oil. Serve hot.

Serving Suggestion:
I like to serve the *Fricandelas* with *Puré de Papas* (Mashed Buttermilk Potatoes, p. 180) and *Ensalada de Lechuga* (Lettuce and Red Onion Salad, p. 163).

Pan de Carne
MEAT LOAF WITH CHICKEN LIVERS AND PISTACHIO NUTS

Serves 10

I developed this recipe from traditional Chilean recipes with the influence of Cordon Bleu terrine ingredients (pistachio nuts). My aunt Ema Neale Silva de Welt had a similar recipe. The addition of soy sauce, which is not common in Chile, is the contribution of my former mother-in-law, Panchita Llona de Huidobro. Panchita lived abroad and traveled around the world, and thus acquired a cosmopolitan cuisine style. She showed me, among other things, how to use soy sauce in this and other recipes. She taught me how to expand my horizons with new ideas from foreign cultures while we were living together in Buenos Aires. For this I am grateful to her. Panchita also prepared a wonderful meatloaf while elegantly entertaining at home.

½	**pound lean ground beef**
½	**pound ground pork butt**
2	**large eggs**
½	**cup pistachio nuts, peeled**
6	**slices bacon**
1	**tablespoon olive oil**
6	**whole chicken livers**
3	**cloves garlic, peeled**
1	**small onion, finely chopped**
½	**cup celery, finely chopped**
½	**cup carrot, finely chopped**
1	**cup bread crumbs**
½	**cup port or red wine**
	black pepper, freshly ground, to taste
1	**tablespoon soy sauce**
2	**cups *Salsa de Tomates* (Tomato Sauce, pp. 212–213)**

1. Preheat the oven to 350 degrees.
2. Mix the beef and pork with the eggs and pistachios.
3. Chop 3 slices of bacon into small pieces and sauté them in the olive oil. Add the bacon to the meats and save the rendered fat.
4. Sauté the chicken livers and the garlic in the bacon fat and save.
5. Sauté the onion, celery, and carrot in the remaining bacon fat and add to the meats.

6. Soak the bread crumbs in the port and add it to the meats. Add the pepper and soy sauce, and mix well.
7. Line the bottom of a loaf pan with the remaining three bacon slices. Fill half the pan with the meat mixture. Add a row of chicken livers and garlic the in middle of the pan. Fill the rest of the pan with the remaining meat mixture. Cover the pan with parchment paper first and then aluminum foil to seal.
8. Bake the loaf for 1½ hours.
9. Remove the loaf from the oven; place a heavy object on top for about 15 minutes to press down and thus release the fat. Discard the fat and turn the loaf over into a serving dish.
10. Warm up the *Salsa de Tomates.* Serve hot with the *Salsa* on top.

Serving Suggestion:
Serve the meat loaf with boiled potatoes as a side dish.

Costillar a la Parrilla
GRILLED RACK OF PORK

Serves 8

Parrilladas (grilled cookouts) are common in Chile during summer. There are many recipes for *parrilladas;* this one is the type most commonly used for pork ribs, pork roasts, or pork chops. The recipe is also adaptable to indoor baking.

1   **whole slab of meaty rack of pork**
1   **cup *Adobo para Costillar***
    (Rack of Pork Marinade, p. 210)

Remove the tenderloin from the rack and save it for *Chanchito Lechón* (Pork Baked in Milk, p. 154). What you have left should still be meaty. Simmer the rack of pork in water for 20 to 30 minutes. Spread the *Adobo para Costillar* all over the ribs and marinate for about 2 to 3 hours. Grill the whole rack over a charcoal fire or under the broiler until golden. Serve hot.

Serving Suggestion:
Serve with *Puré Picante* (Spicy Mashed Potatoes, p. 180) and *Tomates a la Chilena* (Chilean Tomato and Onion Salad, p. 161).

Pino
BEEF AND ONION FILLING
Serves 10

This is another recipe from my aunt Emma Bascuñán's treasures. *Pino* is a juicy and spicy meat filling used in several of the classic Chilean *criolla* recipes such as *Empanadas* (see pp. 38, 52–53), *Pastel de Choclo* (Corn and Beef Casserole, pp. 84–85), *Pastel de Papas* (Potato and Beef Casserole, p. 86), and *Papas Rellenas* (Potatoes Stuffed with Beef and Onion, p. 179). *Pino* is what makes *Empanadas Chilenas* so different from the *empanadas* made in Spain and other Latin American countries.

3	tablespoons butter, unsalted
2	tablespoons olive oil
2	large onions, peeled and finely chopped
3	cloves garlic, peeled and chopped
1	tablespoon *Ají de Color* or Spanish paprika
1	teaspoon cumin powder
1	tablespoon dried oregano, crushed
	black pepper, freshly ground, to taste
1	teaspoon *Pasta de Ají* (Aji Paste optional, p. 207)
1	pound lean ground beef
1	tablespoon flour
⅔	cup *Caldo* (Beef Stock, p. 66)
½	cup golden raisins
24	pitted black olives
	salt, to taste

In a large frying pan melt half the butter with the oil and sauté the onions and garlic until translucent. Add the paprika, cumin, oregano, black pepper, and *Pasta de Ají*; set aside. In another pan, sauté the beef in the remaining butter and oil; do not brown or overcook. Combine the onion and beef mixture in the larger pan. Dissolve the flour in the *Caldo* and add it to the mixture. Cook the mixture over low heat, stirring until thickened; the end result should be juicy. Add the raisins and olives and salt to taste. Cover and store overnight in the refrigerator.

Riñones al Jerez
KIDNEYS IN SHERRY SAUCE

Serves 2

Kidneys were not very popular in my mother's home; she did not like them and so she never served them. I tasted kidneys at aunt Emma's and Great-aunt Julia's tables and learned to use kidneys from them. This recipe is from my Great-aunt Julia's cookbook. *Riñones al Jerez* is a very popular dish in Spain, and surely that is where this recipe originates from. However, as usual it has been modified to add a Chilean flavor, namely *Pasta de Ají* (Aji Paste). Traditionally, this recipe is accompanied by white rice. Other tender beef cuts may also be used.

2	whole beef kidneys
	black pepper, freshly ground, to taste
3	tablespoons olive oil
1	large onion, peeled and finely chopped
3	cloves garlic, peeled and finely chopped
1	tablespoon flour
1	cup dry sherry
1	teaspoon soy sauce
1	teaspoon *Pasta de Ají* (Aji Paste optional, p. 207)
1	pinch fresh, flat-leaf parsley, chopped

Clean the kidneys, remove all fat and skin, and wash them thoroughly in cold water. Cut the kidneys into 1/4-inch slices, sprinkle them with the pepper, and sauté them in the oil. After they have browned, add the onion and garlic and sauté them until they are soft. Add the flour, stir, and sauté a few more minutes to brown the flour. Add the sherry, soy sauce, and *Pasta de Ají*. Turn off the heat and allow the preparation to rest a few minutes. Do not overcook the kidneys because they may turn tough. Sprinkle the parsley on top and serve hot.

Serving Suggestion:
Serve with *Arroz Graneado* (p. 183).

Guatitas

TRIPE AND MUSHROOM STEW

Serves 6

This is another dish that my mother did not care for, so I never had tripe at home. I had it at my Great-aunt Julia's instead. *Guatitas* is often served with *Papas Fritas,* the french-fried potatoes described in *Bistec a lo Pobre* (Chilean Style Beefsteak, p. 146). If you don't like tripe, you can substitute any other inexpensive beef cut that requires long cooking for tenderizing. You can substitute other dried mushrooms for the dried Chilean mushrooms.

1	pound beef tripe
2	medium onions, peeled
3	large carrots
1	stalk celery, coarsely chopped
1	bay leaf
4	whole black peppercorns
2	pinches *Aliño* (Mixed Dried Herbs, pp. 206–207)
1	cup dried Chilean mushrooms
1	cup dry white wine
2	tablespoons olive oil
3	cloves garlic, peeled and chopped
8	medium plum tomatoes, peeled and chopped
1	teaspoon *Pasta de Ají* (Aji Paste optional, p. 207)
1	teaspoon soy sauce
2	tablespoons flour
	black pepper, freshly ground, to taste
	salt, to taste

1. Fill a stock pot with 2 cups of water, tripe, 1 quartered onion, 1 carrot cut into large pieces, the celery cut into large pieces, and the bay leaf, peppercorns, and *Aliño.* Bring this to a boil and simmer for 3 hours, or until the tripe is tender.
2. Save the cooked tripe, discard the vegetables, and reduce the stock to about 1 cup.
3. Soak the mushrooms in the wine and reduced stock for about 1 hour. Remove the mushrooms; chop and save them. Strain the wine mixture to remove any sand that the mushrooms might have left behind and reserve the mixture.
4. Cut the tripe into julienne strips.

5. Sauté 1 finely chopped onion in oil until transparent.
6. Add the garlic, tomatoes, 2 grated carrots, *Pasta de Ají,* tripe strips, mushrooms, soy sauce, and reserved wine mixture.
7. Simmer for about 20 minutes and then add the flour. Stir until thickened, adding more stock if the sauce is too thick.
8. Add pepper and salt to taste and serve hot.

Bistec de Pana
LIVER STEAK

Serves 6

This liver steak is one of my husband's favorite dishes. This is how I prepare it at home.

1½	**pounds beef or calf liver**
3	**tablespoons vinegar**
1	**large egg, beaten**
2	**tablespoons milk**
	black pepper, freshly ground, to taste
1	**cup fine bread crumbs**
½	**cup frying vegetable oil**

Soak the liver in 1 cup of salted water for about 1 hour. Remove the outer skin, wash well, and soak in water with vinegar for another 15 minutes. Cut the liver into six thin steaks. Prepare an egg wash with the beaten egg and milk; add pepper to taste. Coat the steaks with the egg wash and then with bread crumbs. Fry the steaks quickly to brown both sides, but do not overcook because the liver will become tough. Serve immediately.

Serving Suggestion:
Serve with fried potatoes and *Tomates a la Chilena* (Chilean Tomato and Onion Salad, p. 161).

Chanchito Lechón
PORK BAKED IN MILK

Serves 6

This recipe is based on one my mother used to prepare. *Chanchito* is a little pig in Chile. *Lechón* means it is a suckling pig, but also refers to the fact that it is cooked in milk (*leche*). I have replaced whole milk with buttermilk, which is not used in Chile but is an excellent addition to this recipe and another southern U.S. influence in my recipes.

2 pounds pork loin
2 tablespoons vegetable oil
2 tablespoons butter
1 medium onion, finely chopped
2 cups buttermilk
2 teaspoons cornstarch dissolved in water
1 tablespoon *Mostaza* (Mustard Sauce, p. 208)
   or Dijon mustard
   black pepper, freshly ground, to taste
   salt, to taste

Preheat the oven to 325 degrees.

Remove most of the pork's fat. In a covered roasting pot or Dutch oven, heat the oil and butter and brown the pork on all sides. Add the onion and sauté. Add the buttermilk and bake for 1 hour or until done. (Check with a meat thermometer.) Remove the juices from the pot; purée and filter them to eliminate any remaining lumps. Reheat this sauce and thicken it with cornstarch. Remove from the stove and add the *Mostaza* and mix well. Season with pepper, check for needed salt, and serve the sauce over the sliced pork.

Serving Suggestion:
Serve as a main course with *Puré de Porotos Picantes* (Spicy Bean Purée, p. 182) and *Guiso de Repollo Morado* (Red Cabbage and Apple Stew, p. 173).

Arrollado
SPICY ROLLED PORK ROAST

Serves 8

There are two ways of preparing this most typical of Chilean roasts. The *huasos* (Chilean cowboys, horsemen, and farmhands) prepare it by cutting a pork butt in long strips; seasoning with garlic, cumin, oregano, *ají,* vinegar, salt, and pepper; rolling and tying the strips in pork skin; and slowly boiling until tender. Then they remove the roll from the skin, slice, and serve at room temperature. The *arrollado* recipe described below, which uses a flat cut of pork, is the one I know best.

½	cup red wine vinegar
6	cloves garlic, minced
1	tablespoon cumin
1	tablespoon *Pasta de Ají* (Aji Paste, p. 207)
1	tablespoon oregano
1	tablespoon ground black pepper
1	tablespoon thyme
1	whole pork flank or boneless country-style whole rib
1	pound bacon, sliced

Mix the vinegar with all the seasonings. Spread the seasoning mixture over the large, thin, and flat piece of pork. Spread the bacon slices over the seasonings. Roll the meat tightly and tie it with butcher's twine. Let the meat marinate for two days in the refrigerator. Preheat the oven to 350 degrees. Place the pork in a covered dish and bake for 3 hours. Let it cool to room temperature. Remove the twine, slice, and serve at room temperature.

Serving Suggestion:
Serve with a salad such as *Tomates a la Chilena* (Chilean Tomato and Onion Salad, p. 161).

Corderito Asado
ROASTED LAMB WITH GRAPE JELLY SAUCE

Serves 8

In the south of Chile, in the provinces of Aisén and Magallanes, in the regions of Patagonia, and in the island of Tierra del Fuego, lamb is the principal source of meat. Large sheep ranches are the main agricultural activity in those southern regions where the winter weather is very severe. Grilling and baking marinated lamb is the usual cooking practice. This is my version of roasted lamb, which was inspired by a recipe from the *Cordon Bleu Cookery Course* cookbook.

2	tablespoons *Mostaza* (Mustard Sauce, p. 208)
½	cup ginger, freshly grated
3	tablespoons honey
	black pepper, freshly ground, to taste
1	tablespoon *Pasta de Ají* (Aji Paste, p. 207)
1	leg of lamb
6	cloves garlic, peeled
2	tablespoons flour
1	small onion, finely chopped
1	small carrot, finely chopped
3	cloves garlic, finely chopped
2	tablespoons olive oil
3	cups *Caldo* (Beef Stock, p. 66)
	or *Consomé de Ave* (Chicken Stock, p. 64)
1	cup *Salsa de Tomates* (Tomato Sauce, pp. 212–213)
1	cup port or red wine
1	stalk fresh rosemary
2	tablespoons wine or sherry vinegar
½	cup grape or other fruit jelly
10	leaves fresh mint

1. Make a paste with the mustard, ginger, honey, pepper, and *Pasta de Ají*.
2. Trim the lamb and remove most of the fat.
3. Spread the paste all over the lamb and insert whole garlic cloves throughout the meat. Let the meat marinate overnight.

4. Preheat the oven to 400 degrees. Sprinkle the flour through a sifter, over the lamb. Roast the lamb for 1 hour.

5. In the meantime, in a nonreactive saucepan, sauté the onion, carrot, and garlic in the oil. Add the *Caldo, Salsa de Tomates,* port, and rosemary; bring to a boil. Simmer to reduce the liquid to about half. Add the vinegar and jelly and mix well.

6. After 1 hour of roasting in the oven, pour the sauce over the roast, and continue roasting for another 30 minutes. Check the roast with a thermometer; it should be about 130°F in the center. Let the roast rest and keep it warm while finishing the sauce.

7. Deglaze the roasting pan with the wine and mix the juices with the sauce.

8. Serve the slices of lamb hot with the sauce on top. Garnish with the chopped mint.

Serving Suggestion:

Serve with *Arroz Graneado* (p. 183) or *Papitas Asadas* (p. 178) as a main course.

Chuletas de Chancho a la Parrilla
GRILLED PORK CHOPS

Serves 6

I prefer to precook pork. The final charcoal cooking is mainly for flavor.

6   1-inch thick pork chops
1   cup *Adobo de Mostaza* (Mustard Marinade, p.209)

Remove excess fat and cut the silver tissues that shrink during cooking and make the chop curl up. In a large pot with plenty of water simmer the pork chops for about 20 minutes. Remove them from the water and dry them. In a large plastic bag, mix the chops and *Adobo de Mostaza*. Let the chops marinate for about 1 hour. Grill the chops over charcoal about 4 minutes per side. Discard excess marinade.

Serving Suggestion:

The traditional side dish for pork is *Puré Picante* (Spicy Mashed Potatoes, p. 180). and a salad such as *Ensalada de Repollo y Zanahoria* (Cabbage and Carrot Salad, p. 166).

Anticuchos
MEAT GRILLED ON SKEWERS

Serves 4

Anticuchos is very similar to the famous Peruvian barbecue, which uses a variety of meats (innards) cut into bite-sized pieces and grilled over a wood fire. In Chile, we use chorizo, pork, beef, or lamb. My bachelor cousin Alvaro Welt prepared this particularly lavish combination when he had Royce and me to lunch.

    1   cup red wine vinegar
    2   tablespoons *Pebre* (Green Sauce, p. 204)
    1   pound beef tenderloin, cut into 1-inch cubes
    1   pound chorizo, sliced into 1-inch pieces

Mix the vinegar and *Pebre*. Marinate the beef in this mixture for 30 minutes. Prepare the skewers, alternating beef and chorizo. Grill the meat on the skewers over a wood fire, using the rest of the marinade to baste. Turn the skewers frequently because the meat and chorizo will cook quickly (between 5 to 10 minutes depending on the fire).

Serving Suggestion:
Serve hot over *Arroz Graneado* (Pilaf, p. 183).

ENSALADAS Y VERDURAS VARIAS

SALADS AND
VEGETABLE SIDE DISHES

This section features recipes for salads and vegetables meant to accompany the main course. The great majority of these are vegetarian and many may also be served as vegetarian main courses.

Tomatoes figure prominently in Chilean salads and side dishes. Any Chilean will tell you that *Tomates a la Chilena* (Chilean Tomato and Onion Salad, p. 161) is the quintessential Chilean salad. However, the more familiar I become with the cuisines of the world, the more I realize that everybody has a tomato salad like ours, and they are always delicious. On the other hand, *Tomaticán* (Tomato and Corn Stew, p. 170), is a luscious, uniquely Chilean, tomato stew that I have enjoyed since childhood.

The common red tomato (*Solanum lycopersicon*) originated in the Andes and spread throughout the continent long before the arrival of the conquistadors. The tomatoes we know today are derived from a genus of weedy Andean plants that produced red, orange, or green cherry-sized berries. In pre-Columbian Chile, the wild varieties of the small tomato (*S. Lycopersicon chilensis*) were probably gathered for food. The tomato was first noticed by the Spaniards in Mexico, and the word *tomato* derives from the Nahuatl name *tomatl.*

Also conspicuous in Chilean salads and side dishes is the humble potato. Dishes such as *Papas Rellenas* (Potatoes Stuffed with Beef and Onion, p. 179) and *Puré Picante* (Spicy Mashed Potatoes, p. 180) are mouth-watering classics of the Chilean *criolla* cuisine. Potatoes are native to the Andes, where they have been cultivated for about 8,000 years. More than 200 different types of potatoes are cultivated in the Andean regions, and they are adapted to a wide range of climates, altitudes, and seasons. In Chile, the potato is of the Andigena variety (*Solanum tuberosum*), which is adapted to grow in the long daylight hours and cool temperatures of the southern summer. This Chilean potato is believed to have been exported to Spain in the 1500s, later reaching the rest of Europe and North America. The central and southern Chilean climate and agricultural conditions resemble those of Europe, and thus the Chilean potato adapted very well to Spain and to northern and eastern Europe. In Chile we call the potato *papa* which is the Quechua word for *Solanum tuberosum.*

Tomates a la Chilena
CHILEAN TOMATO AND ONION SALAD

Serves 6

This is the most common summer salad served in Chile. It is held in such high esteem that sometimes it is simply called *Ensalada Chilena* (Chilean Salad) as if no other salad is worth mentioning. This recipe is my own version of this all-time favorite. You can replace the aji pepper with jalapeño pepper.

- **3 large ripe tomatoes, peeled**
- **1 medium onion, peeled and julienned**
- **½ cup extra virgin olive oil**
- **1 medium lemon**
- **1 small fresh *aji*, seeded and finely chopped**
- **1 teaspoon fresh parsley, chopped**
- **1 teaspoon finely chopped fresh cilantro**
- **salt, to taste**
- **freshly ground black pepper, to taste**

Plunge the tomatoes into boiling water for 10 seconds. Remove them from the boiling water and immediately immerse them in cold water; then peel them. Slice the tomatoes into ¼-inch slices, and place them in a glass or ceramic serving plate. Wash the onion slices first in hot water and then in cold water; dry and place them over the tomato slices. Drizzle the oil and lemon juice and sprinkle the *aji*, herbs, salt, and pepper over the salad. If the tomatoes are too tart, eliminate the lemon juice. Marinate the salad for 15 minutes and serve at room temperature.

Porotitos Verdes
GREEN BEAN SALAD WITH LEMON HERB DRESSING

Serves 6

Green bean salad is a staple in Chilean summer menus and buffet meals. It is usually served with a tomato salad. I like to make green bean and tomato salad sandwiches as a summer snack, a meatless version of the famous *Chacarero* (Steak and Vegetable Sandwich, p. 261).

1	**pound baby green beans (*haricots vert*)**
½	**large onion, peeled and julienned**
⅓	**cup *Aliño para Ensaladas* (Lemon Herb Dressing, p. 203)**

If the beans are big, slice them lengthwise in the French style. Cook the beans in boiling water for about 6 minutes; they should be *al dente* and bright green. Do not overcook. Remove them from the hot water and immerse them in cold water to cool; drain and let them dry. Wash the onion under hot water to remove the sharpness. Mix the onions, beans, and *Aliño para Ensaladas* in a nonreactive bowl. Serve immediately because the acid from the *Aliño para Ensaladas* tends to discolor the bright green beans.

Ensalada de Choclo con Tomate
CORN AND TOMATO SALAD

Serves 4

I developed this salad during the hot summer months in Chapel Hill when tomatoes and corn, our New World crops, are abundant. The *Pebre* (Green Sauce) adds the Chilean touch to this salad.

2	**large ripe tomatoes, peeled and cubed**
1	**cup corn kennels, precooked**
1	**tablespoon *Pebre* (Green Sauce, p. 204)**

Mix all the ingredients together in a salad bowl about 30 minutes before serving so that they have time to marinate in the *Pebre*.

Ensalada de Lechuga
LETTUCE AND RED ONION SALAD

Serves 6

This humble salad is popular the world over. I include it here because my mother used to serve it for hot summer lunches as a first course. The romaine lettuce in Chile is known as *lechuga de Concón*. Concón is a seaside fishing village and summer vacation destination for people from Santiago. It is located just north of Valparaíso, where the Aconcagua river meets the ocean. In 1543, the conquistador Don Pedro de Valdivia ordered the construction of the first Chilean shipyard in this location. The shipyard and its one ship were promptly destroyed by the cacique Michimalongo, the chief of the local native tribe. The *lechuga de Concón* is grown in the fields behind the village along the banks of the river.

3   **heads young romaine lettuce**
1   **large red onion, peeled**
6   **tablespoons *Aliño para Ensaladas***
    (Lemon Herb Dressing, p. 203)
1   **pinch cilantro, finely chopped**

Remove and discard the outer leaves of the lettuce. Cut the leaves into ½-inch slices and discard the core. Wash them thoroughly in cold water to remove any dirt, then pat them dry. Slice the onion in rings and wash in hot water to remove the sharpness. Marinate the onion in the *Aliño para Ensaladas* for 30 minutes. Mix together the onions and lettuce with the cilantro and serve immediately.

Ensalada de Porotos
BEAN SALAD WITH LEMON HERB DRESSING

Serves 6

My mother serves a similar salad for lunch on hot summer days. The common bean (a lima bean) originated in the New World and was first cultivated about 7,000 years ago. The common bean has developed into literally hundreds of varieties, including the well-known navy, black, pinto, field, and kidney beans. *Porotos* (beans) have been cultivated in Chile for thousands of years. Some of the varieties common in Chile are *granados, burros*, and *pallares*. Fresh, ripe, summer beans are a real treat. In Chile you can buy them in the shell at the neighborhood farmer's market. The same salad can be prepared with fava beans or blackeyed peas. Other variations to this recipe include adding diced green and red peppers and using a mustard vinaigrette.

4 **cups fresh ripe beans, precooked**
½ **cup onion, peeled and diced**
½ **cup green onions, chopped**
½ **cup celery, finely diced**
½ **cup carrots, finely diced and blanched**
½ **cup plum tomatoes, peeled and diced**
⅓ **cup *Aliño para Ensaladas* (Lemon Herb Dressing, p. 203)**

Mix all the vegetables together in a glass or ceramic bowl, and marinate them in the *Aliño para Ensaladas* for at least 1 hour before serving.

Ensalada del Nuevo Mundo
NEW WORLD SALAD WITH GREEN SAUCE

Serves 6

I developed this salad as a variation on *Ensalada de Porotos* (Bean Salad with Lemon Herb Dressing, above), which my mother prepares using fresh ripe beans. The name comes from the New World ingredients: beans, corn, and peppers.

2 cups fresh ripe beans, precooked
½ cup red onion, peeled and diced
½ cup green onions, chopped
1 cup corn kernels, precooked
½ cup sweet green pepper, diced
½ cup sweet red pepper, diced
1 tablespoon *ají* or other hot pepper, finely diced (optional)
⅓ cup *Pebre* (Green Sauce, p. 204)

Mix all the ingredients together in a glass or ceramic bowl, and marinate them in the *Pebre* for at least 1 hour before serving.

Apio con Palta
AVOCADO AND CELERY SALAD

Serves 6

My mother used to serve this salad in the summer. *Palta* is a variety of avocado that grows in northern and central Chile. Quillota, my father's hometown, is famous for its avocado groves. *Paltas* have a smooth green or black skin, are very buttery, and taste fabulous. But avocados from California do very well in this recipe. This salad makes a fine complement to grilled meats, poultry, or fish.

10 stalks fresh celery
6 fresh green onions
3 large ripe avocados
⅓ cup *Aliño para Ensaladas* (Lemon Herb Dressing, p. 203)

Peel the celery stalks and be sure to remove the tough fibers in the outer side of the stalks. Cut the stalks into 2 pieces and cut strips into the pieces without going all the way through. Do the same to the green onions. Put the celery and onions in a bowl of cold water for at least 1 hour; this will make them curl. Peel the avocados, cut them into wedges, and add to them the *Aliño de Ensaladas*. Combine all the ingredients together in a glass or ceramic bowl, and marinate for 30 minutes.

Ensalada de Repollo y Zanahoria
CABBAGE AND CARROT SALAD

Serves 4

My aunt Emma Bascuñán served me this salad the last time I was at her home for lunch. It reminds me of the North American classic, coleslaw, but I am sure my dear aunt has never heard of such a thing. The ingredients are all in season during the winter months, so this is a nice fresh taste in a dull season.

- 1 **small cabbage**
- 3 **medium carrots, peeled and finely julienned**
- 3 **tablespoons extra virgin olive oil**
- 1 **medium lemon, juiced and peel grated**
- ½ **cup cilantro, finely chopped**
  freshly ground black pepper, to taste
  salt to taste

Separate and wash the cabbage leaves, and remove the thick ribs leaving only the tender part of the leaves. Roll the leaves together and cut very thin (⅛ inch) slices. Put the shredded cabbage in cold water for 30 minutes or more. Blanch the carrots in boiling water for just 1 minute and then immerse in cold water to stop the cooking. Mix all the ingredients together in a salad bowl and marinate for 30 minutes before serving.

Ensalada de Beterragas con Cebolla
BEET AND ONION SALAD

Serves 6

My mother has become very fond of this salad; during my last visit to Santiago she served it almost every day we had lunch together! It contributes a fresh taste in winter because its ingredients are all available at that time.

4   medium beets
1   large red onion, peeled and finely sliced in rings
3   tablespoons *Aliño para Ensaladas*
    (Lemon Herb Dressing, p. 203)

Wash the beets and cook them in boiling water for about 40 minutes or until tender. Let the beets cool to room temperature and then slice them into ¼-inch thickness. Wash the onion slices in hot water to remove the sharpness. Mix the ingredients together on a salad platter and let them marinate for about 30 minutes before serving.

Papas con Mayonesa
POTATO SALAD

Serves 6

This is a delicious way to prepare potatoes. It is a common salad in Chile, as well as in Europe and the United States. This is my own version with olive oil and cilantro. It can be served as a first course, and it also makes a good side dish with pork roast.

6   large potatoes
6   small spring onions, sliced
3   small pickled cucumbers, chopped
1   tablespoon *Mayonesa* (Mayonnaise, p. 205)
1   tablespoon *Mostaza* (Mustard Sauce, p. 208)
1   tablespoon olive oil
1   tablespoon fresh cilantro, chopped

Place potatoes in cold water, bring to a boil, and simmer for 20 to 30 minutes or until tender. Drain the potatoes, peel them, and cut them into 1-inch cubes. Mix the potatoes with the onions and pickles in a glass or ceramic bowl. In a separate bowl mix the *Mayonesa, Mostaza,* and oil. Add the dressing to the potatoes, mix well and garnish with cilantro. Serve warm or cold.

Ensalada de Arroz
RICE AND AVOCADO SALAD

Serves 8

This recipe is a variation on a salad from Isabel Allende Llona, friend of my youth, my former sister-in-law, and world-famous author. In the 1960s Isabel used to make a similar salad for summer outdoor lunches on Sundays. It can be served as a first course or as a side dish with a roast.

1½	cups converted long grain rice
1	package frozen peas
1	large ripe avocado
1	small lemon, juiced
¾	cup *Mayonesa* (Mayonnaise, p. 205)
2	large sweet red peppers, roasted
12	large stuffed green olives, sliced into circles
1	tablespoon olive oil
1	pinch fresh flat-leaf parsley, cilantro, or basil, chopped

1. Cook the rice in 3 cups of water for 20 minutes or until dry. Let the rice cool to room temperature.
2. Cook the peas in boiling water for 3 minutes and immediately strain and run cold water over them so that they stay bright green.
3. Peel and dice the avocado and toss it with the lemon juice.
4. Dice one of the red peppers and mix it with the rice, avocado, peas, *Mayonesa*, and all but a few of the sliced olives in a large glass or ceramic bowl.
5. Slice the other red pepper into strips.
6. Prepare an oiled ring mold or bread loaf mold lined with oiled parchment paper (avoid aluminum or cast iron molds). At the bottom of the mold arrange the strips of red peppers and reserved olive circle in a geometric pattern so that when you unmold there will be a decorative design on top of the rice.
7. Transfer the rice mixture to the mold, pressing down firmly to eliminate any air bubbles. Cover and refrigerate for at least 1 hour or overnight. Invert the mold onto a serving dish and decorate with the fresh herbs.

VERDURAS Y VARIOS
VEGETABLES AND SIDE DISHES

Tomates al Horno
BAKED STUFFED TOMATOES

Serves 6

There are many variations on the filling for these tomatoes, including some with seafood, chicken, or ham. This one is vegetarian and is an ideal summer side dish.

6	large ripe tomatoes
6	small plum tomatoes
2	large onions, peeled and finely chopped
1	large sweet green pepper, chopped
6	cloves garlic, peeled and chopped
½	cup fresh, flat-leaf parsley or cilantro, chopped
3	tablespoons olive oil
3	medium eggs
1	cup bread crumbs
1	cup Parmesan cheese, grated
	freshly ground black pepper, to taste
	salt, to taste

Preheat the oven to 375 degrees.

Cut off the tops of the large tomatoes and remove the pulp. Discard the seeds and chop the pulp. Peel, seed, and chop the plum tomatoes. Sauté the onions, pepper, garlic, and parsley in oil. Add the chopped tomato and sauté for another 10 minutes. Remove from the heat and pour the mixture into a bowl. Add the beaten eggs to the onion/tomato mixture. Add the bread crumbs and ½ cup of the cheese. Season with pepper and add salt to taste. Stuff the large tomatoes with the mixture and top with Parmesan cheese. Place in a buttered baking dish and bake for 30 minutes. Serve hot.

Tomaticán
TOMATO AND CORN STEW

Serves 6

I adapted this recipe from my Great-aunt Julia's cookbook. This recipe is a typical example of the Chilean *criolla* cuisine. The ingredients are mainly from the New World, and the name and preparation method suggest an ancient native origin. This can be served as a side dish with meat, chicken, or fish or as a vegetarian main course.

- 1 large onion, peeled and julienned
- 3 cloves garlic, peeled and chopped
- 2 tablespoons olive oil
- 3 large plum tomatoes, peeled and diced
  freshly ground black pepper, to taste
- 8 ounces fresh or frozen corn kernels
  salt, to taste
- 1 pinch fresh, flat-leaf parsley, chopped

In a large saucepan sauté the onion and garlic in hot oil. Add the tomatoes and pepper and cook covered for 5 minutes. Add the corn and cook for another 3 minutes. Add salt to taste, garnish with parsley, and serve hot.

Zapallitos Saltados
SAUTÉED ZUCCHINI OR SUMMER SQUASH

Serves 6

In the summer zucchinis are abundant in Chile. They are versatile and lend themselves to a wide range of preparations. This is one of the many side dish recipes for squash that I found in my mother's notebooks.

1   large onion, peeled and sliced
3   cloves garlic, peeled and chopped
2   tablespoons olive oil
1   pound zucchini or summer squash, sliced
1   pinch *Aliño* (Mixed Dried Herbs, pp. 206–207)
    freshly ground black pepper, to taste
    salt, to taste

In a large skillet heat the oil and sauté the onion and garlic in oil until soft. Add the squash, *Aliño*, and pepper. Cover and cook over low heat for 5 to 7 minutes. Add salt to taste and serve hot.

Guiso de Acelgas
SWISS CHARD STEW

Serves 6

Acelgas (Swiss chard) and *espinacas* (spinach) are common winter vegetables in Chile. They are used in many different dishes including omelets, stews, soups, and salads. This recipe is similar to the one in my mother's cookbook, and can be prepared with spinach, collard greens, or kale. You can also add chopped ham or bacon to the sautéed onions, which makes a heartier dish. Serve as a side dish with a meat main course.

6	cups Swiss chard leaves
2	tablespoons olive oil
1	medium onion, peeled and finely chopped
3	cloves garlic, peeled and finely chopped
1	cup carrot, grated
1	pinch fresh, flat-leaf parsley, chopped
	freshly ground black pepper to taste
¼	cup Parmesan cheese, grated

Wash the chard leaves thoroughly in cold water and remove the stems. Plunge in the leaves into boiling water for just 1 minute to wilt and soften them. Remove them from the hot water and immediately rinse with cold water. Squeeze the leaves to remove most of the water and chop them coarsely; set aside. In a large pan heat the oil and sauté the onions, garlic, and carrot. Add the chard, parsley, and pepper; mix well and cook over low heat for about 5 minutes, stirring occasionally. Serve hot, topped with cheese.

Guiso de Repollo Morado
RED CABBAGE AND APPLE STEW

Serves 6

Guiso de Repollo Morado is similar to some German recipes for cabbage and was probably brought to Chile by the German immigrants who settled in the Chilean south. It is traditionally served as a side dish with pork roasts such as *Chanchito Lechón* (Pork Baked in Milk, p. 154).

3	tablespoons olive oil
1	medium red cabbage, shredded
2	large sour apples, peeled and sliced
1	medium onion, julienned
½	cup red wine vinegar
1	tablespoon brown sugar
1	pinch nutmeg, freshly grated
	freshly ground black pepper, to taste
6	whole cloves
	salt, to taste

In an enameled or stainless steel pan, heat the oil and sauté the cabbage, apples, and onion for about 5 minutes. Add the other ingredients and cook covered over low heat for about 20 minutes or until tender. Check for needed salt and serve hot.

Guiso de Berengenas y Tomate
EGGPLANT AND TOMATO STEW

Serves 6

There are many recipes for preparing eggplants in Chilean cookbooks. This is my own variation on ratatouille. Eggplants are abundant in summer in Santiago. When they are young and tender, there is no need to salt them before cooking.

3	tablespoons olive oil
2	pounds eggplants, cubed
1	large onion, peeled and sliced
3	cloves garlic, peeled and chopped
1	pound plum tomatoes, peeled, seeded, and diced
2	leaves bay
1	pinch dried oregano
	freshly ground black pepper, to taste
	salt, to taste

In a saucepan heat the oil and sauté the eggplant until it is lightly brown. Add the onion and garlic and sauté until the onion is soft. Add the tomatoes, herbs, and pepper. Cover and simmer for about 30 minutes. Taste for needed salt and serve hot.

Serving Suggestion:
This side dish can also be served as a vegetarian main course.

Humitas en Olla
TAMALES IN STEWPOT

Serves 6

Corn stews like this one were prepared in Chile long before the arrival of the Spanish conquistadors. This version of *Humitas* is from my mother's cookbook. Prepare it if good, large corn leaves are not available for tamale pouches, or if you have leftover corn mix from a *Pastel de Choclo* (Corn and Beef Casserole, pp. 84–85). It is reminiscent of the North American grits, but more flavorful. This stew makes a lovely side dish for roasts such as *Asado Jugoso* (Marinated Juicy Roast Beef, p. 143).

6   **large corn ears**
2   **tablespoons olive oil**
1   **large onion, peeled and finely chopped**
1   **tablespoon *Ají de Color* or Spanish paprika**
    freshly ground black pepper, to taste
    ***Pasta de Ají* (Aji Paste, p. 207) to taste**
1   **pinch dried oregano, crushed**
½   **cup fresh basil, chopped**
    salt, to taste
3   **tablespoons butter, unsalted**
    milk as needed

Traditionally this dish is prepared by grating the corn, but you can also do it with some modern help. Cut the corn kernels from the cob and grind them in the food processor. In a saucepan heat the oil and sauté the onion. Add the paprika, pepper, *Pasta de Ají*, herbs, and salt to taste. Add the onion mixture to the corn and transfer to a heavy casserole. Cook slowly over low heat, stirring constantly, for about 20 minutes. Add some milk if the mixture is too thick. Finish the dish by stirring in the butter. Serve hot.

Variation:
Pour the cooked corn mixture into a buttered baking dish, cover with Parmesan cheese, and bake at 400 degrees for 30 minutes until golden brown.

Mote con Zapallo
HOMINY WITH PUMPKIN

Serves 6

Mote is a common ingredient in popular Chilean cuisine. It is a special type of whole corn kernel and is similar, though not identical, to hominy. This is one of many recipes that include *mote,* which together with pumpkin makes a nutritious meal, substantial enough to be served as a vegetarian main course. Both corn and pumpkin were ingredients available to the original inhabitants of Chile, and the mode of cooking is also ancient, so this may be a modified version of one of the recipes of the native peoples of Chile.

1   can white hominy, precooked
2   cups milk
1   large onion, peeled and finely chopped
3   cloves garlic, peeled and chopped
¼   cup olive oil
1   tablespoon *Ají de Color* or Spanish paprika
1   pinch *Aliño* (Mixed Dried Herbs, pp. 206–207)
3   cups pumpkin, cooked and puréed
½   cup Parmesan cheese, grated
    salt, to taste
    freshly ground black pepper, to taste

Cook the hominy in the milk until tender. Heat the oil in a frying pan and sauté the onion, garlic, and paprika. Add the onion mixture and *Aliño* to the hominy. Add the pumpkin and cook slowly until creamy, stirring constantly. Add the cheese and salt and pepper to taste. Serve hot.

Papas con Mote
POTATOES WITH HOMINY

Serves 8

Together with potatoes, *mote* makes another complete and nutritious vegetarian meal that can be served as a main course. Corn and potatoes were cultivated by the original inhabitants of Chile long before the arrival of the conquistadors. The ingredients and cooking technique suggest this dish has an ancient pre-Columbian origin. Fresh *ají,* or other hot pepper, is often added to the finished dish for extra spice.

10	medium potatoes, peeled, and quartered
1½	cups white hominy, precooked
	salt, to taste
3	tablespoons olive oil
1	large onion, peeled and finely chopped
1	medium sweet red pepper, diced
3	cloves garlic, chopped
2	tablespoons *Ají de Color* or Spanish paprika
1	tablespoon fresh, flat-leaf parsley, chopped

Cook the potatoes and hominy in boiling water for about 20 minutes; add salt to taste. There should be almost no water left; if there is, drain it off. In a frying pan heat the oil and sauté the onion, pepper, and garlic with the paprika. Add this mixture to the potato and hominy mixture. Garnish with parsley and serve hot.

Papitas Asadas
ROASTED POTATOES

Serves 4

Potatoes are a favorite side dish in my house. They are very nutritious, so I have found many ways to prepare them. This recipe was adapted from a Cordon Bleu recipe. It can be served as a side dish with a meat main course.

- 4 **large potatoes, peeled and thinly sliced**
- 4 **tablespoons olive oil**
  freshly ground black pepper, to taste
- 1 **pinch nutmeg, freshly grated**
  salt, to taste

Preheat the oven to 400 degrees.

Coat the potato slices with the olive oil. Oil a round baking pan. Arrange one layer of potato slices on the bottom of the pan. Sprinkle with pepper and nutmeg. Continue arranging potato layers with pepper, nutmeg, and salt to taste. Cover with oiled parchment paper and place an ovenproof dish on top. Put a weight on the dish to press down the potatoes. Cook over medium heat for 10 minutes. Uncover and transfer the pan to the oven for 30 minutes. Invert onto a serving dish for presentation. Serve hot.

Variation:

My mother's way of roasting potatoes is simpler:

- 4 **large potatoes, peeled and cut into 1-inch cubes**
- 4 **tablespoons olive oil**
  freshly ground black pepper, to taste
  salt, to taste

Preheat the oven to 400 degrees.

Coat the potato cubes with olive oil, sprinkle with pepper and salt and toss to mix well. Arrange the potato cubes in one layer in a shallow, ovenproof dish. Roast for about 50 minutes. Serve hot.

Papas Rellenas
POTATOES STUFFED WITH BEEF AND ONION

Serves 6 to 8

This recipe is a classic example of the Chilean *criolla* cuisine that I found in my mother's cookbook. It is one of my favorite ways to fix potatoes, perhaps because of the fond childhood memories it evokes. It has practically the same ingredients as *Pastel de Papas* (Potato and Beef Casserole, p. 86) but it is assembled and cooked in a different way.

2   cups *Pino* (Beef and Onion Stuffing, p. 150)
1   large egg, beaten
2   cups potatoes, precooked, peeled, and puréed
1   cup flour
1   tablespoon cream
    freshly ground black pepper, to taste
1   pinch nutmeg, freshly grated
1   cup vegetable oil
1   tablespoon confectioners sugar (optional)

Prepare the *Pino* the day before. The following day, mix the egg with the potatoes. To this mixture add the flour, cream, and seasonings; mix well. Take 1 tablespoon of the purée mixture in your floured hand, put 1 tablespoon of *Pino* in the center and enclose the *Pino* in the purée to form a ball in the shape of a potato. Sprinkle with flour, set in a floured dish, and continue making the stuffed potatoes. When they are all finished, heat the oil in a large frying pan. Fry the potatoes until golden brown on all sides. Serve hot, sprinkled with confectioners sugar.

Puré de Papas
MASHED BUTTERMILK POTATOES

Serves 4

In Chile, milk or cream would be used instead of buttermilk; this recipe is my own version of this classic. A variation of this recipe is *Puré Picante* (Spicy Mashed Potatoes, p. 180), which involves the addition of red hot *ají* sauce at the end.

- 4 **large potatoes**
- ½ **cup buttermilk, warmed**
- 1 **tablespoon olive oil**
  freshly ground black pepper, to taste
- 1 **pinch fresh, flat-leaf parsley, finely chopped**
  salt, to taste

Peel the potatoes and keep them in a bowl covered with water, to prevent oxidation and browning, until ready to cook. Boil the potatoes for 20 to 30 minutes until tender. Strain and purée. Add the warm buttermilk, oil, pepper, and parsley. Check for needed salt and serve hot.

Puré Picante
SPICY MASHED POTATOES

Serves 6

This recipe of my Great-aunt Leonie's is a variation on classic mashed potatoes. In Chile this is often served with pork dishes, such as *Chanchito Lechón* (Pork Baked in Milk, p. 154) For *Ají Picante* Sauce you can substitute a smooth hot chili sauce or a mixture of paprika and Tabasco sauce to taste.

- 3 **cups freshly prepared *Puré de Papas***
  (Mashed Buttermilk Potatoes, p. 180)
- 3 **tablespoons *Ají Picante* Sauce (hot red pepper sauce)**

Prepare the potato purée. Just before serving, stir in the *Ají Picante* and mix well. The result should be a pink purée. Serve hot.

Papitas Duquesa
LITTLE FRIED POTATO BALLS

Serves 6

This is one of the dozens of recipes for potatoes as a side dish. This recipe is from my mother's cookbook. She also calls this recipe *Papitas Soufflé,* but in restaurants they are called *Duquesa.* I don't know what the *Duquesa* (duchess) refers to, since titles of nobility were abolished in Chile after independence in 1810. Perhaps this recipe was developed in Europe, where titles of nobility are still used. This is an excellent side dish to accompany meats and it's a good way to use leftover *Puré de Papas.*

6   tablespoons *Puré de Papas* (p.180)
1   pinch nutmeg, freshly ground
      freshly ground black pepper, to taste
2   large eggs, separated
1   pinch cream of tartar
½   cup flour
½   cup frying oil

Season the *puré* with nutmeg and black pepper. Beat the egg yolks, add to the *puré,* and mix well. Whip the egg whites with the cream of tartar into stiff peaks and then fold them into the potato purée. Form small balls of the mixture about the size of walnuts. Coat the balls with flour and deep fry them until golden brown.

Puré de Porotos Picantes
SPICY BEAN PURÉE

Serves 6

Puré de Porotos Picantes is probably very ancient, as similar recipes are found in many of the cuisines of pre-Columbian America. This is an excellent way to serve winter beans as a side dish. Serve with beef or pork roasts.

2   cups precooked beans
2   tablespoons olive oil
1   medium onion, finely chopped
3   cloves garlic, minced
1   tablespoon *Pasta de Ají* (Aji Paste, p. 207)

Purée the beans and pass them through a sieve to obtain a smooth consistency and eliminate the skins. In a saucepan heat the oil and sauté the onions and garlic. Add *Pasta de Ají*. Add the onion mixture to the bean purée. Stir well and serve hot.

Arroz Graneado
PILAF

Serves 6

My mother prepares this dish with just onions and carrots, but I like to add mushrooms and peppers. More elaborate pilaf recipes are also common. The kind and amount of vegetables added depends on availability; this recipe is very flexible. Converted rice is not usually available in Chile, but I have become accustomed to it in the United States and use it in all my rice recipes.

1	tablespoon olive oil
1	medium onion, peeled and chopped
1	large carrot, sliced
1	stalk celery, sliced
1	medium sweet red pepper, chopped
1	medium sweet green pepper, chopped
6	cloves garlic, peeled and chopped
½	cup mushrooms, chopped
1	cup converted rice
2	cups *Caldo* (Beef Stock, p. 66) or *Consomé de Ave* (Chicken Stock, p. 64), boiling
1	pinch *Aliño* (Mixed Dried Herbs, pp. 206–207) freshly ground black pepper, to taste
1	bay leaf fresh or dried salt, to taste

In a saucepan, heat the oil and sauté the vegetables. Add the rice and sauté until it changes color. Add the boiling *Caldo* and the rest of the ingredients. Bring to a boil, lower the heat to a slow simmer, cover and cook for 20 minutes or until dry. Check for needed salt and serve hot.

Arroz Amoldado
MOLDED RICE

Serves 4

This recipe comes from the collection of my aunt Ema Neale Silva de Welt. In Chile, the most common type of rice used is the short grain *Valenciano*. In the United States, I have become accustomed to converted long grain rice and have adapted all my rice recipes to this type, as it works very well. You can substitute dried porcini or shiitake mushrooms for the Chilean dried mushrooms. Dried mushrooms must be soaked before use. They often contain some sand that collects at the bottom of the soaking bowl, but it is easy to discard. The soaking liquid is very flavorful and should not be discarded. Add it to the rice instead of water or save it for another dish. This is an elegant side dish for the main course.

2	tablespoons olive oil
1	cup converted rice
2	cups *Consomé de Ave* (Chicken Stock, p. 64), boiling
½	cup dried Chilean mushrooms, soaked, rinsed, and chopped
3	large red pimentos, roasted and chopped
1	pinch *Aliño* (Mixed Dried Herbs, pp. 206–207) freshly ground black pepper, to taste
2	tablespoons butter, unsalted
⅓	cup Parmesan cheese, grated

Heat the oil in a saucepan and sauté the rice. Add the boiling *Consomé,* mushrooms, pimentos, *Aliño,* and black pepper. Cover and simmer the rice for 20 minutes. Add butter and cheese and mix well. Butter 4 small, single-portion molds and place a piece of parchment paper in the bottom of each, buttering the parchment paper as well. Transfer the rice mixture to the buttered molds and keep them warm in a bain-marie in the oven until ready to unmold. Serve warm.

Fideos con Salsa de Nueces
NOODLES WITH WALNUT SAUCE

Serves 4

I think that pasta was introduced to Chile only recently by the newer European immigrants. But noodles are certainly very popular, often served *a la Italiana* (Italian style) with *Salsa de Tomates* (Tomato Sauce, pp. 212–213) and Parmesan cheese. This excellent preparation from my aunt Ema Neale Silva de Welt can be a side dish for beef or pork roast.

1	cup crustless white bread cubes
1	cup milk
1	cup walnuts, chopped
	freshly ground black pepper, to taste
1	pinch fresh flat-leaf parsley, chopped
1	pinch dried oregano, crushed
2	tablespoon olive oil
1	tablespoon butter, unsalted
3	cloves garlic, peeled and chopped
1	pound angel hair noodles
	salt, to taste
½	cup Parmesan cheese, grated

Preheat the oven to 375 degrees.

Soak the bread in the milk. In the food processor, grind the walnuts. Add the pepper, parsley, oregano, oil, butter, garlic, and soaked bread. Blend until well mixed and smooth. Cook the noodles al dente. Warm the sauce over low heat and check for salt. Add the sauce to the noodles, place the mixture in an oiled baking dish, top with the cheese, and bake until golden brown on top. Serve hot.

PANES

BREADS

Most urban centers in Chile have easily accessible local bakeries that provide the daily breads. Only in rural homes do people bake their own breads such as Pan Amasado (Kneaded Yeast Bread, p. 190). Here I have collected a few recipes of the most common Chilean breads. All of them use wheat flour. The ancient potato and corn flour breads have all but disappeared in Chile, although in isolated areas in the south the Mapuches still bake a potato bread called Milcao (Mapuche Potato Bread, p. 194).

Bread has long been regarded as basic nourishment and essential for human survival. It is a symbol that represents the fundamentals of life. Some time ago I came across a superb poem written by the Chilean poet Pablo Neruda entitled "Ode to Bread." It starts like this:

Bread,
you rise
from flour,
water
and fire.

Dense or light,
flattened or round,
you duplicate
the mother's womb,
and earth's twice-yearly
swelling.

Later it continues:

O bread familiar to every mouth,
we will not
kneel before you:
men
do not
implore
unclear gods
or obscure angels:
we will make our own bread
out of sea and soil,
we will plant wheat
on our earth and planets,
bread for every mouth,
for every person,
our daily bread.
Because we plant its seed
and grow it
not for one man
but for all,
there will be enough:
there will be bread
for all the peoples of the earth.

Toward the end it goes like this:

Then
life itself
will have the shape of bread,
deep and simple,
immeasurable and pure.
Every living thing
will have its share
of soil and life,
and the bread we eat each morning,
everyone's daily bread
will be hallowed
and sacred,
because it will have been won
by the longest and costliest
of human struggles.

In 1971 Pablo Neruda was awarded the Nobel Prize for literature for this and other fabulous, moving poems about simple things such as love, freedom, and the beauty of our native land. Neruda was born in Parral, Chile, in 1904 and traveled the world while conceiving what I consider to be the most splendid poems ever written, including this one for the baker in me. He died in Santiago during the worst month of my life: September 1973, during which time the long-held Chilean democracy was crushed in a bloody military coup. The tragic events of that month, my democratic convictions, and my loyalty to the constitution forced me to resign my faculty position at the University of Santiago and begin my long and painful journey into exile.

Pan Amasado
KNEADED YEAST BREAD

Serves 8

Pan Amasado is a Chilean country bread, usually baked in a traditional, outdoor, cone-shaped adobe oven fueled with wood or coal. The bread is advertised on country roads by flying a white flag at the driveway entrance to the farmer's home. On an early spring day, when the *aromos* (mimosa trees) are blooming and the air is filled with their perfume, you can take a drive from Santiago up into the Maipo Canyon. There, along the road, you will find *Pan Amasado* advertised with the white flag. You may also find along that road another type of country bread called *Tortillas de Rescoldo* (flat country bread also baked in the adobe oven). This is a wonderful tradition, and modern Chileans prize those who know the art and craft of making this bread. This recipe is my adaptation for modern kitchens.

3 ½	**cups all-purpose flour**
1	**teaspoon salt**
½	**cup shortening, softened**
2	**packages yeast**

1. Preheat the oven to 375 degrees.
2. In the electric mixer bowl with a dough hook, mix the flour and salt for 15 seconds and scrape the walls of the bowl.
3. Add the softened shortening and knead slowly for one minute.
4. Dissolve the yeast in ¾ cup of warm water (110°F or 45°C) and add it to the bowl.
5. Knead for another two minutes until the dough is soft and smooth. Adjust water or flour as necessary.
6. Allow the dough to rest and rise in an oiled bowl, covered with plastic wrap, for 1 to 3 hours in a warm place (about 85°F) until it doubles in volume.
7. Punch down and knead the dough until soft and smooth.
8. Form small rolls about 3 inches in diameter and ½ inch tall, with a very smooth top surface. Place on a non-stick baking sheet, prick the tops with a fork, and allow to rest for 30 minutes.
9. Bake the rolls for about 20 minutes or until lightly browned.

Hallullas
SPECIAL BREAD

Serves 24

In my mother's neighborhood bakery, *hallullas* are called *Pan Especial* or "special bread" to distinguish them from *Marraquetas* (pp. 193–194) which is the ordinary everyday bread. My mother buys *hallullas* every day for teatime, and what is left over gets toasted for dinner. This recipe is my home version of this bakery jewel.

2½ cups milk
6 ounces butter
1½ teaspoons baking powder
2 teaspoons baker's yeast
8 cups all purpose flour

Preheat the oven to 400 degrees.

Mix all the ingredients to form a loose, soft dough. Knead the dough until it becomes spongy. Roll the dough to a thickness of one inch. Cut the dough into 3-inch squares. Make horizontal cuts along the edges of the squares so that the dough will separate and rise straight up while baking. Bake the squares for 15 to 20 minutes. Serve warm.

Pan Rápido
QUICK BREAD

Serves 8

This recipe is a variation of a recipe in my mother's cookbook. It is a fast recipe because it does not use yeast, which requires time to rise. Instead, it uses baking powder. It can be used as a breakfast or tea bread by replacing the flavorings and cheese with raisins and honey, see *Pan Rápido Dulce* (p. 25).

1	cup buttermilk or milk
½	cup corn oil
1	tablespoon *Pasta de Albahaca* (Basil Paste, pp. 204–205)
2	cups all purpose flour
2	tablespoons baking powder
1	pinch nutmeg, freshly grated
1	tablespoon Parmesan cheese, grated

Preheat the oven to 450 degrees.

In a bowl mix the buttermilk, oil, and *Pasta de Albahaca* first. In a separate bowl, mix the flour, baking powder, nutmeg, and cheese. Add the buttermilk mixture to the flour mixture and stir with a wooden spoon, do not overmix. The batter should be relatively thin. Pour the batter into a greased and floured loaf pan and bake for 5 minutes. Reduce the heat to 325 degrees and bake another 35 minutes or until done. Check with a toothpick for doneness. Let the bread cool on a rack before slicing.

Marraquetas
FRENCH STYLE ROLLS

Serves 6

This recipe is my adaptation of a classic bread recipe for the modern home kitchen. *Marraquetas* is the most common bread found in the Chilean bakeries. Sometimes it is called *Pan Frances* (French bread) because of the type of dough, but the distinctive shape is uniquely Chilean. My mother's local bakery starts baking at about 4 A.M. every morning, and by breakfast time the smell of freshly baked bread fills the air. By midafternoon, fresh sweet breads are for sale in time for *Onces* (afternoon tea). *Marraquetas* are served for breakfast, lunch, and dinner. This recipe, and several others in this chapter, call for bread flour instead of all-purpose flour. Bread flour has a much higher protein content, in the form of gluten, than does regular flour. The gluten polymerizes during kneading and thus helps make the dough more elastic so it can rise as the yeast ferments.

1	package yeast
1	teaspoon sugar
1	teaspoon salt
3	cups bread flour
2	tablespoons corn oil
1	small egg white

1. In a bowl combine 1 cup warm water, yeast, and sugar and set aside.
2. Mix the salt and flour in an electric mixer with a dough hook for about 15 seconds. Slowly add the yeast mixture to the flour until a stiff dough is formed.
3. Knead the dough for about 2 minutes or until it is no longer sticky (add extra flour if necessary) and the dough clings to the hook and pulls away from the mixing bowl.
4. Let the dough rest for 5 minutes and then knead for another 2 minutes.
5. Put the dough in an oiled bowl; turn it over so that the oil coats the top. Cover the bowl and let the dough rise in a warm place for 1 to 3 hours to double its volume.
6. Deflate the dough and separate it into 6 portions. Shape oblong rolls and place them on a baking sheet. With a knife, make a trench across the middle of each roll to form two attached loaves. Brush the rolls with egg white. At this time they can be stored in the refrigerator until ready to bake.
7. Place the rolls in a cold oven; place a pan of water on the bottom shelf; set the oven to 425 degrees and bake the rolls for 25 to 30 minutes. Serve hot.

Milcao
MAPUCHE POTATO BREAD

Serves 8

Milcao is a very ancient bread recipe of Mapuche origin. It is prepared in the southern regions where the Arauco nation is more prevalent. This type of bread was probably prepared in pre-Columbian times using the native wild potato. Some recipes indicate that the dough should be baked in an oven, as in this recipe, but others call for frying the dough like potato pancakes, and it can also be steamed while preparing *Curanto* (Mapuche Seafood Casserole, pp. 118–119). An added flavor is *chicharrones* or cracklings prepared by rendering the fat out of cubed bacon.

5   **pounds cooked potatoes, peeled and mashed**
5   **pounds potatoes, grated and strained**
¼   **pound lard, at room temperature**
⅓   **pound cracklings**

Preheat the oven to 400 degrees.

Mix the mashed and grated potatoes with the lard to make a soft dough. In your hands form 2 to 3 inch rolls with a few cracklings inside. Place the rolls in an oiled pan and bake for about 20 to 30 minutes until golden brown on top. Serve hot.

Pan Candeal
BAKERY-STYLE YEAST BREAD
Serves 8

Pan Candeal is common in Chilean bakeries. The tradition of baking this type of bread comes from Spain.

         3¾ **cups bread flour**
          1 **package yeast**
          1 **teaspoon salt**
          1 **whole egg white**

1. Mix 3 cups of flour with 1 cup of warm water in the bowl of an electric mixer with a dough hook.
2. Knead the dough for 1 minute, adjust the flour or water for a smooth texture. Let the dough rest for 5 minutes.
3. Knead the dough for another minute and transfer it to another bowl. Dust the dough with flour, cover the bowl with foil and set aside in the pantry for two days. The dough should expand a little and have a slightly sour aroma.
4. Dissolve the yeast in ¼ cup of warm water and add ¾ cup of flour. Mix this dough with the dough you prepared two days before.
5. Knead the dough for 1 to 2 minutes, incorporating the salt and adjusting the flour and water to end up with a smooth, elastic dough.
6. Place the dough in an oiled bowl, cover the bowl, and let the dough rise for 2 to 3 hours. Punch the dough down and knead for another minute or two.
7. Form the rolls with smooth tops, place in a baking sheet, and let them rest for another hour.
8. Preheat the oven to 425 degrees and bake the rolls with a water pan in the bottom of the oven. After 5 minutes remove the water pan, brush the tops of the rolls with egg white, and bake another 15 minutes until golden brown. Serve hot or cold.

Pan Fino
FINE DINNER ROLLS

Serves 8

These rolls are served on special occasions; they are richer than the more common *Marraquetas* (French Style Rolls, pp. 193–194).

½	**cup warm milk**
¼	**cup unsalted butter, melted**
2	**packages dry yeast**
2	**teaspoons sugar**
3½	**cups bread flour**
1	**teaspoon salt**
1	**small egg white**

1. In a bowl combine ½ cup warm water, milk, and butter.
2. Mix the sugar and yeast, add it to the liquid mixture, and set aside.
3. Mix the flour and salt in an electric mixer with a dough hook. Slowly add the liquid mixture to the flour and knead for 2 minutes.
4. Put the dough in an oiled bowl and let it rise in a warm place for 2 hours. Deflate the dough and knead it for 2 minutes.
5. Separate the dough into 8 portions. Form the rolls and let them rise for another hour or so. Coat the tops with egg white, being careful not to deflate the rolls.
6. Preheat the oven to 400 degrees and bake the rolls for 20 minutes, or until golden brown on top. Serve hot.

Pan Favorito
FAVORITE HERB BREAD

Serves 12

This is my variation of *Pan Fino* (p. 196). I have simplified the original recipe and replaced milk with buttermilk and butter with oil. Buttermilk is not available in Chile, but I have learned to use and appreciate it in the southern United States.

2	packages dry yeast
2	teaspoons sugar
4	cups bread flour, approximately
1	teaspoon salt
¼	cup olive oil
1	cup buttermilk
	black pepper, freshly ground (optional) to taste
1	tablespoon *Aliño* (Mixed dried herbs, p. 205, optional)

1. In the electric mixer bowl, dissolve the yeast and sugar in ½ cup warm water using the mixing paddle. Add 2 cups of flour and the salt and oil and mix gently. Slowly add the rest of the flour alternating with the buttermilk.

2. Add the optional flavorings at this time. Adjust the amount of flour to produce a dough that is not sticky. Change to the dough hook and knead the dough for about 5 minutes.

3. Transfer the dough to an oiled bowl and cover; put the bowl in a warm place to rise for about 1½ hours.

4. Punch down the dough and put it back into the mixer bowl to knead for another 2 minutes.

5. Take out the dough and divide it to form 4 elongated loaves. Put the loaves on a baking sheet. At this point the dough can be stored in the refrigerator until ready to cook. Let the dough rise again at room temperature for about 1 hour until it doubles in volume.

6. Preheat the oven to 400 degrees and bake the loaves for about 30 minutes. Remove the bread from the oven and let it cool on a rack. You can also use this recipe to make small rolls, which cook much faster (about 15 minutes at 375 degrees).

ALIÑOS, SALSAS, ADOBOS, Y BETUNES

DRESSINGS, SAUCES, MARINADES, AND BATTERS

This section deals with condiments, flavorings, and enhancements. Seasonings and *Aliños,* such as garlic, cilantro, parsley, oregano, sweet basil, thyme, mint, lemon balm, and spices, such as black pepper, cumin, saffron, vanilla, cinnamon, cloves, and nutmeg are frequently used in Chilean recipes for strong, or milder and subtler tastes. But the singular most important condiment in Chilean cuisine is, without a doubt, the *ají* pepper.

Hot and sweet peppers are believed to have originated in the Andean region that is now Bolivia and were used for flavoring as much as 7,000 years ago. They spread throughout America in ancient times, and the Spaniards encountered them in Mexico. From Mexico the Spanish galleons took them to the Philippine Islands, and from there they spread to Southeast Asia, India, and the rest of the world. Today many pepper varieties are cultivated around the globe; they are one of the New World's most important flavor gifts. The Andean pepper most common in Chile is called *ají,* of which there are hot and sweet types. *Ají* is the species *Capsicum Baccatum,* but the Chilean *ají* is a distinct variety. The hot Chilean *ají* grows from white flowers to a yellow, elongated form, about 3 inches long. It is usually used at the yellow stage of maturation. When ripe it turns bright red and is so hot that it is inedible, at least to my taste. It is often eaten fresh in salads or added to provide heat to casseroles, stews, and meats. When my mother eats *ají* she always carefully removes all the seeds and the white ribs that hold the seeds; in spite of these precautions *ajíes* can still be quite hot. Some people who boast about their ability to tolerate the heat, like to rub the whole *ají* between their hands before cutting it open. This causes the capsaicin (the chemical that causes the burning sensation) in the seeds to invade the entire fruit, making it far hotter. I am not one of those people. Fresh *ajíes* are in season only during the summer, so in winter people use a preserved form called *Pasta de Ají* (Aji Paste, p. 207). A commercial preparation called *Ají Picante* is also widely available year-round in the markets throughout Chile; I am surprised that this product has not yet been marketed in the United States. Although the Chilean *ají* peppers have a unique and distinctive flavor, you can substitute any other hot pepper in these recipes.

Another typical Chilean flavoring is *Ají de Color,* or Chilean paprika powder, which is made from the sweet *pimiento porrón.* In the Central Market in Santiago, you can find *Ají de Color* in large (kilogram) bags, and it is not uncommon to see home cooks buy it in these large quantities since it is used in almost every *criolla* cuisine recipe. It is often fried together with onions and garlic and added to stews and casseroles. It is one of the crucial ingredients of *Pino* (Beef and Onion Filling, p. 150), the meat filling for *Empanadas Chilenas* (Chilean Meat Turnovers, pp.52–53), *Pastel de Choclo* (Corn and Beef Casserole, pp. 84–85) and *Papas Rellenas* (Potatoes Stuffed with Beef and Onion, p. 179). If you can't get *Ají de Color,* use Spanish paprika.

Chilean mushrooms are another original flavoring in Chilean cuisine. Chilean mushrooms are called *Callampas* and while fresh they resemble Portobello mushrooms. In the dried form, they are sometimes confused with several European mushrooms, but they are a distinct species. Chilean mushrooms are usually used dried, and in that way they produce a very concentrated, wonderful flavor. When soaked in warm water, Chilean mushrooms yield an intensely flavorful liquor that can be used on its own, as in *Salsa de Callampas* (Mushroom Sauce, p. 213), or with the swollen mushrooms for a bolder flavor. Dried Chilean mushrooms often carry some sand, so after soaking you must remove it by straining the liquor through cheesecloth.

I have organized this chapter by placing recipes used primarily in cold dishes, salad dressings, and associated recipes at the beginning. They are followed by recipes used mostly, but not exclusively, in hot dishes such as casseroles and stews. Next you will find recipes for meat marinades; sauces; and, finally, the frying batters. Most of the recipes can be used in a variety of preparations, so feel free to explore and experiment!

Vinagre Aromático
FLAVORED VINEGAR

This is a variation on my mother's flavored liqueurs (pp. 276–277). The basic principle of the preparation is that you extract the essential flavors of the additive by slowly refluxing the solvent (in this case the vinegar) over a long period of time. With exposure to the sun, the solvent gently heats up and stirs, thus aiding the extraction process. You can use this flavored vinegar in salad dressings and marinades.

> 1   pint white wine vinegar
> 1   cup fresh dill, tarragon, or *ají*

Pour vinegar into a clean glass jar and add the flavoring agent (one or both herbs, the hot pepper, or both). Close the jar and set it on a sunny windowsill. Allow 2 months for the vinegar to extract flavors before using.

Variation:
Other popular flavoring ingredients include raspberries, basil, ginger, and orange or lemon peel. To prepare use the same quantities.

Aceite Aromático
GINGER AND GARLIC–FLAVORED OIL

This is a way to preserve fresh ginger and is ideal for stir-fried dishes. Ginger is not a common ingredient in Chilean recipes, but recent influences from the Orient have prompted some cooks to experiment with it. I first came across Oriental cuisine while studying for my doctorate in London. Although I was only a graduate student on a scholarship, I was lucky enough to be invited to some of the famous Chinese restaurants in London. These new flavors and cooking techniques were immediately appealing to me. Since then, I have made an effort to learn more about the cuisines of the Orient. The principle of flavoring oil is the same as the one used to flavor vinegar (p. 202) and liqueurs (pp. 276–277). Other flavoring agents can be garlic, herbs, and orange or lemon peel. Use this oil in salads or for sautéing vegetables, meats, or fish.

2 cups corn oil
1 head garlic, peeled
1 tablespoon fresh ginger, peeled and chopped

Put all the ingredients in a clean glass bottle. Close the bottle and set it on a sunny window sill. Let the extraction process take place for at least one month.

Aliño para Ensaladas
LEMON HERB DRESSING

My mother would call this dressing *vinagreta*. Olive oil and lemon juice are the only salad dressings my mother ever used. I sometimes use a flavored vinegar instead of lemon juice.

1 tablespoon lemon juice, freshly squeezed
3 tablespoons extra virgin olive oil
   freshly ground black pepper, to taste
1 pinch fresh, flat-leaf parsley or cilantro, chopped
   salt, to taste

In a glass or ceramic bowl, use a whisk to mix all the ingredients and beat well to form an emulsion. Pour over salad 15 minutes before serving to allow for marinating.

Variation:
For a more sweet-and-sour taste, add 1 teaspoon of *Mostaza* (Mustard Sauce, p. 208) and 1 tablespoon honey (optional) and reduce the lemon juice to 1½ teaspoons. I call this Mustard Vinaigrette.

Pebre

SALSA VERDE, GREEN SAUCE

This is a classic condiment of the Chilean *criolla* cuisine. It is called either *Pebre* or *Salsa Verde*. Preparations served with this sauce are called *al Pil Pil,* such as *Locos al Pil Pil* (Chilean Abalones with Green Sauce, p. 46). It is usually served over seafood or cold meats. I also like it with salads or on toasted bread.

> 1   **bunch fresh, flat-leaf parsley**
> 1   **bunch fresh cilantro**
> 1   **small onion**
> 3   **cloves garlic**
> 2   **tablespoons extra virgin olive oil**
> 2   **tablespoons lemon juice**
> 1   **teaspoon *Pasta de Ají* (Aji Paste, p. 207)**
>   **freshly ground black pepper, to taste**
>   **salt, to taste**

Finely chop the parsley, cilantro, onion, and garlic. This chopping can be done in the food processor but be careful not to purée. Mix the ingredients in a glass or ceramic container. Add the oil, lemon juice, *Pasta de Ají,* and pepper, salt to taste. Mix well and marinate for at least 1 hour before using, or even better, overnight.

Pasta de Albahaca

BASIL PASTE

This is a variation of one of my mother's recipes. Basil is one of the many herbs the Spaniards brought to Chile. It is often used in dishes of the Chilean *criolla* cuisine. This paste is a convenient way to preserve and store fresh basil; if you freeze it it remains flavorful for up to a year. It is used in marinades and casseroles and is mixed with cheese to spread on bread. You can prepare a similar paste with any other fresh herb or mixed herbs such as parsley and cilantro. This paste can also be used as a flavoring in salad dressings.

4   cups fresh basil leaves
1   cup olive oil

Wash and dry the basil leaves, remove the stems. Transfer the leaves to the food processor and add the olive oil. Chop the mixture to a paste consistency; it does not need to be very smooth. Store in glass jars in the freezer.

Mayonesa
HOMEMADE MAYONNAISE

I learned this recipe from my mother. Mayonnaise is a very common dressing and garnish in Chilean salads and cold first courses. This recipe calls for raw eggs, so if you suspect salmonella contamination in the eggs in your area, avoid this recipe or any other recipe that requires raw or soft-cooked eggs. This recipe can be used as a salad dressing or over meat, fish, or bread.

2   large egg yolks
¾   cup olive oil
1   medium lemon
3   cloves garlic, peeled and crushed
    salt, to taste
    freshly ground black pepper, to taste

In a small, deep, glass or ceramic bowl, mix the 2 yolks with one beater of an electric hand mixer at slow speed. Very slowly add the oil and continue to mix at slow speed. After all the oil is added, the mixture should be thick and a light yellow color. Add the lemon juice, garlic, salt, and pepper and stir. Store in the refrigerator in a glass or ceramic container.

Variation:
I make a "lighter" modification of my mother's recipe with 1 whole egg instead of the yolks, ¼ cup extra virgin olive oil, ½ cup canola oil, ½ a medium lemon and the same amount of garlic, salt, and pepper. It still tastes like homemade mayonnaise!

Mayonesa sin Yemas
YOLKLESS MAYONNAISE

I developed this mayonnaise as a no-cholesterol alternative to the traditional home-made *Mayonesa* (p. 205). This recipe works because there is enough emulsifier in the egg white and mustard to produce the oil suspension characteristic of mayonnaise. Serve as a dressing like any other mayonnaise.

> 1 large egg white
> 1 teaspoon yellow mustard
> 1 clove garlic
> ½ cup olive oil
> 1 teaspoon lemon juice
>   freshly ground black pepper, to taste
>   salt, to taste

In the food processor, mix the egg white, mustard, and garlic until completely homogenized. With the processor running, add the oil very slowly until all of it is incorporated. Add the lemon juice and the pepper and salt to taste. Refrigerate.

Aliño
MIXED DRIED HERBS

The word *aliño* means seasoning, flavoring, or dressing. In Chile, it is common to season fish, meats, and poultry with an *Aliño*. Following is my own preferred mixture of herbs for flavoring in sauces, stews, casseroles, soups, and marinades. It is also a convenient way to store dried herbs and have them ready to use. The kind of ingredients and their amounts change according to availability. If you have a little space in your backyard, use it to grow your own herbs; or grow them in containers in a sunny window or on a balcony. That way, you will always have fresh herbs without having to pay a fortune for them. Growing herbs is easy; these plants are actually ancient weeds and they are not usually bothered by insects or other pests.

1   tablespoon dried thyme (*tomillo*) leaves
1   tablespoon dried rosemary (*romero*) leaves
1   tablespoon dried oregano leaves
1   tablespoon dried sage (*salvia*) leaves
1   tablespoon dried mint (*menta*) leaves (optional)
1   tablespoon dried lemon balm (*toronjil*) leaves (optional)
1   tablespoon dried marjoram (*mejorana*) leaves (optional)
1   tablespoon dried tarragon (*estragón*) leaves (optional)

Mix and crush the herbs. Store them in an airtight, dry container in the dark.

Pasta de Ají
AJI PASTE

My mother used to make a paste similar to this one, and she taught me to wear gloves when handling hot peppers. This recipe is a convenient way to preserve and store *ají* peppers. This paste adds flavor and heat to any dish, and it is always used as an optional flavoring. Royce grows *ají* and other hot peppers in our vegetable garden every summer; he likes to make sandwiches of cheese and this paste. You can use this paste to add heat and flavor to soups, stews, casseroles, breads, marinades, and so on.

12   whole *ají* peppers
1   cup olive oil

Open up the peppers and remove the seeds very carefully (they are very hot, so use gloves). You can also remove the whitish vein where the seeds are attached to the shell. Chop the peppers coarsely. Transfer to the food processor, add the oil and chop to form the paste. A smooth consistency is not necessary. Store in glass jars in the freezer.

Rábano Picante
HORSERADISH SAUCE

This recipe is a variation on pickled radishes, from my mother's cookbook. Horseradish is not common in Chile, but little red radishes are. Royce grows our own horseradish in a halved whiskey barrel in the vegetable garden. Serve with red meats, salmon, or poultry.

2 **cups horseradish roots, cut into small pieces**
¼ **cup white vinegar**
½ **cup olive oil**

Clean the horseradish roots with a coarse, hard brush until they are white on the outside. Cut them into smaller pieces. Purée them in the food processor together with the vinegar and oil. Store in the refrigerator in a clean glass, ceramic, or plastic container.

Mostaza
MUSTARD SAUCE

Mustard in Chile is usually purchased ready-made. It was popularized by German immigrants and is used with pork dishes, sausages, and ham or cold cuts sandwiches. You can substitute Dijon mustard, but somehow your own mustard has a special, different flavor. Use over meats, in sandwiches, and in marinades.

1 **cup mustard seeds**
½ **cup white wine vinegar**
½ **cup dry white wine**
½ **teaspoon salt**
1 **tablespoon honey**

Mix all the ingredients together in the blender and grind until the seeds are crushed; its up to you how smooth you want the mustardto be. Age the mixture in a sealed glass or ceramic container at room temperature for at least 4 weeks and then store in the refrigerator.

Adobo de Mostaza
MUSTARD MARINADE

This is an adaptation of a popular Chilean meat marinade. Use on pork or beef roasts.

2   tablespoons *Mostaza* (Mustard Sauce p. 208)
6   cloves garlic, peeled and chopped
3   tablespoons olive oil
1   tablespoon *Vinegre Aromatico*
1   teaspoon cumin powder
    freshly ground black pepper, to taste
1   teaspoon *Ají de Color* or Spanish paprika

Mix all the ingredients in a glass or ceramic bowl. Spread them over the meat. Marinate the meat for at least 2 hours, preferably overnight.

Adobo para Asado
ROAST MARINADE

The word *adobo* in Spanish means either seasoning or marinade, whether it is meant to flavor the meat, tenderize it, or both. I developed this recipe for oven roasting and grilling. This marinade works well with roast beef, roast pork, and roast lamb. In Chile, some kind of *adobo* is always used to marinate before roasting.

3   tablespoons honey
2   tablespoons *Mostaza* (Mustard Sauce, p. 208)
6   cloves garlic, peeled and crushed
1   tablespoon *Pasta de Albahaca* (Basil Paste, pp. 204–205)
1   tablespoon *Pasta de Ají* (Aji Paste, p. 207)
1   tablespoon soy sauce
1   tablespoon Worcestershire sauce
½   cup *Vinagre Aromatico* (Flavored Vinegar, p. 202)
½   cup port, sherry, or cabernet savignon

Mix the ingredients thoroughly and cover the meat with it. For best results, put the meat in a large plastic bag, pour in the marinade, and close the bag leaving in as little air as possible. Marinate the meat for at least 1 hour, preferably overnight, turning the bag over occasionally.

Adobo para Costillar
RACK OF PORK MARINADE

This marinade is used primarily with pork. *Costillar de Chancho* (Rack of Pork Roast) is a favorite of Chileans. In Chile, you can usually buy the pork already marinated from the neighborhood butcher or at the specialized *pulperia* in the *Mercado Central* (the downtown food market). Sometimes the rib bones are removed, the meat marinated, rolled with flavorings and vegetables inside, and tied up. This is called *Arrollado* (Spicy Rolled Pork Roast, p. 155) and can be roasted in the oven or outdoors over charcoal.

2 tablespoons *Ají de Color* or Spanish paprika
  red *ají* powder or hot chili powder to taste
1 tablespoon black pepper, freshly ground
1 teaspoon cumin powder
1 tablespoon dry oregano leaves, crushed or ground
1 head garlic, peeled and finely chopped
3 tablespoons olive oil
2 tablespoons red wine vinegar

In a blender mix together all the ingredients to form a paste; adjust the amounts of oil and vinegar if necessary. Apply to all sides of the pork roast and marinate the meat for at least 2 hours or overnight.

Adobo para Parrillada
BARBECUE SAUCE

This recipe was inspired by my dear friend Emily Spiegle, who lived in Chapel Hill for a few years, and now lives in Cambridge, Massachusetts. The use of honey and tomato purée in marinades is not common in Chile; this resembles a North Carolina barbecue sauce. This sauce can be used to marinate chicken and pork.

   freshly ground black pepper, to taste
½ cup honey
3 tablespoons tomato purée

1   tablespoon Worcestershire sauce
1   tablespoon soy sauce
1   tablespoon *Pasta de Albahaca* (Basil Paste, pp. 204–205)
1   tablespoon *Pasta de Ají* (Aji Paste, p. 207)
½   cup red wine or port
½   cup *Vinagre Aromatico* (Flavored Vinegar, p. 202)

In a glass or ceramic container, mix all the ingredients together thoroughly and spread on the meat. Marinate the meat for a few hours before baking over charcoal.

Salsa Blanca
WHITE SAUCE

My aunt Emma Bascuñán showed me how to make this sauce, which is similar to the traditional béchamel, but much thicker. It is used like a roux to thicken other sauces. Chilean cooks use it in many dishes, especially those including chicken and fish.

½   cup butter
½   cup flour
1   cup milk
    white pepper, ground, to taste
1   pinch nutmeg, freshly grated
    salt, to taste
1   pinch fresh parsley, chopped

Melt the butter in a saucepan. Add the flour and stir and cook for 5 minutes over low heat. Slowly add the milk, stirring with a whisk. Bring to a boil, add the pepper, nutmeg, salt, and parsley. You can store the sauce in the refrigerator for a few days until ready to use.

Salsa de Palta
AVOCADO SAUCE

This sauce is from my mother's cookbook. The amount of milk to be added depends upon the desired thickness of the sauce. If you want a thick sauce, add only half the milk specified. You can spice it up with *Pasta de Ají* (p. 207) or add herbs such as cilantro or basil. You may serve this sauce warm over pork or seafood. Avocados are native to the northern regions of Chile and are very popular in Chile, so many recipes that include avocados have been developed there. However, this is one of the very few that call for a warm preparation. High temperatures increase the avocado's oxidation which causes them to turn gray, so don't cook the avocado and avoid aluminum or cast iron containers.

> 3 tablespoons *Salsa Blanca* (White Sauce, p. 211)
> 1 cup milk
> 1 medium ripe avocado
> 1 small lemon
>   salt, to taste

Dissolve the *Salsa Blanca* in the milk. Bring it to a boil and keep it warm. Peel and purée the avocado (in a blender or by hand with a fork) and add the lemon juice. Warm the sauce and just before serving add the avocado purée and salt to taste. Serve immediately.

Salsa de Tomates
TOMATO SAUCE

My mother used to prepare a similar sauce with Chilean dried mushrooms and use it over noodles like an Italian red sauce. I like to add soy sauce to this preparation. You can use this sauce with pastas, *Pan de Carne* (Meat Loaf with Chicken Livers and Pistachio Nuts, pp. 148–149), vegetable casseroles, and so on. Fresh mushrooms can be replaced by dried Chilean mushrooms for a richer flavor.

> 2 tablespoons olive oil
> 1 medium onion, peeled and chopped
> 1 cup fresh mushrooms, chopped
> 1 large red pepper, chopped

2 pounds very ripe plum tomatoes, peeled and chopped
3 bay leaves
2 tablespoons dried oregano, crushed
½ cup red wine
1 tablespoon soy sauce
6 cloves garlic, peeled and chopped
freshly ground black pepper, to taste

In saucepan heat the oil and sauté the onions until soft and translucent. Add the mushrooms and pepper and sauté them until soft. Add the tomatoes and all the other ingredients except the garlic and black pepper. Bring to a boil and simmer slowly for about 1 hour or until reduced to the desired thickness. At the last minute add the chopped garlic and freshly ground pepper.

Salsa de Callampas
MUSHROOM SAUCE

This recipe was inspired by a Cordon Bleu recipe. I like to serve it with *Asado Jugoso* (Marinated Juicy Roast Beef, p. 143). I use the dried Chilean mushrooms that have a wonderful smoky, woodsy flavor. If you can't find them, you can use other dried mushrooms; each type of mushroom will impart its own flavor to the sauce. Be sure to remove the sand that sometimes accumulates in the bottom of the soaking bowl.

1 quart *Caldo* (Beef Stock, p. 66)
½ cup port
1 cup dried mushrooms
1 cup *Adobo para Asado* (Roast Marinade, p. 209)
3 tablespoons olive oil
1 cup fresh mushrooms, sliced

Reduce the *Caldo* to about 1 cup. Add the port and simmer for about 5 minutes to evaporate the alcohol. Soak the dried mushrooms in 1 cup of hot water for half an hour. Filter the mushroom juice and add it to the sauce; save the mushrooms for another dish. Add the *Adobo para Asado* and simmer for 10 minutes. In a sauté pan, heat the oil and sauté the fresh mushrooms. Add the mushrooms to the sauce and keep warm until ready to serve

Salsa de Carne
MEAT-BASED SAUCE

I learned this sauce from my mother. I use it over noodles with Parmesan cheese on top or in vegetable dishes.

- 3 tablespoons olive oil
- 1 pound lean ground beef
- 1 medium onion, peeled and chopped
- 3 cloves garlic, peeled and chopped
- 3 cups *Salsa de Tomates* (Tomato Sauce, pp. 212–213)

In a frying pan heat the oil and sauté the meat until brown. Add the onions and garlic and sauté until soft. Add the *Salsa de Tomates* and simmer for about 1 hour.

Betún de Cervesa
BEER BATTER

In Chile, egg and flour batters are used for frying fish, especially conger eel steaks, and vegetables, such as eggplant slices. This recipe is from my husband, Royce, who uses batters for frying vegetables, as is typical in the southern United States. The leftover batter makes wonderful pancakes to serve with the meal. Use the batter for frying eggplant, green tomatoes, peppers, and so on.

- 1 cup all-purpose flour
- 1 teaspoon baking powder
- 1 large egg
- 2 teaspoons corn oil
- 1 cup beer (preferably dark)

Mix the flour and baking powder thoroughly. Beat the egg with the oil and add it to the flour. Add the beer and stir to smooth the mixture. Dip the vegetables or fish into the batter and fry in a small amount of oil.

Betún para Frituras
FRYING BATTER

This recipe, from my Great-aunt Julia's cookbook, is a traditional Chilean batter rooted in the Spanish tradition of frying fish and vegetables. This batter can be used for frying fish such as conger eel steaks and whole small fish, such as trout or *pejerreyes*. It also can be used to fry sliced vegetables such as eggplant, zucchini, and summer squash.

1 medium egg
¾ cup all-purpose flour
½ cup milk
   freshly ground black pepper, to taste
1 pinch *Aliño* (Mixed Dried Herbs, pp. 206–207)

In a bowl combine all the ingredients and mix well. Dip the pieces to be fried into the batter to coat on all sides. Place in a hot, oiled frying pan.

POSTRES Y ONCES

DESSERTS AND
TEATIME DELIGHTS

Chileans are known for their sweet tooth. This is certainly true of my mother. Her specialties are custards and pastries and I discovered that the majority of the recipes in her personal cookbooks were, in fact, sweets. When sugar is optional, such as in *Pastel de Choclo* (Corn and Beef Casserole, pp.84–85) or *Empanaditas Fritas* (Little Fried Turnovers, p. 38) she makes it mandatory. And when no one is looking, I have even caught her adding sugar to her wine! Of course my mother also has a sweet and loving nature. I, on the other hand, find it appealing to have just a small sweet something at the end of a meal.

Sugar cane, which originated in the South Pacific, is now the most common source of sugar around the world. It was first extracted as raw sugar in India, and it was brought to Europe by the Moors when they invaded Spain in the eighth century A.D. There are so many fine foods for which we have to thank the Moors! Sugar was a luxury until the 18th century, when the sugar cane plantations in the Caribbean began large-scale production and export. Sugar was unknown in the pre-Columbian New World; instead, honey and tree sap syrups were used as sweetening agents. Sugar cane is not cultivated in Chile; sugar is refined from the locally grown sugar beet.

Chancaca (Molasses Syrup, p. 242), *Miel de Palma* (Palm syrup), and honey are the most common sweet syrups used in Chile. The *Chancaca de Paita* from Quillota is the most famous and delicious of these syrups. *Chancaca* is also the name for the solid form of raw sugar used in preparing the syrup. *Miel de Palma* is extracted from the *Palmera Chilena* (*Jubaea chilensis,* the Chilean palm tree) in the same manner as maple syrup is obtained in North America. The native Chilean honey is produced by the *aveja caupolicana,* the native black honeybee, which gathers pollen from Andean wildflowers to produce its exceptionally flavored honey. The Chilean bee has the distinction of being named after Caupolicán, the renowned Mapuche leader who courageously fought the conquistadors and died under brutal torture at the hands of the invaders. Caupolicán is honored today with a larger-than-life bronze statue that adorns the top of the Santa Lucia hill (the Huelén hill in Mapuche) in downtown Santiago.

Desserts or *postres* in Chile usually consist of a custard or pudding such as *Leche Asada* (Flan, p. 232) or *Maicena con Leche* (Cornstarch Pudding, p. 235). We often serve fruits, either fresh or preserved, such as *Chirimoya Alegre* (Merry Chirimoya, pp. 220–221) and *Papayas en Almibar* (Papayas in Syrup, p. 222) after a meal, never pastries or tortes, which are reserved for *Onces.*

Onces is a small meal served at about 5 P.M. Its origin is obscure. I have heard that during colonial times, there was a break in the working day at 11 (which in Spanish is *once*) in the morning. Later, this break was moved to the afternoon, but the name persisted, and thus we have *Onces* at 5 P.M.

Pastries and tortes, such as *Alfajores* (Chilean Pastries with Caramel Spread, p. 238) and *Torta de Lúcuma* (Lucuma Torte, p. 259), are served at *Onces.* The pastries are accompanied by beverages such as *Té con Leche* (Tea and Milk, p. 19) or *Café Helado* (Iced Coffee, p. 278) in the summer. If you plan for an elaborate affair such as a birthday party at teatime, you can add to the menu small sandwiches, cheeses, ham, sweet breads, and preserves. Some people prefer a snack or sandwich for *Onces,* so I have added a few classic Chilean sandwiches, such as *Churrasco* (Marinated Steak Sandwich, pp. 260–261) and *Barros Garpa* (Ham and Cheese Sandwich, p. 263).

My childhood birthday parties were always celebrated at *Onces*. Sometimes this was at home, and other times in a fancy downtown tearoom. When celebrated at home, my mother would hire a temporary pastry cook to make *Pasteles Chilenos* (Chilean Pastries), such as *Alfajores* and *Empolvados* (Dusted Pastries with Caramel Spread, pp. 238 and 239) by the dozens. My aunt Erika would bring her fabulous *Cujens,* and I would invite all my schoolmates and cousins, including Aunt Erika's children, Alex, Rudy, and Karen. When I was a teenager, my father arranged for a very special treat. For my fifteenth birthday, he took me and my boarding school classmates to the Goyescas, an elegant and famous restaurant and tearoom in downtown Santiago. The entertainment for the afternoon party was none other than the rock-and-roll teenage idol Ricky Nelson, who was touring South America at the time. With a front row table, I had one of the most memorable birthday parties at *Onces*. Unfortunately, the Goyescas, like so many other things, is no longer there.

Chirimoya Alegre
MERRY CHIRIMOYA

Serves 4

My mother prepares this dessert when *chirimoyas* are in season. *Chirimoya* (*Annona cherimola*) also known as *cherimoya* or custard apple, derives its name from the Quechua name *chirimuya*. It is the Chilean national fruit, and its trees are native to the warm valleys north of Santiago. *Chirimoya* is regarded as a premium fruit, "the pearl of the Andes." Mark Twain once called it "deliciousness itself"! The fruit is 4 to 6 inches in diameter and covered with a green skin. The flesh is creamy and white; has a custardlike texture, and is juicy, sweet, and delectable. It has several, easy-to-remove, ¼-inch black seeds. Its unique flavor is a subtle blend of papaya, pineapple, and banana. A mixture of these fruits can be used as a substitute. *Chirimoyas* are now commercially grown in Southern California, and are available in West Coast markets and by mail order throughout the United States.

1   large fresh, ripe *chirimoya*
1   large sweet Valencia orange
1   tablespoon Grand Marnier

Peel the fruit, remove the seeds, and cut the *chirimoya,* or its substitutes, into 1-inch cubes. Squeeze the orange and add the juice to the cubes. Mix in the Grand Marnier and let it rest for 15 minutes in the refrigerator. Serve in cool fruit glasses.

Substitution:
Replace 1 *chirimoya* with ½ cup of cubed papaya, ½ cup of cubed banana, and ⅓ cup of cubed pineapple.

Variation:
Other fruits that can be prepared in the *Alegre* style include *tunas,* or prickly pears, which are very popular in Chile. Another excellent substitute is a mixture of strawberries and raspberries, but of course, the taste will be quite different.

Mote con Huesillos
HOMINY WITH DRIED PEACHES

Serves 6

Mote is a special type of corn kernels used in Chile long before the arrival of the Spanish conquistadors. The corn kernels are cooked whole and become soft and chewy. The best approximation I can think of is hominy. *Duraznos* is the Spanish name for fresh peaches, but in Chile, dried ones are called *huesillos,* which literally means "little bones." This can be either a dessert or a summer snack, and it is always served cold. Before ice cream was common, *Mote con Huesillos* was sold in the streets of Santiago on hot summer days. Legend has it that in 1814–1817, the famous Revolutionary War hero Manuel Rodriguez would disguise himself as Ño Goyo, an old shabby peasant, selling *Mote con Huesillos* in the streets of Santiago. He would place himself with his dilapidated cart near Government House where he would watch and listen to the comings and goings of government officials. Thus, he gathered vital information for the revolutionary cause, all the while hiding from the royalist police who had placed a price on his head. Today, *Mote con Huesillos* is frequently offered in restaurants. My mother prepares the *huesillos* without the *mote,* which is an excellent winter dessert.

8   **ounces dried peaches**
1   **cup sugar**
2   **cups white hominy, precooked**

Boil the peaches in 4 cups of water with the sugar for 30 minutes; let them cool to room temperature. Add the *mote,* stir, and refrigerate. Serve cold in glasses, as a dessert or a refreshing snack in the summer.

Papayas en Almibar
PAPAYAS IN SYRUP

Serves 6

My mother prepares many fruits *en almibar*, including pears, apples, peaches, cherries, and apricots. But papayas are my favorites. Papayas are five-sided yellow fruits, 6 to 8 inches long, with small round seeds. The Chilean papaya is smaller than its tropical cousin, tolerant of cold weather, and very fragrant. It also contains the papain enzyme, which is a meat tenderizer. It is grown principally in northern Chile, down to about La Serena. This is one of the many delicious ways of preparing papayas.

> 6 **large fresh ripe papayas**
> 2 **cups sugar (equal to fruit weight)**

Wash and soak the papayas in water for about 2 hours or until they puff up; this makes them easier to peel. Peel them, slice them into quarters, and remove the seeds. Save the seeds and peels for *Miel de Papaya* (p. 244). Simmer the fruit in about 6 cups of water for 5 minutes. Remove the fruit and add the sugar to the water, bring to a boil, and reduce to make a syrup. Return the fruit to the syrup and simmer for about 1 hour or until soft. Store in sterile glass containers for 3 days before eating so that the sugar has time to penetrate the fruit. If you want *Papayas Confitadas* (Candied Papayas), which are very popular in Chile, after a week take the papayas out of the syrup and dry them in the sun.

Serving Suggestion:
Serve topped with whipped cream.

Pepino Dulce en Almibar
SWEET PEPINO IN SYRUP

Serves 6

Pepino or *Pepino Dulce* (*Solanum muricatum*) is an egg-shaped fruit about 5 inches long. The skin is yellow with purple streaks; the flesh is sweet, juicy, and pink and tastes like melon. *Pepino dulce* can be eaten raw and is fabulously refreshing on a hot summer day. The Quechua name for *pepino* is *cachun* and its Aimará name is *kachuma*. In Chile *pepino dulce* is grown principally in the Longotoma Valley, near La Ligua north of Santiago. It is currently available in the United States by mail order. This recipe from my aunt Emma Bascuñán is a good way to savor this delicious fruit.

6 large fresh *pepinos*
2 cups sugar (equal to fruit weight)

Peel the *pepinos* and cut them into quarters lengthwise. Remove and discard the seeds. Simmer the fruit in about 6 cups of water and sugar for 15 to 20 minutes or until tender. Refrigerate and serve cold.

Substitution:
Cantaloupe can be substituted for *pepinos*.

Peras en Vino Tinto
PEARS IN RED WINE

Serves 6

This dessert is common in Chile and Spain, and is also known as *Peritas Borrachas* (Drunken Little Pears). I adapted it from a Cordon Bleu recipe.

½ cup sugar
1 bottle red wine such as cabernet
1 pinch lemon rind, grated
6 whole cloves
6 large ripe pears
1 tablespoon cornstarch, dissolved in 1 teaspoon of water

In a nonreactive saucepan, dissolve the sugar in the wine, add the lemon rind and cloves, and bring to a boil. Peel the pears and core them with an apple corer. Put the pears into the wine mixture and poach them until tender, 20 to 30 minutes. Remove the pears to a serving dish. Discard the lemon peel and cloves. Reduce the liquid by half, add the cornstarch, and stir to thicken into a syrup. Pour the syrup over the pears, and serve cold.

Serving Suggestion:
Serve the pears with whipped cream or vanilla ice cream.

Turrón de Vino
WINE MERINGUE

Serves 10

This dessert, from my mother's cookbook, is of Spanish origin, and is now considered part of the Chilean *criolla* cuisine. You can add a dollop of whipped cream on top for that extra something.

1	cup sugar
1 ½	cups red wine, such as cabernet
6	large egg whites
1	pinch cream of tartar
2	teaspoons vanilla extract
1	cup walnuts or almonds, chopped

Dissolve the sugar in the wine, bring to a boil, and simmer until you obtain a syrupy consistency and the volume is reduced by about half. Beat the egg whites with the cream of tartar to form stiff peaks. Put the beaten egg whites over a bain-marie. Slowly add the hot wine syrup, beating constantly until it is fully incorporated and the egg whites are cooked. Add the vanilla. Remove from the heat and continue to beat over ice until cool. Add the chopped walnuts and serve cool in wine glasses.

Note:

When whipping egg whites, I recommend using a copper bowl, as this will increase the volume and stability of the meringue.

Espuma de Frambuesas
RASPBERRY FOAM

Serves 8

I found similar recipes for this in my mother's great-aunts' cookbooks. This is tradition-ally prepared with chirimoyas or *lúcumas,* but raspberries or strawberries can be used instead. Don't use raw pineapple or papaya; the enzyme in these fruits, papain, will prevent the gelatin from setting. Fresh raspberries can be used for garnish.

1 cup *Salsa de Frambuesas* (Raspberry Sauce, p. 243)
1 cup sugar
1 teaspoon corn syrup
1 package unflavored gelatin (¼ ounce)
4 large egg whites
1 pinch cream of tartar
1 cup fresh raspberries

Prepare the *Salsa de Frambuesas.* Dissolve the sugar and corn syrup in 5 table-spoons of water and bring to a boil. Simmer until the sugar mixture becomes a syrup (*almibar*) and forms a hair when poured from a spoon (*almibar de pelo*). Dissolve the gelatin according to the package instructions. Whip the egg whites with the cream of tartar into stiff peaks. When whipping egg whites, it is recommended that you use a copper bowl to increase the volume and stability of the meringue. Slowly add the hot syrup to the whites and continue to whip until cold. Fold in the gelatin and the fruit sauce. Pour into a mold or individual glasses and store in the refrigerator for at least 4 hours until set. To unmold, warm the outside of the mold for a few sec-onds in hot water.

Bavarois de Frutas
BAVARIAN FRUIT CUSTARD

Serves 12

Bavarois (also called *Bávaro*) refers to a German (Bavarian) dessert that has been adapted and widely used in Chile. I adapted this recipe from one in my Great-aunt Julia's cookbook. Similar recipes appear in my mother's, and Great-aunt Leonie's cookbooks. You can use fruits such as berries, apricots, bananas, peaches, oranges, apples, chestnuts, chirimoyas, and *lúcumas*, but not raw pineapple or papaya.

1½	packages unflavored gelatin
¼	cup Grand Marnier
1½	cups *Crema Pastelera* (Pastry Cream, p. 246)
2	cups seasonal fresh or frozen fruits, puréed
½	cup whipping cream, chilled
5	large egg whites
1	pinch cream of tartar
1	cup confectioner's sugar

1. Soak the gelatin in the Grand Marnier for a few minutes. Place over a bain-marie until it dissolves, and keep warm until ready to use.
2. Combine the *Crema Pastelera* with the fruit purée.
3. Whip the cream until it begins to stiffen and fold it into the fruit mixture.
4. Add 1 tablespoon of fruit mixture to the dissolved gelatin and mix, then pour this mixture back into the fruit mixture.
5. Whip the egg whites with the cream of tartar to form stiff peaks and slowly add the confectioner's sugar. When whipping egg whites, it is recommended to use a copper bowl to increase the volume and stability of the meringue.
6. Fold the meringue into the fruit mixture.
7. Pour the *Bavarois* into parfait glasses or a ring mold and put in the refrigerator for at least 4 hours.
8. Unmold if necessary by dipping the mold into hot water for a few seconds; do not let hot water get into the dessert. Transfer the dessert to a serving dish.

Serving Suggestion:
Serve cold with some whole or sliced fruits for decoration.

Budín Porteño
BREAD PUDDING

Serves 8

This recipe is from my Great-aunt Julia who married an Irishman, Guillermo (William) Neale. This recipe is a modified English bread pudding. And its name is connected to England in a way as well. *Porteño* refers to its origin in the Port of Valparaíso, which received many English immigrants. Furthermore, in early colonial times, Valparaíso was often attacked by buccaneers and pirates trying to break the Spanish trade monopoly. Among them was the infamous Francis Drake (Sir Francis to some), who, as people in Valparaíso still remember, raided the port city in 1577 and stole the treasured gold relics from the Iglesia de la Matriz church. When Royce and I visited the Federico Santa Maria Technical University perched on the cliffs above Valparaíso bay, we toured the beautiful campus overlooking a gloriously blue Pacific ocean. On a prominent edge of the cliff, surrounded by an ancient stone wall, were the old canons that used to defend the port against outlaws like Drake.

2	cups sugar
1	pound white bread
4	cups milk
4	medium eggs, beaten
1	cup raisins
1	cup walnuts, chopped
1	teaspoon lemon rind, grated
1	pinch cinnamon powder
1	pinch nutmeg, freshly grated

1. Preheat the oven to 375 degrees.
2. Melt 1 cup of the sugar and let it caramelize, but do not burn. For more details see the recipe on page 23.
3. Pour the hot caramel into a ring baking mold, swirl it around to coat the sides, and let it cool and solidify.
4. Soak the bread in 2 cups of the milk.
5. Mix the rest of the milk and the sugar with the beaten eggs.
6. Add the egg mixture and the raisins, walnuts, lemon rind, cinnamon, and nutmeg to the bread.
7. Pour the mixture into the prepared mold.

8. Bake the pudding in a bain-marie for 45 minutes. Allow to cool.
9. After it is completely cooled, unmold onto a serving dish so that the caramel is on top.

Delicia de Manzanas
APPLE DELIGHT

Serves 6

This recipe appears in my mother's cookbook simply as *Postre de Manzanas* (Apple Dessert). A similar dessert also appears in my Great-aunt Julia's cookbook although the apples are not grated but sliced. You can serve this dessert either warm or cold.

4	medium apples, peeled and grated
3	large separated eggs
1	can sweetened condensed milk
1	tablespoon baking powder
½	cup walnuts, chopped
1	pinch cream of tartar
½	cup confectioner's sugar

Preheat the oven to 375 degrees.

Peel, core, and grate the apples. In the food processor, mix the apples, egg yolks, milk, baking powder, and walnuts. Pour the mixture into a buttered baking dish and bake for 40 minutes. Beat the egg whites with the cream of tartar to form stiff peaks and add the sugar. When the apples are done, spread the egg whites on top and put under the broiler for 60 seconds to brown. Serve cold.

Budín de Manzanas
APPLE PUDDING

Serves 8

Apples, pears, and oranges were brought to Chile from Europe and have all become popular winter fruits. This recipe is one of the many apple desserts in my Great-aunt Julia's cookbook. This dessert can be served warm or cold.

1	**cup sugar**
3	**large eggs**
14	**ounces sweetened condensed milk**
12	**ounces evaporated skim milk**
1	**pinch orange peel, grated**
1	**teaspoon vanilla extract**
9	**slices white bread**
½	**cup golden raisins**
2	**large apples, peeled, cored, and sliced**

1. Preheat the oven to 350 degrees.
2. Prepare a caramel by placing the granulated sugar in a small shallow metal pan; some cooks add water to the pan, but I do not. Heat the pan until the sugar melts, stir a little to melt evenly. The melted sugar will begin changing color and caramelize very quickly. Be careful not to burn it.
3. Pour the caramel into a tall baking or pudding mold; set aside and let the caramel cool and solidify.
4. In the blender, mix the eggs, milks, orange peel, and vanilla.
5. Cut the bread into triangles and arrange one layer of bread over the caramel, overlapping the slices to create a decorative pattern. Follow with a layer of apples, sprinkle on some raisins, and pour in some of the egg mixture. Continue layering and finish with a layer of bread. Press down with your hands to eliminate air.
6. Bake in a bain-marie for 45 minutes or until golden on top. Allow to cool, unmold, and serve cold.

Manzanas Asadas
ROASTED APPLES

Serves 6

As a child I learned to prepare this popular Chilean dessert in home economics class. It can be served warm or cold and is always scrumptious.

6   large apples
1   can sweetened condensed milk

Preheat the oven to 350 degrees.

Core the apples and peel the top half. Stand the apples in a buttered baking dish and fill them with milk. Bake them for 45 minutes or until golden brown on top.

Huevo Mol
EGG YOLK CANDY

Serves 6

This wonderfully rich dessert is known in Spain as *Yemas.* In Chile it is also known as *Huevo Molle,* and it is used as a candy or as filling for *Alfajores* (Chilean Pastries with Caramel Spread, p. 238), *Empolvados* (Dusted Pastries with Caramel Spread, p. 239), and other Chilean pastries.

5   large egg yolks
2   cups sugar
1   teaspoon corn syrup

Beat the yolks until they turn pale yellow. Make *Almibar de Pelo* (syrup to the hair state) by boiling the sugar, corn syrup, and ¼ cup of water until a hair is formed when you pour the syrup from a spoon. Pour the syrup over the yolks, beating vigorously with a whisk. Cook the mixture carefully over a bain-marie for a few minutes until thickened; keep the heat very low to avoid ending up with scrambled eggs. Pour the smooth cream over a piece of buttered parchment paper on a cookie tray. Spread it in a ½-inch layer and allow it to cool. Sprinkle with confectioner's sugar and cut into cubes. For a filling use it while still warm.

Huevos Falsos
FALSE EGGS

Serves 6

This is another common Chilean dessert my mother used to prepare, and it was a childhood favorite of mine. As the name implies, you pretend to serve sunny-side-up fried eggs on the dessert plate. For a lighter version you can replace the cream with meringue.

2 cups *Crema Chantilly* (Cream and Meringue Blend, p.247)
1 can peach halves, drained

Place 4 tablespoons of *Crema Chantilly* on a flat dessert plate. Place one half peach, round side up, over the cream. Serve cold.

Leche Asada
FLAN

Serves 8

This recipe is from my mother's cookbook. Flan is a custard of Spanish origin and is well known in the Spanish-speaking world. The numerous variations include additions of cream, cheese, coconut, and chestnuts. This version is the basic custard, and I have a weakness for it. You can serve this dessert with fresh fruits such as strawberries or raspberries as a garnish.

1½ cup sugar
6 large eggs
4 cups milk
1 tablespoon vanilla extract

Preheat the oven to 350 degrees.

Melt 1 cup sugar in a saucepan until it caramelizes to golden brown (see p. 230 for details on preparing caramel). Quickly pour the caramel into 8 small cups and let it cool. In the blender, mix the eggs with the milk, vanilla, and remaining sugar. Pour the mixture over the caramel in the cups. Put the cups in a bain-marie, with a kitchen towel in the bottom, and bake for 40 minutes. Serve at room temperature.

Leche Nevada
SNOWED MILK

Serves 4

This is my mother's recipe, and another childhood favorite. The origin of this very common Chilean dessert is probably Germany. You can serve it cold or warm.

4	**large eggs, separated**
1	**pinch cream of tartar**
1¼	**cups sugar**
4	**cups milk**
1	**vanilla bean, or ½ teaspoon vanilla extract**

1. Whip the egg whites and cream of tartar into stiff peaks; add ½ cup of the sugar and mix well. When whipping egg whites it is recommended that you use a copper bowl to increase the volume and stability of the meringue.
2. Boil the milk with the vanilla and remaining sugar.
3. While the milk is slowly simmering, spoon the egg whites into the milk. Don't crowd the spoonfuls, four at a time is about right. Cook the meringue balls on all sides by turning them slowly. They are cooked when they look shiny and firm; it takes about 4 minutes.
4. With a large slotted spoon, remove the cooked meringues to a serving dish and continue to cook the rest of the meringue.
5. When you are finished, remove the milk from the heat.
6. Beat the egg yolks to mix well; pour a few tablespoons of the hot milk over the yolks and stir, then pour the yolk mixture back into the hot milk, stirring vigorously with a whisk.
7. Return the milk to low heat to cook the yolk, about 5 minutes. The custard is ready when it coats the back of a spoon. Be sure not to overcook and scramble the yolks.
8. Pour the custard around the egg white balls and let it cool. Serve cold in individual plates.

Camotillos
SWEET POTATO CANDY

Serves 20

This is my mother's recipe for this typical *Dulce Chileno* (Chilean Sweet), one of the many Chilean *criolla* cuisine recipes for sweet potatoes. *Camotes* (sweet potatoes) are native to the New World and were cultivated in Chile long before the arrival of the Spanish. The word *camote* derives from the Aztec word *camotli*, and the conquistadors first found them in Mexico. *Camotes* were imported to Spain and Europe on Columbus's first voyage.

Camotes are well adapted to the Chilean climate and are very popular, especially in winter. The Chilean sweet potato is golden yellow inside, while the sweet potato available in the United States is more of a pumpkin color, but the flavors are similar. *Camotes* are very high in sugar (up to 6 percent), and the sugar content increases with storage because they contain the enzymes that convert starch to sugar. Serve *Camotillos* as a winter dessert.

2 **pounds sweet potatoes**
3 **cups sugar**
1 **teaspoon corn syrup**
1 **teaspoon vanilla extract**
1 **teaspoon cinnamon powder**

1. Preheat the oven to 325 degrees.
2. Cook unpeeled, whole sweet potatoes in simmering water for 30 to 40 minutes (time depends on the size of the root) until tender.
3. Peel the cooked potatoes, purée them in the food processor for several minutes until very smooth.
4. Prepare a syrup with the sugar, corn syrup, and ⅓ cup of water. Add the syrup to the potato purée.
5. Cook the mixture for a few minutes until it doesn't stick to the bottom of the pan (it should be fairly thick).
6. Allow the purée to cool to room temperature and add the vanilla and cinnamon.
7. Use 2 tablespoons to form the *Camotillos* into oval-shaped *knoedels* or dumplings and drop them onto buttered parchment paper on a baking sheet. Traditionally the *Camotillos* are egg-shaped with a ridge on top, but you can mold them to any shape.
8. Bake the *Camotillos* for about 45 minutes until they dry. Let them cool overnight before serving.

Maicena con Leche
CORNSTARCH PUDDING

Serves 6

I love this dessert! This traditional Chilean dessert combines a native product, cornstarch, and products of Old World origin, milk and sugar. It was presented weekly at my boarding school; of the options available at the time it was my preferred choice. It can be prepared with *maicena* (cornstarch), or *glucena* (cornmeal), or *sémola* (semolina). I usually use cornstarch because it yields a smoother texture.

8   tablespoons cornstarch, white cornmeal, or polenta
6   tablespoons sugar
4   cups milk
1   medium lemon or orange rind, grated
1   teaspoon vanilla extract
1   cup *Miel de Vino* (Wine Syrup, p. 244)

Mix the cornstarch and sugar and dissolve the mixture in the milk. Add the lemon rind; and slowly bring the mixture to a boil. The custard will begin to thicken quickly so stir constantly to avoid sticking. Simmer for about 3 minutes and remove from the heat. Remove the lemon rind, add the vanilla, and stir. Pour into moistened individual molds and let them cool until the pudding sets. Unmold and serve at room temperature.

Serving Suggestion:
Serve topped with syrup and with fruit or raisins on the side.

Arroz con Leche
RICE PUDDING

Serves 10

I adapted this recipe from Great-aunt Leonie's cookbook, using converted rice instead of the short grain *Valenciano* type. As a result, the pudding is less sticky.

1	**cup converted rice**
5	**cups milk**
½	**cup sugar**
1	**tablespoon vanilla extract**
1	**tablespoon lemon rind**
1	**cup raisins**
½	**cup whipping cream**
1	**cup honey or syrup (optional)**

Simmer the rice with the milk, sugar, vanilla, and lemon rind for about 40 minutes. Add the raisins and let the rice cool to room temperature. Whip the cream to double in volume and fold it into the cooled rice.

Serving Suggestion:
You can serve this pudding with *Miel de Papaya* (Papaya Syrup, p. 244) or honey on top for extra sweetness, as my mother would do.

Dulce de Almendras
ALMOND SWEET

Serves 24

Another name for this sweet is *Piñonete.* You can use it as a filling for *Empolvados* (Dusted Pastries with Caramel Spread, p. 239), or cut into little squares as a candy or sweet for teatime. Almond sweets similar to these were brought from Spain and were fashionable in colonial Chile during the 1600s and 1700s. The ingredients and procedure are similar to those for marzipan, so these sweets may well be the precursors of the modern marzipan.

1½	cups almonds, peeled
3	cups sugar
1	teaspoon corn syrup
2	large egg whites
1	pinch cream of tartar
1	cup confectioner's sugar (optional)

1. Grind the almonds to a fine paste in the blender or food processor.
2. Prepare a syrup by adding ⅓ cup of water to the sugar and corn syrup. Bring the syrup to a boil and reduce the liquid without browning it; it is not necessary to form a very thick syrup.
3. Add the almond paste to the syrup. Cook the mixture over low heat for 2 to 3 minutes, stirring with a wooden spoon, remove from the heat, and set aside.
4. Beat the egg whites with the cream of tartar into stiff peaks. Carefully fold the egg whites into the almond paste.
5. Return to low heat, continue whisking, and cook until you can see the bottom of the pan.
6. Remove from the heat and continue beating until the paste is barely warm. Spread the paste over a torte or pastry.
7. If prepared as a candy, spread over buttered parchment paper on a cookie sheet and allow to cool and dry; this can take several days depending on the amount of water left in the mixture and the humidity. I prefer to do this in the refrigerator. Sprinkle with confectioner's sugar and cut into small squares or triangles.

Alfajores
CHILEAN PASTRIES WITH CARAMEL SPREAD

Serves 12

My mother learned to make *Dulces Chilenos* (Chilean pastries) from a specialized cook who, on special occasions, would provide these pastries and others such as *Melindres, Principitos, Cocadas, Hojuelas,* and *Calzones Rotos. Alfajores* and *Empolvados* (Dusted Pastries with Caramel Spread, p. 237) are some of the more traditional of *Dulces Chilenos.* They are probably of ancient Spanish origin, and they are very popular at teatime and at birthday parties.

 10 tablespoons all-purpose flour
  2 medium egg yolks
  1 tablespoon *pisco, aguardiente,* or *eau-de-vie* (liqueurs)
  1 cup *Manjar Blanco* (Caramel Spread, p. 243)
 ½ cup confectioner's sugar

Preheat the oven to 450 degrees.

Mix the flour, egg yolks, and pisco to form a dry, soft, smooth dough. Roll the dough very thin (⅛ inch) with rolling pin. Cut 1-inch circles and place them on a buttered baking sheet. Prick the circles with a fork to keep them flat while cooking and bake for about 8 minutes. Remove them from the oven and let them cool. Assemble pairs of circles with *Manjar Blanco* in between, sandwich style. Sprinkle confectioner's sugar on top.

Empolvados
DUSTED PASTRIES WITH CARAMEL SPREAD

Serves 12

This recipe is one of the classic Chilean pastries (*Dulces Chilenos*) that I adapted from my mother's cookbook. The name *Empolvado* derives from *polvo* (dust), meaning covered with sugar dust. There are some variations: for example, the filling can be made with two-thirds *Manjar Blanco* (Caramel Spread, p. 245) and one-third *Crema Pastelera* (Pastry Cream, p. 246), or half *Manjar Blanco* and half *Huevo Mol* (Egg Yolk Candy, p.231), or half *Manjar Blanco* and half *Dulce de Almendras* (Almond Sweet, p. 237).

½   recipe *Bizcochuelo* batter (Sponge Cake, p. 255)
½   recipe *Manjar Blanco* (Caramel Spread, p. 245)
1   tablespoon butter
1   tablespoon flour
½   cup confectioner's sugar

1. Preheat the oven to 325 degrees.
2. Prepare the *Manjar Blanco* and the *Bizcochuelo* batter according to the separate recipes.
3. Butter and flour 2-inch round pastry molds.
4. Place the *bizcochuelo* batter, one tablespoon at a time, into the molds. Sprinkle the dough in the molds with confectioner's sugar.
5. Bake for about 20 minutes. When done, they should be little cakes, 2 inches in diameter and about ½ inch tall, cooked inside and pale on the outside.
6. Let the cakes cool. To form the *Empolvados,* take two cakes and join them, using the *Manjar Blanco* as glue.
7. Sprinkle more confectioner's sugar on top.

Picarones
CHILEAN DOUGHNUTS WITH MOLASSES SYRUP

Serves 12

Some people use yeast in this recipe (and allow for fermentation overnight), but my mother uses baking powder instead. I think this is an easier recipe, and it tastes delicious.

1	cup cooked pumpkin
2½	cups flour
1	cup milk
2	teaspoons baking powder
	salt, to taste
2	cups vegetable frying oil
2	cups *Chancaca* (Molasses Syrup, p. 242), heated

Remove any extra water from the cooked pumpkin. Purée the pumpkin and pass it through a sieve. Mix the pumpkin purée with the flour, milk, baking powder, and salt. Knead the mixture until the dough separates from the bowl. (This can also be accomplished in an electric mixer.) In a frying pan, heat the oil. Form the doughnuts in your floured hands and carefully drop them into the hot oil. Fry the doughnuts until golden brown on all sides. Dip the doughnuts into hot *Chancaca* and serve hot.

Sopaipillas
PUMPKIN FRITTERS WITH MOLASSES SYRUP

Serves 8

Sopaipillas are perfect for cold winter afternoon snacks. They are traditionally served with *Chancaca* (Molasses Syrup) on top. It is common to soak *sopaipillas* in warm *Chancaca* to soften them; this is called *Sopaipillas Pasadas*.

1	cup pumpkin, peeled, and diced
2½	cups all-purpose flour, sifted
½	teaspoon baking powder
2	tablespoons warm vegetable lard
1	pinch salt
1	cup corn oil
2	cups *Chancaca* (p. 242)

1. Cook the pumpkin in enough water to cover it, until tender, about 20 minutes.
2. Remove any extra water from the cooked pumpkin. Purée the pumpkin and pass it through a sieve.
3. In a bowl, mix the pumpkin purée with the sifted flour, baking powder, lard, and salt. Mix with a wooden spoon, until the dough separates from the bowl, adding more flour if necessary. (This can be done in an electric mixer.)
4. Spread the dough with a rolling pin to ¼ inch thickness. Cut the *sopaipillas* into 2-inch circles.
5. In a large frying pan, heat the oil and fry the *sopaipillas* on both sides until golden brown; when ready they will rise to the surface.
6. Remove them from the oil and drain them on paper towels.
7. Serve hot with *Chancaca* or other syrup on top.

MIELES Y ALMÍBARES
SYRUPS

Chancaca
MOLASSES SYRUP

Chancaca is one of the most common sweet syrups used in Chile. *Chancaca* is also the name for the solid form of raw sugar used in preparing the syrup. I have substituted molasses, which is the best United States approximation I could find. *Chancaca* is served over *Sopaipillas* (Pumpkin Fritters with Molasses Syrup, p. 241) and *Picarones* (Chilean Doughnuts with Molasses Syrup, p. 240).

1   cup molasses
1   cup granulated sugar
1   teaspoon vanilla extract
1   pinch orange rind

In a bain-marie, simmer all the ingredients in ½ cup of water until the sugar is dissolved. Keep it warm until ready to serve. Do not boil.

Miel de Melón
MELON SYRUP

Melons are so perfumed that the aroma of the kitchen, when I make this syrup, reminds me of my mother's kitchen and my early childhood. This recipe is made with leftovers of *Dulce de Melón* (Melon Preserve, p. 23).

    1   **large melon**
    1   **cup sugar**

Use only the seeds and green pulp next to the skin. Save the ripe pulp for eating fresh or for *Dulce de Melón*. Peel the skin and dice the green pulp. Mix the cubes with the seeds, fibers, and juices that surround the seeds. Bring to a boil with no added water; simmer for 10 minutes. Pour into a cheesecloth and squeeze out the juices. Add 1 cup of sugar for every 3 cups of juice. Bring the juice to a boil and simmer until it is reduced by half and syrupy and golden. The syrup can be stored in a sterile, sealed container for months without refrigeration.

Serving suggestion:
Serve it cold over toast or with ice cream as a dessert.

Salsa de Frambuesas
RASPBERRY SAUCE

I developed this recipe as a way to preserve surplus home-grown raspberries. You can also prepare this sauce with blueberries or strawberries. I serve it as a dessert topping.

    2   **cups fresh or frozen raspberries**
    ½   **cup sugar**
    ½   **cup Grand Marnier**

Put the raspberries through a strainer to remove the seeds; make sure you recover all the pulp and juices. Blend the raspberry purée with the sugar and Grand Marnier. Adjust the sugar to taste, this depends on the ripeness of the fruits. Store in the freezer.

Miel de Papaya
PAPAYA SYRUP

I adapted this recipe from my mother's cookbook. This syrup is made with the left-overs of *Papayas en Almibar* (Papayas in Syrup, p. 222). I like to serve this syrup over ice cream, *Arroz con Leche* (Rice Pudding, p. 236), or toast.

- 6 **large papayas, seeds and peels only**
- 2 **cups sugar**

Slowly simmer the papaya seeds and peels in 6 cups of water, uncovered, for about 1 hour until the liquid reduces to about 1 cup. Discard the seeds and peels, and add the sugar. Simmer for another 10 minutes. Serve cold. Store in a sterile glass container.

Miel de Vino
WINE SYRUP

Wine-based desserts are popular in Chile because of the abundance of good, inexpensive wines. You can serve this syrup over *Maicena con Leche* (Cornstarch Pudding, p. 235) or other custard desserts.

- 1 **bottle red wine such as cabernet sauvignon**
- ½ **cup sugar**
- 1 **slice lemon rind**
- 1 **teaspoon vanilla extract**

Boil the wine with the sugar and lemon rind for about 30 minutes or until the liquid has reduced by about half. Add the vanilla, remove the lemon rind, and let it cool. Serve cold.

CREMAS Y RELLENOS
CREAMS AND FILLINGS

Manjar Blanco
CARAMEL SPREAD

I adapted this recipe from one of Ms. Rosario Guerrero's, who was the late Mrs. Felicia Montealegre de Bernstein's (Leonard Bernstein's wife) Chilean chef. Similar recipes are in my mother's and Great-aunt Julia's cookbooks. In Spain, this sweet is called *Dulce de Leche.* In Chile, the milk used in this recipe would be whole and unhomogenized. *Manjar Blanco* can also be made by boiling an unopened can of sweetened condensed milk for 1 hour, but it will not taste quite the same.

- **6 cups whole milk**
- **1½ cups sugar**
- **1 vanilla bean**

Bring all the ingredients to a boil, lower the heat and simmer slowly. Stir the mixture frequently until it begins to thicken (about 45 to 60 minutes). After that, stir constantly until done (another 30 to 40 minutes). The cooking time depends on the type of milk used and the simmering conditions. It is safer to go slow and avoid burning at the bottom, so be patient. At the end, it will be reduced to about 1 ½ cups, have the consistency of custard, and be a light caramel color.

Serving Suggestions:
Serve on buttered bread or as a pastry filling for *Dulces Chilenos* (Chilean Pastries).

Crema Pastelera
PASTRY CREAM

Crema Pastelera is found in many French, Spanish, and Italian recipes so its origin is Old World. It is widely used in Chilean pastries. You can use this cream to decorate pastries or stuff a layer cake such as *Torta de Cumpleaños* (Birthday Torte, p. 257).

> 2 **cups whole milk**
> 1 **vanilla bean (or 1 tablespoon vanilla extract)**
> 5 **large egg yolks**
> 1 **cup sugar**
> ½ **cup all-purpose flour**
> 1 **tablespoon brandy**
> 1 **tablespoon Grand Marnier**
> 1 **tablespoon butter, unsalted, melted**

1. Simmer the milk with the vanilla bean for 5 minutes; cover and keep warm; remove the vanilla bean and save it, you can reuse it. (If you are using vanilla extract simply heat the milk.)
2. Beat the egg yolks with the sugar until the mixture is light yellow. Stir in the flour. Pour the hot milk over the egg mixture, beating constantly with a whisk. Pour the mixture back into the saucepan and bring to a slow simmer, stirring constantly. Lower the heat and cook for 2 minutes stirring vigorously, then remove from the stove.
3. If you are using vanilla extract instead of vanilla bean, add the extract at this point. Add the brandy and the Grand Marnier and mix well. Pour the cream into a bowl and spread melted butter over it to prevent the formation of a crust. Cover the cream with parchment paper until you are ready to use it.

Crema Chantilly
CREAM AND MERINGUE BLEND

In spite of the name, this cream should not be confused with the classic French *Crème Chantilly,* which is lightly whipped cream with sugar. I don't know the origin of this cream, but my Great-aunt Julia used it with Chilean pastries. This cream is used with *Crema de Lúcuma* (Lucuma Cream, p. 248), *Huevos Falsos* (False Eggs, p. 232), and as a filling for pastries and layered tortes.

> 4 **large egg whites**
> 1 **pinch cream of tartar**
> ¾ **cup confectioner's sugar**
> 1 **cup whipping cream**

Whip the egg whites with the cream of tartar into stiff peaks. Add ½ cup of sugar, whip to homogenize, and set aside. In a separate bowl, whip the cream to the same consistency as the meringue. Add ¼ cup of sugar and whip to homogenize. Fold the meringue into the whipped cream. Store in the refrigerator until you are ready to use it. It will hold for up to 6 hours.

Crema de Lúcuma
LUCUMA CREAM

Lúcuma trees (*Pouteria lucuma*) are native to the warm valleys north of Santiago and can grow up to 30 meters tall. They start producing fruits after fifteen years. *Lúcuma* is a delicious fruit, about 3 inches in diameter, with dark green skin, golden yellow flesh, and a large brown seed in the middle. The flavor strikingly resembles butterscotch and is not too sweet. It is often used in milk shakes and ice cream. In Chile, *lúcuma* purée is sometimes available in a can, and it is perfectly adequate for this recipe instead of fresh *lúcumas*. In the United States, you can substitute canned chestnut purée. I hope some day *lúcuma* trees will grow in the United States. Southern California has the perfect climate for them. You can use this cream as a filling for pastries and layered tortes, such as *Torta de Lúcuma* (Lucuma Torte, p. 259), but it also makes a wonderful dessert served in parfait glasses.

4   large *lúcumas* (or 10 ounces of canned chestnut purée)
1   cup *Crema Pastelera* (Pastry Cream, p. 246)
     sugar, to taste
1   cup *Crema Chantilly* (Cream and Meringue Blend, p. 247)

Peel and seed the *lúcumas* and press the pulp through a metal sieve or vegetable strainer. Blend the *lúcuma* purée into the *Crema Pastelera* and add sugar to taste. Fold about a third of the *Crema Chantilly* cream into the *lúcuma* cream to loosen it up and then fold in the rest of the *Crema Chantilly* cream.

Crema de Chocolate
CHOCOLATE CREAM

This cream is used as the filling in *Torta de Chocolate* (Chocolate Torte, pp. 258–259). It is similar to a chocolate mousse, so you can also serve it as a dessert with fresh fruits such as raspberries or strawberries.

8	ounces semisweet chocolate
6	large egg whites
1	pinch cream of tartar
1	cup confectioner's sugar
1	cup whipping cream

Melt the chocolate over a bain-marie; set aside and allow it to cool almost to room temperature. (Do not overheat the chocolate.) Whip the egg whites with the cream of tartar into soft peaks. Add the confectioner's sugar to the egg whites and whip to form stiff peaks; set aside. Whip the cream to a stiff consistency and add the melted chocolate while still whipping. Fold the egg whites into the chocolate mixture; adding a third first to loosen up the cream and then the rest, trying not to deflate the volume. Refrigerate until ready to serve.

CÚJENES
TARTS

Cujen de Fresas
KUCHEN, FRESH BERRY TART

Serves 8

Cujen is the Spanish phonetic spelling for the German word *kuchen,* and that is how it appears in my mother's recipes. *Cujen (kuchen)* is of German origin and is very common in Chile. There is a large Chilean population of German origin in the southern provinces. This *cujen* is particularly good with strawberries. The large strawberries *(Fragaria chilensis)* are native to southern Chile. In the early eighteenth century, a Frenchman named Frezier, who was visiting Chile, took this large berry variety back to Europe. It gave rise to the large strawberries we all enjoy today. The berries for this *cujen* can be raspberries, strawberries, or blueberries. *Cujenes* are served at teatime. I have not included a recipe for pie crust because it can be found in any general cookbook or can be purchased ready-made.

    1   10-inch pie crust
    2   tablespoons sugar
    2   tablespoons brandy
    1   cup fruit jelly
    1   cup *Crema Pastelera* (Pastry Cream, p. 246)
    1½   cups fresh berries, such as strawberries, raspberries,
         or blueberries

Preheat the oven to 400 degrees.

Transfer the pie dough to a buttered *cujen* mold (similar to a quiche mold, 8 inches in diameter and 1 inch tall). Prick the dough all over with a fork and bake for 12 minutes. Let it cool and remove it to a serving dish. Add the sugar and brandy to the jelly and bring to a boil to make a glaze. Spread some of the glaze over the pie crust to seal the bottom. Spread the *Crema Pastelera* about ½-inch thick over the pie crust. Arrange the fruit in a decorative pattern over the cream and spread the remaining glaze over the fruit. Serve cold.

Cujen de Frutas
KUCHEN, FRUIT TART

Serves 8

This is one of the many recipes for *cujen* in Great-aunt Leonie's cookbook. The recommended fruits for this *cujen* are apples, quince, apricots, pears, strawberries, and peaches; do not use blueberries or other juicy fruits.

1	cup all-purpose flour
1	teaspoon baking powder
6	tablespoons confectioner's sugar
6	tablespoons butter, unsalted
2	large eggs
2	cups very ripe fruit, peeled and sliced
1	cup milk
½	cup sugar (amount depends on sweetness of fruit)
1	teaspoon vanilla extract
1	tablespoon cornstarch, dissolved in 1 tablespoon of cold water
1	pinch cinnamon powder

1. Preheat the oven to 375 degrees.
2. Butter a *cujen* mold (similar to a quiche mold).
3. Mix the flour, baking powder, confectioner's sugar, butter, and one egg to form a dough.
4. Spread the dough in the mold. Using your floured fingers, extend it all over the bottom of the dish and up the edges.
5. Cover the dough with the fruit and set aside.
6. Boil the milk with the sugar and vanilla. Add the dissolved cornstarch to the milk, stir, and simmer for 5 minutes. Remove the milk from the heat and let it cool a bit.
7. Beat the remaining egg and add it to the milk, stirring rapidly. Pour this custard over the fruit. Sprinkle with a little sugar and the cinnamon.
8. Bake 50–60 minutes. Serve cold.

Cujen Millahue
APPLE *KUCHEN*, APPLE TART

Serves 8

A *cujen* like this one is served at the Hotel Millahue, a vacation resort located up in the Andes in the Maipo Canyon. This recipe is what I remember of the Müller family recipe, owners of Millahue. I spent many happy summer vacations at Millahue and went to boarding school with the Müller sisters (Linda, Mirta, Edith, and Ema), my childhood best friends. Summers were unforgettable. One January, the Chilean former heavyweight champion Don Arturo Godoy (who was defeated only once by Rocky Marciano) was vacationing there and decided to shape up us children. He organized fitness classes for all the kids at the resort—gymnastics in the mornings and after siesta, swimming lessons—whether we wanted to or not. It was not easy to argue with the Champion, and crying was not allowed. But we returned to school fitter than ever.

1	cup butter, unsalted
6	large sweet apples, cored, peeled, and sliced
1	cup sugar
½	teaspoon nutmeg, freshly ground
1	teaspoon cinnamon powder
⅓	cup kirsch
½	cup confectioner's sugar
2	large eggs
1½	cups all-purpose flour
1	tablespoon baking powder

1. Preheat the oven to 375 degrees.
2. In a frying pan, melt about 3 tablespoons of the butter and sauté the apples for about 10 minutes. Continue to cook the apples slowly until they turn golden.
3. Remove from the heat, add the sugar, nutmeg, cinnamon, and kirsch, and set aside.
4. Mix the remaining butter with confectioner's sugar until light and fluffy.
5. Add the eggs, one at a time, and mix well.
6. Sift in the flour and baking powder and mix to form a dough.
7. In a buttered *cujen* mold (similar to a quiche mold), pat the dough over the bottom and up the sides.
8. Pour the apples over the dough.
9. Bake about 30 minutes or until the edges of the dough turn brown. Serve warm or cold.

Relleno para Cujen
FRESH BERRY PIE FILLING

Serves 8

I developed this recipe based on similar recipes for *cujen* (or *kuchen*) fillings. Traditional Southern pies that use blueberries (which are unknown in Chile) and raspberries were part of the inspiration for this recipe. This filling can be used with store-bought pie crust. I do not include a recipe for pie crust since it can be found in any general cookbook.

½   **cup all-purpose flour**
⅓   **cup cornstarch**
¾   **cup sugar**
1   **teaspoon cinnamon**
1   **teaspoon nutmeg, freshly grated**
4   **cups blueberries or raspberries, fresh or frozen**

Preheat the oven to 375 degrees.

In a bowl mix the dry ingredients well. Add the mixture to the berries. Stir thoroughly and pour into the pie crust. Bake for about 45 minutes.

Queque
JENNIE HERD'S TEA CAKE

Serves 10

Jennie Herd was Royce's maternal Great-aunt. Mrs. Samuel L. Creswell, Royce's grandmother from Birmingham, Alabama, wrote this recipe down presumably the way Aunt
Jennie told it: no procedure, just ingredients. As with many family recipes, you learned
the procedure hands-on, thus there was no need to write it down. So I have adapted
my interpretation of the tea cake to this recipe. In my mother's cookbook, there is a
cake similar to this, but milk is used instead of buttermilk. She calls it *Queque Casero*
(Homey Cake). The word *queque* is, of course, the Castilian spelling for the English
word *cake.* Serve it with afternoon tea or for breakfast.

1	cup sugar
½	cup butter, unsalted
1	large egg
1 ¾	cups low protein flour
2	teaspoons baking powder
½	cup buttermilk
1	tablespoon lemon or orange rind, grated
1	teaspoon vanilla extract
½	cup chopped pecans (optional)
1	teaspoon confectioner's sugar

Preheat the oven to 350 degrees.

Mix the sugar and butter until light and fluffy. You can use an electric mixer for
this. Add the egg and mix well. Stir in the flour and baking powder, alternating with
the buttermilk. Add the lemon rind, vanilla, and pecans and stir to mix. Pour the batter
into a buttered and floured loaf pan. Bake 40 to 45 minutes. Check with a toothpick
for doneness. Remove from the baking pan and sprinkle with the confectioner's sugar.

Bizcochuelo

SPONGE CAKE

Serves 10

Bizcochuelo is a variation on sponge cake or genoise. It is the base for preparing *Tortas* (see pp. 257 and 259) and pastries such as *Empolvados* (Dusted Pastries with Caramel Spread, p. 239). For *Tortas,* the cake is usually cut into three layers and filled with either *Manjar Blanco* (Caramel Spread, p. 245), *Crema Chantilly* (Cream and Meringue Blend, p. 247), *Crema de Lúcuma* (Lucuma Cream, p. 248), *Crema Pastelera* (Pastry Cream, p. 246), butter creams, marmalades, fruits (pineapples, chirimoya, papaya, strawberries) or combinations of these and other fillings. The top of the *torta* is covered with the same cream used between the layers and is decorated with fruits.

- **5   large separated eggs**
- **1   pinch cream of tartar**
- **1   cup confectioner's sugar**
- **1   cup all-purpose flour, sifted before measuring**

1. Preheat the oven to 350 degrees.
2. Butter and flour two 10-inch round cake pans. Place buttered parchment or wax paper in the bottom to prevent sticking.
3. Beat the egg whites with cream of tartar into stiff peaks; set aside.
4. Mix the sugar and egg yolks until they turn pale yellow and form a ribbon; slowly add ½ cup hot (not boiling) water. Stir the yolk mixture over a bain-marie until the batter coats the back of a spoon. Be careful not to overcook and scramble the eggs. Remove the yolk mixture from the heat and continue to stir until cool.
5. Add the flour to the yolk mixture, folding gently.
6. Add a third of the egg whites to the yolk mixture to loosen it up, and then carefully fold in the rest of the egg whites so that they don't lose volume.
7. Pour the batter into the mold, leaving plenty of room for rising.
8. Bake about 35 minutes. Check with a toothpick for doneness. Let the cake cool before unmolding and cutting.

Pan de Pascua
CHRISTMAS FRUIT CAKE

Serves 24

My mother got this recipe from my aunt Erika, who is of German descent, so its origin is most likely German. As my mother did for as long as I can remember, I prepare this cake the first week in December and allow it to age for a week or so. It tastes better the longer you wait for it. This recipe makes two large 10-inch cakes; you can cut the recipe in half for just one cake. You can serve this cake alone or with tea, coffee, or *Cola de Mono* (Chilean Eggnog, pp. 274–275).

1 cup golden raisins
1 cup currants
1 cup brandy or rum
4 cups assorted glazed fruits, chopped into small cubes
1 cup almonds, peeled
1 cup walnuts
5 cups low protein flour, sifted
2 cups butter, unsalted
3 cups confectioner's sugar
6 large separated eggs
2 tablespoons baking powder
2 tablespoons white vinegar
1 teaspoon cinnamon powder
1 teaspoon nutmeg, freshly grated
1 teaspoon ground cloves
1 teaspoon vanilla extract
1 pinch cream of tartar

1. Preheat the oven to 350 degrees.
2. Soak the raisins and currants in the brandy and set aside.
3. Mix the glazed fruits, almonds, and walnuts with 1 cup of the flour to coat them, and set aside.
4. Butter and flour, two 10-inch tube pans.
5. Blend the butter with ½ cup of water until smooth.
6. Add the sugar to the butter and blend until smooth.
7. Add the egg yolks to the batter and mix well.

8. Add the raisins and fruit mix to the batter.
9. Add the rest of the flour and the baking powder, vinegar, spices, and vanilla.
10. Beat the egg whites to form soft peaks with the cream of tartar.
11. Carefully fold the egg whites into the cake batter. First mix in a third of the egg whites to soften the mixture and then the rest.
12. Pour the batter into the pans.
13. Bake about 1 hour. Test with a toothpick for doneness.

Torta de Cumpleaños
BIRTHDAY TORTE

Serves 10

I developed this recipe from my mother's *Torta de Amor* (Love Torte); she got it from Aunt Erika. Mother prepared this torte for my birthdays. The original recipe calls for the same layering and filling but does not use a sponge cake, instead it calls for individually baked, 10-inch *galletas* (thin, crusty, round, cookies) as layers. The *Licor de Frambuesas* (Raspberry Liqueur) can be replaced by other liqueurs or brandy or rum.

> 1 10-inch *Bizcochuelo* (Sponge Cake, p. 255) or yellow sponge cake
> 1 cup *Licor de Frambuesas* (pp. 276–277)
> 2 cups *Crema Pastelera* (Pastry Cream, p. 246)
> 1 cup quince, raspberry, blueberry, or grape jelly

1. Prepare the *Bizcochuelo* and let it cool on a rack.
2. Let the *Crema Pastelera* cool completely before using.
3. Level the top of the cake so it is perfectly flat. Cut a thin layer of cake and place it in the serving dish. (You will need 6 cake layers.)
4. Soak the layer with the liqueur. Spread on a layer of the jelly (if using raspberry preserve, make sure it is the seedless kind).
5. Add another layer of cake, soak it with liqueur and spread on a layer of cream. Continue layering and soaking the cake.
6. Cover the top and sides of the torte with cream. Use a fork to create a stripe design on the top and sides. Let the *torta* rest overnight before serving.

Torta de Chocolate
CHOCOLATE TORTE

Serves 16

"No recipe collection is complete without a chocolate torte," says my stepdaughter Debra, who likes anything that contains chocolate. So I went back to Great-aunt Julia's cookbook, and there it was. I served it to Royce's children last Christmas dinner, and there were no leftovers. This cake is a variation on *Bizcochuelo* (Sponge Cake, p. 253). You can replace the *Licor de Frambuesas* with rum or brandy and the fruit with apricots or peaches.

½	cup low protein flour, sifted
½	cup potato starch, sifted
2	teaspoons baking powder, sifted
3	tablespoons cocoa powder, sifted
1	cup sugar
1	tablespoon corn syrup
6	large eggs, separated
1	pinch cream of tartar
½	cup walnuts, ground
½	cup *Licor de Frambuesas* (Raspberry Liqueur, pp. 276–277)
1	cup seedless raspberry or strawberry jam
2	cups *Crema de Chocolate* (Chocolate Cream, p. 249)
½	cup chocolate shavings
½	cup fresh raspberries or strawberries

1. Preheat the oven to 350 degrees.
2. Butter and flour two 8-inch baking pans. You can line the bottoms of the pans with buttered parchment or wax paper to avoid sticking and to help with unmolding.
3. Sift all the dry ingredients together.
4. Prepare the syrup (*Almibar*) by heating the sugar, corn syrup, and ½ cup of water until dissolved and transparent.
5. Whip the egg whites with the cream of tartar into stiff peaks. Slowly add the hot syrup to the egg whites while you continue whipping until the meringue is cool.
6. Whip the egg yolks and fold them into the egg whites.
7. Fold the flour mixture into the eggs.
8. Fold in the walnuts.

9. Pour the batter into the pans, leaving enough room for rising.
10. Bake for 35 minutes on the middle rack of the oven. Check with a toothpick for doneness. Allow the cakes to cool.
11. Remove the cakes from the pans and cut into 2 equal layers each.
12. Assemble the torte in a springform to help you with the stability of the torte. Start with a cake layer at the bottom, sprinkle with *Licor de Frambuesas,* spread a generous layer of jam, then another cake layer sprinkled with liqueur and spread with *Crema de Chocolate,* and so on. Leave some *Crema de Chocolate* for spreading on the outside of the torte.
13. Refrigerate overnight before removing the springform sides. Cover the unmolded torte with *Crema de Chocolate* and decorate with chocolate shavings and fresh fruits.

Torta de Lúcuma
LUCUMA TORTE

Serves 12

This is a scrumptious, rich torte. Some people prepare it with meringue layers instead of *Bizcochuelo,* which is also very good. This is a perfect example of the adaptation of an Old World recipe (the torte) to New World ingredients (the lucuma). You can replace the *Crema de Lúcuma* with a chestnut cream.

1   10-inch *Bizcochuelo* (Sponge Cake, p. 255)
½   cup rum or brandy
2   cups *Crema de Lúcuma* (Lucuma Cream, p. 248)
1   cup *Crema Chantilly* (Cream and Meringue Blend, p. 247)

1. Let the *Bizcochuelo* cake cool before cutting.
2. Cut the cake into three even layers. Save the best layer for the top.
3. Place one layer at the bottom of your serving dish. Sprinkle the layer with rum, and cover it with a generous layer of *Crema de Lúcuma.* Follow with another cake layer sprinkled with rum and covered with *Crema de Lúcuma.* Do not press down, the cake will settle after a while.
4. Finish with the best of the cake layers, and cover the top and sides of the *torta* with the *Crema Chantilly.* Decorate with any remaining *Crema de Lúcuma.* Refrigerate the torte until ready to serve.

Churrasco
MARINATED STEAK SANDWICH

Serves 2

Churrasco is the quintessential Chilean sandwich offered in every *Fuente de Soda* (akin to soda fountain stores where carbonated beverages and ice cream are served), bistro, cafeteria, or restaurant in the country. It is the basic beef sandwich, served always in a white Pullman loaf bread with the crust removed. This sandwich can be served with some toppings. For example, if you add mayonnaise and avocado purée the sandwich is called *Churrasco Palta-Mayo,* and if you add mayonnaise, mustard, avocado purée, sliced tomatoes, and fresh, chopped *ají,* it is called a *Churrasco Completo.* The sandwich would always be served to you cut once down the long side of the bread and then twice in the other direction, thus creating six, juicy, square, bite-sized morsels that you pick up with your fingers and let the juices run down your hand. (You can always wash up later.) This is a great recipe to surprise your teatime guests.

½   **pound beefsteak meat**
2   **tablespoons red wine vinegar**
2   **cloves garlic, minced**
1   **teaspoon cumin**
1   **small fresh *ají* or jalapeño pepper,**
      deseeded and finely chopped
4   **large slices of Pullman or firm sandwich loaf bread**
1   **tablespoon olive oil**
      salt, to taste
      freshly ground black pepper, to taste

Slice the meat very thin (⅛ inch thick). Mix the vinegar, garlic, cumin, and pepper and marinate the meat in this mixture for at least 1 hour. Remove the crusts from the bread slices. Spread the oil on a very hot griddle, and toast the bread on both sides. Then sauté the meat on the hot griddle for just a minute or two, adding the remaining marinating juices at the end. Do not overcook the meat; it will be done quickly because it is sliced so thin. Assemble the sandwich, picking up all the juices from the griddle. Cut the sandwich into six bite-sized morsels and serve immediately.

Chacarero
STEAK AND VEGETABLE SANDWICH

Serves 2

The *Chacarero* is a *Churrasco* (pp. 260–261) with vegetables on it. The name derives from the word *chacra* or *chacara* which is a vegetable garden or small isolated farm where the *chacarero* or field laborer works. The vegetables raised in the *chacra* are added to the basic *churrasco* to create this absolutely fabulous sandwich. This was my favorite snack in the cafeteria at the University of Chile's School of Sciences where I obtained my degree in Chemistry. I will never forget the days, weeks, and months when I had to stay late at night in the lab, pursuing some elusive experiment, with nothing to eat. A run down to the cafeteria for a *Chacarero* always felt like going to the most desirable gourmet restaurant in the world.

½   **pound beefsteak meat**
2   **tablespoons red wine vinegar**
2   **cloves garlic, minced**
1   **teaspoon cumin**
2   **small fresh *ají* or jalapeño peppers,**
    deseeded and finely chopped
1   **tablespoon olive oil**
4   **large slices of Pullman or sandwich loaf bread**
    salt, to taste
    freshly ground black pepper, to taste
1   **large tomato, very ripe, peeled and sliced**
1   **cup green beans, cooked**

Prepare the sandwich the same way as the *Churrasco* (pp. 260–261). When assembling it, add the tomato, green beans, and chopped fresh *ají*. Cut the sandwich into six bite-sized morsels and serve immediately.

Barros Luco

STEAK AND CHEESE SANDWICH

Serves 2

This is another variation on the famous *Churrasco* sandwich (pp. 260–261), this time with added cheese. The cheese used in Chile would be *mantecoso,* which I have replaced with Monterey Jack. Don Ramón Barros Luco was the president of Chile between 1910 and 1915. How this delicious sandwich got its name from this conservative president, I do not know.

½   pound beefsteak meat
2   tablespoons red wine vinegar
2   cloves garlic, minced
1   teaspoon cumin
2   small fresh *ají* or jalapeño peppers,
    deseeded and finely chopped
1   tablespoon olive oil
4   large slices of Pullman or sandwich loaf bread
    salt, to taste
    freshly ground black pepper, to taste
2   slices Monterey Jack cheese

Prepare the sandwich the same way as the *Churrasco* (pp. 260–261). When assembling the sandwich, add a slice of cheese, cover with the top bread slice and return to the griddle to melt the cheese. Cut the sandwich into six bite-sized morsels and serve immediately.

Barros Jarpa
HAM AND CHEESE SANDWICH

Serves 2

This delightful sandwich is another of the most preferred snack foods served in the *Fuente de Sodas,* cafeterias, and informal bistros in Chile. The cheese used in Chile would be *mantecoso,* which I have replaced with Monterey Jack. Don Ernesto Barros Jarpa was a representative in Congress in the 1920s. He was deported and went into exile during the first government of president Don Carlos Ibañez del Campo. How this, and the previous, perfectly respectable and delectable sandwiches got their names mixed up in national politics is a mystery to me.

1	**tablespoon olive oil**
4	**large slices of Pullman or sandwich loaf bread**
2	**slices cooked ham**
2	**slices Monterey Jack cheese**
1	**small fresh *ají* or jalapeño pepper, deseeded and finely chopped**

Heat the oil on a griddle. Assemble the sandwich with a slice of ham, one of cheese, and a sprinkle of the pepper on top. Toast the sandwich on both sides over the hot griddle until the cheese melts. Serve hot.

APERITIVOS, BAJATIVOS, Y BEBIDAS

COCKTAILS, LIQUEURS, AND BEVERAGES

In Chile, as in many countries around the world, it is customary to gather for *aperitivos* (cocktails) before a main meal. The word *aperitivo* refers to the drink's traditional purpose of stimulating the appetite before the meal, and the traditional opening toast in Chile is *Buen Provecho!* (May it benefit you! Cheers!). *Pisco* Sour (p. 272) and *Vaina* (Egg and Port Cocktail, p. 274) are two of the most popular cocktails, and they are among my personal favorites.

Meals are always accompanied by one of our famous Chilean wines. In my opinion they are beyond doubt the best in South America, and they compete very well in the international wine market. Chilean grape vineyards are among the oldest in the Americas. The first Chilean wines were produced in the central valley near Santiago by Franciscan and Dominican friars during colonial times, using Spanish *cepas* (rootstocks) also known as *Del País*. In the sixteenth century, Chile began exporting wines to the Peruvian Viceroyalty. By the 1850s, French rootstocks began to be introduced by Chileans such as Don Silvestre Ochagavía. When *Phylloxera vastatrix,* an insect pest that bores into the roots of grapevines, devastated the European and Californian vineyards in the 1870s, fortunately Chilean vineyards were spared due to its geographic isolation. Chilean growers sent back to France cuttings of the original ungrafted vines to restock the French vineyards. The grapes used to manufacture the choice Chilean wines today include Cabernet Sauvignon, Cabernet Franc, Merlot, Pinot Noir, Semillón, Sauvignon Blanc, Riesling, and Chardonnay. Many brands of Chilean wines are now available in North America, at very reasonable prices.

Several popular beverages prepared from grape juice and wines include *Ponche* (Berry Punch, p. 268), *Vino con Frutillas* (a variation is presented on p. 271), *Chacolí* (Fermented Grape and Orange Juice Punch, p. 269), and *chicha,* a fermented grape juice with a delicious sweet flavor, fruity aroma, and light amber color. *Chicha* fermentation occurs after eight days of simmering in a copper pot coated on the outside with clay. *Chicha* contains 2 to 5 percent alcohol and is sold by the 10- or 15-liter carafe. In the late autumn, my family used to drive over to Quilicura, a small town near Santiago, to buy their famous *chicha.* The word *chicha* is of Quechua origin, and in Peru refers to a fermented corn liquor that has been prepared since pre-Columbian times. *Chicha, Chacolí, Ponche,* and *Vino con Frutillas* are often served at parties and outdoor celebrations, such as the Independence Day celebration, on September 18.

For these celebrations *ramadas* (temporary pavilions of rough wood with thatched roofs) are erected and colorfully decorated with garlands. They have been used for celebrations at least since colonial times and perhaps even earlier. A refinement of the *ramadas* known as *peñas* became popular as clubs or establishments where people congregate to hear folk music and have drinks. In the free, romantic idealism of the 1960s, before terror, pragmatism, and mistrust settled in, a new musical movement was born, becoming known as *La Nueva Canción Chilena* (the new Chilean song). This revived folklore incorporated indigenous musical instruments such as the *quena* (the Andean flute made popular in this country by the song "The Flight of the Condor") along with the Spanish *gitarra* (guitar) and *gitarrón* (large guitar with a double set of strings). The *peñas* were the heart and soul of this new folk music movement. La Peña de los Parra, owned by Angel and Isabel Parra and their mother, the celebrated poet, composer, and folklorist Violeta Parra, was the most famous of all. I will never forget the time I heard Violeta sing her famous song *"Gracias a la Vida,"* later recorded by Joan Baez as "Thanks to Life." Evenings at the *peñas* were full of enthusiasm and optimism. Well-known intellectuals, artists, and politicians mingled with common folk to listen to the new wave of music and ideas. But in the 1970s, during the dark ages of military dictatorship and repression, the *peñas* virtually disappeared. Perhaps in Chile's future there will be another renaissance of music and optimism returning the *peñas* to their full splendor.

In addition to the popular beverages mentioned above, liqueurs called *bajativos* are also common in Chile. Their name is based on the verb *bajar* (descend), meaning that they aid digestion by lowering the food, and these liqueurs are naturally served after dinner. In addition to the traditional brandy, Chileans often drink a sweet or dry (according to taste) *mistela,* a homemade liqueur made with *pisco* or *aguardiente* and flavored with fruits. *Pisco* is a liqueur manufactured from distilled wine, similar to the French *eau-de-vie* and Spanish *aguardiente. Pisco* is prepared in northern Chile where the grapes grow in hot, dry summer weather. Chilean *aguardiente* is prepared south of Santiago with grapes that grow in cooler and rainier climates.

Several members of my family are well known for their fruit-based liqueurs. When I first introduced my husband Royce to my family, my uncle Miguel Neale Silva, the senior member of the extended family, gave Royce a bottle of his own *mistela.* Royce was very grateful for the gift, and since then has encouraged me to continue in this family tradition of liqueur preparation. *Apiado* (Celery Liqueur, p. 276), *Guindado* (cherry liqueur), and *Licor de Frambuesas* (Raspberry Liqueur, pp. 276–277) are a few of my favorites.

Nonalcoholic after-dinner beverages such as *aguitas calientes* (hot herbal teas, p. 277) are also common in Chile. They are drunk after a meal instead of coffee, and at any other time for medicinal purposes. Herbs commonly used are *yerbabuena* or *menta* (mint), *toronjil* (lemon balm), *manzanilla* (chamomile), *ruda* (rue), *apio* (celery), *tilo* (linden tree), and others for which I have no translation, such as *boldo, paico, cedrón, poleo, matico,* and *pailahuen.* I grow my own herbs, so I have fresh ones available year round. A well-planned herb garden should include parsley, cilantro, oregano, basil, lemon balm, mint, rosemary, thyme, sage, chives, lavender, and bay. In Chile, medicinal properties are attributed to many of these herbs, and they are sold in the city market as specific remedies for ailments (*tilo* for the common cold and respiratory problems; *boldo* for liver pains; chamomile and mint for indigestion; lemon balm for melancholy, grief, and sadness; and so on). Lemon balm occupies a prominent place in my herb garden, and since it is a spreading plant, occasionally in the surrounding garden as well.

Ponche
BERRY PUNCH

Serves 28

This is an adaptation of the traditional Chilean *Ponche*, which is prepared with red wine and strawberries. In the nineteenth century, *ponche* was called *chincolito,* which means "little sparrow," I presume because those who drink it are inclined to sing like sparrows. I have used this recipe at Thanksgiving dinners with great success (but so far no sparrows).

    3 quarts cranberry juice
    1 teaspoon cinnamon powder
    1 tablespoon nutmeg, freshly grated
   12 whole cloves
    1 whole lemon peel
    1 whole orange peel
    1 bottle cabernet
    1 whole orange

In a large nonreactive pot, simmer the cranberry juice with the cinnamon, nutmeg, cloves, and lemon and orange peels for 15 minutes. Let cool and then discard the cloves and fruit peels. Pour the juice into the punch bowl and add the wine. Cut thin slices of orange with skin and float them in the punch for decoration.

Chacolí
FERMENTED GRAPE AND ORANGE JUICE PUNCH

Serves 12

Chacolí is a popular and refreshing beverage with a small amount of alcohol. It is typical of the Rancagua region, south of Santiago. This region is famous for its agricultural richness and is said to be the heart of *huaso* culture. *Huaso* is the Chilean cowboy, horseman, and farmhand. He is characterized as a strong, proud, and honest man of the country and a superb rider. In his distinctive and elegant attire, he always looks irresistibly handsome. The *huaso* wears an attractive wide and flat brim hat; a short, tightly tailored jacket with a colorful *poncho* over it; and knee-high black leather boots anchored by 5-inch silver spurs. He rides a similarly fair, agile, powerful, and courageous mount, which is descended from the ancient Andalusian war horses and is known as *corralero* for its role in the corralling of cattle. *Huaso* and *corralero* make a tantalizing pair at the rodeos. The most famous of all rodeos is held in Rancagua in March where spectacular shows of horsemanship are a sight to behold. *Chacolí* is generously served at rodeos, often in a hollowed out bull's horn.

The original recipe is prepared with *chicha,* a fermented grape juice. In this recipe I have replaced the *chicha* with hard cider, which is more readily available. You will have to find your own bull's horn.

1   **gallon hard cider**
1   **gallon orange juice**
     ice as needed

Mix the ingredients together, stir and serve cold in tall glasses.

Horchata
ALMOND BEVERAGE

Serves 10

Horchata is an almond beverage of Spanish origin. *Horchata* was always a special treat for children, served when the grown-ups were having cocktails. This recipe is for a concentrated almond extract that is diluted to taste at the time of serving. Serve as a cold refreshment for a hot summer afternoon.

> 1   **pound almonds, peeled**
> ½   **pound sugar**

   Purée the almonds in a grinder, add some water to produce a paste, and stir to mix well. Add more water to form a thick milk. Transfer the almond milk to a saucepan, bring it to a boil, and simmer for 5 minutes. Filter the milk through a sieve, and set aside. Prepare a syrup with the sugar and ½ cup of water. The syrup should be clear and the consistency must be such that when poured from a spoon the liquid solidifies and forms a thin hair (this is called *almibar de pelo*). Add the almond extract to the syrup and mix well. Let the mixture cool. To serve, add water to adjust to the desired thickness, and pour it into a decanter.

Champaña Alegre
MERRY CHAMPAGNE WITH PINEAPPLES

Serves 4

This elegant recipe from my Great-aunt Julia's cookbook is used in Chile to toast the New Year. Other names for it are *Cocktail Primavera* or *Ponche de Champaña*. Serve with appetizers such as *Masitas de Erizos* (Sea Urchin Pastries, p. 34) or *Galletas Picantes* (Spicy Crackers, p. 39).

> 1   **cup canned pineapple juice**
> 1   **cup canned pineapple cubes**

1   bottle dry white wine
1   bottle sparkling wine, chilled

Mix the pineapple juice, the pineapple cubes, and the white wine in a glass decanter and keep cold. To serve, half fill tall champagne glasses with the mixture and top off the glasses with the sparkling wine.

Champaña con Frutillas
STRAWBERRY CHAMPAGNE

Serves 12

I found this sumptuous recipe in Great-aunt Leonie's cookbook. It is an elegant cocktail, appropriate for a special occasion or party. It is a spring and summer cocktail because fresh fruits are necessary. Raspberries can also be used in this drink. Serve with appetizers such as *Bocadillos* (Little Morsels, p. 31).

1   pound fresh strawberries
1   bottle dry white wine, such as Chardonnay
1   bottle dry sparkling wine

Start the preparation a day ahead. Wash and dry the strawberries; reserve ½ cup of whole strawberries for garnish. Slice the rest of the strawberries. In a glass container mix the sliced strawberries with the wine and let them marinate for 24 to 36 hours. Filter the wine into a decanter and refrigerate until ready to serve. Discard the used strawberry slices. Slice the reserved strawberries. Fill champagne glasses about halfway with the wine, top with the chilled sparkling wine, and garnish with the fresh strawberry slices. Serve immediately.

Pisco Sour

Serves 2

Pisco Sour is the most popular cocktail in Chile. Serve it with appetizers like *Canapés de Mariscos* (Shellfish Hors d'oeuvres, p. 33).

2 **jiggers Pisco**
1 **tablespoon sugar**
2 **large egg whites**
2 **teaspoons lemon juice**
   crushed ice to taste

Shake the ingredients in a cocktail mixer to thoroughly incorporate the egg whites. When you pour the drink into glasses a white foam should form on top. Strain the mixture into cocktail glasses.

Pichuncho
CHILEAN MARTINI

Serves 2

This recipe was adapted from one in Great-aunt Julia's cookbook. This is a typical drink from the southern port of Concepción. Our Chilean friends, Hugo and Nora Castillo, formerly from Concepción and now residents of Chapel Hill, served us this cocktail with appetizers before dinner.

2 **jiggers** *aguardiente* **or** *eau-de-vie*
1 **jigger vermouth**
1 **teaspoon sugar**
   crushed ice to taste

Mix the ingredients in a cocktail mixer. Strain into martini glasses.

Ponche de Erizos
SEA URCHIN PUNCH

Serves 1

This unusual drink is not for the faint of heart. It is known in the region of Bio-Bio, Concepción, and Arauco. I have to confess I have never tried it, and it is not in my family's repertoire; I came across the recipe while traveling.

1   jigger *aguardiente* or *eau-de-vie*
1   glass tomato juice
1   teaspoon Tabasco sauce
1   fresh, raw sea urchin tongue or roe
    crushed ice as needed

Shake the ingredients in a cocktail mixer. Strain into cocktail glasses. Add one fresh, raw sea urchin tongue or roe per glass and serve immediately.

Coctel Santiago
SANTIAGO COCKTAIL

Serves 2

Coctel Santiago was developed at the turn of the century in one of the memorable bars in downtown Santiago. Santiago has many elegant and well-attended bars, where "important men" congregate to discuss significant current issues of national relevance. It is still unlikely that you would find a woman in one of them; it is simply not done. The word *coctel* is the Spanish phonetic spelling of the English word *cocktail* and has been adopted in Chile to describe an alcoholic drink.

2   jiggers *aguardiente* or *eau-de-vie*
1   jigger orange juice
2   tablespoons ground fresh peaches
    crushed ice as needed

Shake the ingredients in a cocktail mixer. Strain into cocktail glasses.

Vaina
EGG AND PORT COCKTAIL

Serves 1

In a less expensive version of this drink, called *Malta con huevo,* the port and brandy are replaced by a dark malt beer. In the evenings, Royce and I enjoyed *vainas* at the Pehue Inn bar in Torres del Paine National Park, while admiring the spectacular landscape of snowcapped granite peaks, glacier lakes, and the vastness of the Chilean Patagonia. *Vaina* is often served with *canapés* and other appetizers.

1   **jigger port**
1   **small egg**
1   **teaspoon brandy**
1   **teaspoon Creme de Cacao liqueur**
1   **tablespoon crushed or cubed ice**
1   **pinch cinnamon powder**
    crushed ice to taste

Thoroughly shake the ingredients in a cocktail mixer to incorporate the egg. Strain into sherry glasses; a foam should form on top of the liquid. Sprinkle cinnamon on top of the foam.

Cola de Mono
CHILEAN EGGNOG

Serves 10

My mother prepares *Cola de Mono* every December to welcome friends and family during the traditional holiday visits. This recipe was adapted from my Great-aunt Julia's cookbook. It is akin to the American eggnog. The name literally means "monkey's tail"; obviously another eccentricity of the Chilean speech.

1   **gallon milk**
1   **cup sugar**
1   **vanilla bean**

1   cup whole coffee beans
6   large egg yolks
2½   cups *pisco, aguardiente,* or *eau-de-vie*

Bring the milk to a boil with the sugar, vanilla, and coffee. Let it simmer slowly, stirring occasionally, until the milk turns a light brown. Remove it from the heat, strain, and return to low heat. Add a couple of tablespoons of the hot milk to the egg yolks to dilute and warm them. Stir the yolks back into the hot milk and cook the mixture for a few minutes. Let it cool completely. Add the *pisco* to taste and serve cold. It will keep in the refrigerator for several days. White rum can be substituted for *pisco*. For a shortcut, use ½ cup instant coffee instead of coffee beans.

Licor de Oro
LIQUEUR OF GOLD

Serves 4

This unique drink gets its name from its rich golden color. It is served in the southern port of Puerto Montt. In the long rainy winters there, a drink like this feels very comforting.

4   jiggers dark brandy (Spanish brandy)
4   tablespoons sweetened condensed milk
     crushed ice as needed

Thoroughly shake the ingredients in a cocktail mixer to incorporate the milk. Strain into sherry glasses.

Apiado
CELERY LIQUEUR

Serves 8

Apiado is a *mistela* (homemade liqueur) prepared by several members of my family. My uncle Miguel Silva Neale gave my husband Royce a bottle of his *Apiado* the first time they met. It did not last very long! This liqueur must be prepared 2 to 3 months before using. Celery leaves may be replaced by mint or other fragrant herbs to produce other delicious liqueurs.

1   bottle *pisco, aguardiente,* or *eau-de-vie*
3   stalks fresh celery with leaves

Pour the *pisco* into a large mason jar and put the celery stalks in it. Allow the liqueur to extract the flavors on a sunny windowsill. The gentle warmth of the sun circulates the liquid and facilitates the extraction of flavors. After 2 to 3 months, pour the *Apiado* into a decanter, leaving the celery behind. It is now ready to drink.

Licor de Frambuesas
RASPBERRY LIQUEUR

Serves 8

This is a variation on my mother's recipe for fruit liqueur, which uses dried cherries (*Guindado*), dried apricots, or celery (*Apiado,* p. 276). My mother, of course, uses these liqueurs, strictly for "medicinal" purposes.

1   bottle *pisco, aguardiente,* or *eau-de-vie*
2   cups fresh raspberries
1   cup sugar

Pour the *pisco* into a larger bottle or mason jar and add the raspberries. Close the bottle and place it on a sunny windowsill for about two months to extract the flavors.

After two months, the liquid will have turned raspberry red; strain out the raspberries. Dissolve the sugar in 1 tablespoon of water and bring it to a boil; simmer until the sugar is totally dissolved and still colorless (this is called *almíbar*) and forms a hair when poured from the spoon (this is called *almíbar de pelo*). Pour the syrup into the liqueur and mix well. Pour the liqueur into a decanter, and it is ready to serve.

Café con Malicia
SHREWD COFFEE

Serves 6

This drink is from the southern region of Concepción. It is ideal for cold winter nights when the wind is howling and the rain is pounding, threatening to drown you. The name *"con Malicia"* refers to something clever and hidden. In other words, you may pretend that you are simply drinking an innocent cup of coffee with milk, rather than an alcoholic beverage.

6   **teaspoons instant coffee**
6   **tablepoons sugar**
6   **cups boiling milk**
6   **jiggers *aguardiente* or brandy**

Put 1 teaspoon of coffee and 1 tablespoon of sugar into each of six cups. Add 1 tablespoon of boiling milk per cup, stir to dissolve, and mix until creamy. Half fill the cups with hot milk and add 1 jigger of *aguardiente* per cup. Drink hot.

Café Helado
ICED COFFEE

Serves 6

In the summer, tortes are served with *Café Helado* (iced coffee) instead of tea at teatime. It is a common beverage served in tearooms and ice cream parlors in Chile. It is also a refreshing snack at any time.

6 teaspoons instant coffee
6 scoops vanilla ice cream
6 tablespoons whipped cream
6 pinches cinnamon powder

Dissolve the coffee in 6 cups of boiling water and let it cool. In tall glasses, serve a cup of coffee and a scoop of ice cream topped with 1 tablespoon of cream and sprinkled with cinnamon.

Aguita Caliente
HOT HERBAL TEA

Serves 1

Herbal teas are very common in Chile. They are drunk after a meal instead of coffee or at any other time for medicinal purposes. Herbs are an enhancement to taste, and a cure for everything!

2 leaves fresh or dried herbs or lemon rind
1 cube sugar

Lightly burn the sugar cube over the stove on all sides but not all the way; this is to create a coating of caramel to flavor the tea. (This step is optional.) Place the sugar with the herb leaves (an herbal tea bag can substitute) or lemon rind in a teacup. Pour 1 cup of boiling water over and infuse for 5 minutes. Stir, remove the leaves, and drink hot.

INGREDIENTES ESPECIALES

SPECIAL
INGREDIENTS

This section lists a few ingredients the reader may not be familiar with, but most Chilean recipes do not require special ingredients. When a special ingredient is listed in the recipe, I have generally included some suggested substitutions.

Ají: The Andean pepper most common in Chile is called *ají,* of which there are hot and sweet types. *Ají* is the species *Capsicum Baccatum,* but the Chilean *ají* is a distinct variety. The hot Chilean *ají* grows from white flowers to a yellow, elongated form, about 3 inches long. It is usually used at the yellow stage of maturation. When ripe it turns bright red and is so hot that it is inedible, at least to my taste. It is often eaten raw in salads or sandwiches or cooked in casseroles, stews, and meats.

Callampas: Chilean mushrooms are called *Callampas,* and while fresh they resemble the Italian Portobello mushrooms. In the United States the dried ones are sometimes confused with several European mushrooms, but they are a separate and distinct species. Chilean mushrooms are usually used dried, which concentrates their flavor. When soaked in warm water, they yield an intensely flavorful liquor that can be used on its own.

Centolla: *Centolla* (Patagonian king crab), the southern version of Alaskan crab, is abundant in the Pacific Ocean near the coast of Patagonia and Tierra del Fuego. *Centollas* and Alaskan king crabs are usually sold already cooked so you may not need to bother with the cooking, but they are best when freshly cooked.

Chirimoya: *Chirimoya* (*Annona cherimola*), also known as *cherimoya* or custard apple, derives its name from the Quechua word *chirimuya*. It is the Chilean national fruit and its trees are native to the warm valleys north of Santiago. *Chirimoya* is regarded as a premium fruit, "the pearl of the Andes." Mark Twain once called it "deliciousness itself"! It is approximately 4 to 6 inches in diameter and covered with a green skin. The flesh is creamy and white with a custardlike texture and is juicy, sweet, and delectable. It has several, easy-to-remove, ¼-inch black seeds. Its unique flavor is a subtle blend of papaya, pineapple, and banana. A mixture of these fruits can be used as a substitute. *Chirimoyas* are now commercially grown in Southern California, and are available in West Coast markets and by mail order throughout the United States (Harry and David, P.O. Box 712, Medford, OR 97501, 800-547-3033).

Chuño: *Chuño,* or potato starch, was traditionally manufactured high in the Andes by crushing potatoes and allowing them to freeze-dry during the cold, dry winter nights. It has the appearance of cornstarch or arrowroot, very white and finely ground. When cooked, it thickens to the consistency of light cream and is semitransparent. It is served without flavorings to babies and sick people.

Cochayuyo: *Cochayuyo* is a seaweed found all along the Chilean coast. It grows in green strands as much as 100 meters long. When harvested it is folded into bundles and allowed to dry in the sun, which turns it brown and very hard.

Congrio: *Congrio* is a scaleless, fishlike, conger eel, with a thick body and long, narrow tail. It is found in deep (down to 300 meters), cold ocean waters, and usually sold in sizes between 18 and 30 inches long. There are at least two subspecies of *congrio: congrio colorado* (red conger) and *congrio negro* (black conger).

Corvina: *Corvina* is a fish from deep, cold ocean waters. The meat is wonderful, very white and tender, with a mild fish taste, somewhat like the Atlantic sea bass. Any white fish can be substituted for *corvina.*

Erizos: *Erizos* or sea urchins are an acquired taste, but they are considered a delicacy in Chile. There are at least two subspecies of sea urchins: *erizos colorados* (red urchins) and *erizos negros* (black urchins); only the red ones are edible. Inside the round spiny shell of the urchin there are five, deep orange, 2-inch-long strips that we call tongues. (They are in fact the gonads; in Japanese sushi bars they are called roe or *uni*). This is what you eat. Inside the shell you may also find a small crablike mollusk that lives in symbiosis with the sea urchin; some people think this is the best part of the meal and eat it raw.

Locos: The *Loco* is sometimes called abalone because it resembles the Californian abalone. But *locos* are actually a different species, *C. Concholepas. Locos* have been harvested for food since prehistoric times, and 12,000-year-old mounds of *loco* shells have been found along the coast of Chile. Before 1986, *locos* were plentiful in Chile and were commonly served in salads and stews. Canned *locos* are sometimes available, but they are not nearly as good as the fresh ones.

Lúcuma: *Lúcuma* trees (*Pouteria lucuma*) are native to the warm valleys north of Santiago. They can grow as tall as 30 meters and start producing fruit after fifteen years. *Lúcuma* is a delicious fruit, about 3 inches in diameter, with dark green skin, relatively dry golden yellow flesh, and a large brown seed in the middle. The flavor strikingly resembles butterscotch and is not too sweet. It is often used in milk shakes and ice cream. In Chile, *lúcuma* purée is sometimes available in a can, and it is delicious.

Machas: *Machas* (*Mesodesma donacium*) are a type of razor clam from the Pacific coast of South America. They were harvested in prehistoric times along the coast of Chile and archaeologists have found its shells in large mounds where the native Chileans used to live. The shell resembles an elongated clam, and its meat is pink.

Mate: *Mate* was drunk by the pre-Columbian peoples of Paraguay, Uruguay, Argentina, and Chile. *Yerba Mate* is the dried leaves of a shrub in the holly family that grows wild on the banks of the upper Paraguay River. Like coffee and tea, *mate* contains caffeine. *Mate* has been popular in Chile since colonial times. In the big cities, though, it has been replaced by coffee or tea. *Mate* can be drunk any time of day, and drinking it can be a kind of social ceremony.

Mote: *Mote* is a common ingredient in popular Chilean cuisine. It is a special type of whole corn kernel and is similar, but not identical, to hominy.

Palta: *Paltas* are Chilean avocados. They are slightly different from the California avocado. Chilean *paltas* have thin skins and are smaller than the Californians. They are very buttery, and some are stringy. Quillota, a city about 100 kilometers north of Santiago, is reputed to grow the best *paltas* in the country.

Papayas: Papayas are five-sided yellow fruits, 6 to 8 inches long, with small round seeds. The Chilean papaya is smaller than its tropical cousin, tolerant of cold weather, and very fragrant. It contains the papain enzyme, which is a meat tenderizer. It is grown principally in northern Chile down to about La Serena.

Pejerreyes: *Pejerreyes* are small fish, 8 to 10 inches long, from cold, ocean waters. They are akin to the Arctic Norwegian whiting and are sometimes called smelt. They thrive along the coast of Chile where the cold Humboldt current runs.

Pepinos: *Pepino* or *Pepino Dulce* (*Solanum muricatum*) is an egg-shaped fruit about 5 inches long. The skin is yellow with purple streaks; the flesh is sweet, juicy, and pink and tastes like melon. *Pepino dulce* can be eaten raw and is fabulously refreshing on a hot summer day. The Quechua name for *pepino* is *cachun* and its Aimará name is *kachuma.* In Chile *pepino dulce* is grown principally in the Longotoma Valley, near La Ligua north of Santiago. It is currently available in the United States by mail order catalog (Harry and David, P.O. Box 712, Medford, OR 97501, 800-547-3033).

BIBLIOGRAPHY

Culinary References

Bascuñán, Aida, *Recetas de Cocina,* Vols. I & II, Santiago, Chile, personal notes, 1950–1990.

Beard, James, *Beard on Bread,* New York, A.A. Knopf, 1993.

Becker, L., et al., eds. *Gran Libro de la Cocina Chilena,* São Paulo, Brazil, Editorial Bibliográfica Chilena, 1993.

Behrens, Elsa, *Cooking the Spanish Way,* London, Paul Hamlyn, 1960.

Boisier, Laurie, *Cocinando Para Dos,* Santiago, Chile, L.K., 1972.

Bravo Walker, Mariana, *Cocina Popular,* 23d ed. Santiago, Chile, Editorial Grijalbo, 1992.

Calera, A. M., *Cocina Andaluza,* Leon, España, Editorial Everest S.A., 1984.

Casas, Penelope, *The Foods and Wines of Spain,* New York, A.A. Knopf, 1991.

Círculo Las Gaviotas *Manual de Cocina,* Linares, Chile, Talleres de Imprenta de la Escuela de Artillería, 1959.

Eyzaguirre, Maria Victoria, *Cocina Chilena y Latino Americana,* Santiago, Chile, Editorial Lord Corchane, 1991.

Gordon, Elizabeth, *Cuisines of the Western World,* New York, Golden Press, 1965.

Hesse, Zora, *Southwestern Indian Recipe Book,* Colorado, Filter Press, 1973.

Hume, R., and Downes, M., *Cordon Bleu Cookery Course,* Vols. I–IV, 2d. ed., London, Purnell BPC Publishing, 1968.

Kavasch, Barrie, *Native Harvests, Recipes and Botanicals of the American Indian,* New York, Vintage Books, 1979.

Lagarrigue, Maria Paz, *Recetas de las Rengifo,* Santiago, Chile, Empresa Editora Zig-Zag, 1992.

Leonard, Jonathan Norton, *Latin American Cooking,* New York, Time-Life Books, 1972.

Rojas-Lombardi, Felipe, *The Art of South American Cooking,* New York, Harper Collins, 1991.

Valdes, Ramona, *Cocina Práctica,* Méjico, Ediciones Botas, 1937.

General References

Advisory Committee on Technology Innovation, National Research Council, *The Lost Crops of the Incas,* Washington, D.C., National Academy Press, 1989.

Andrews, Jean, *Peppers, The Domesticated Capsicums,* Austin, University of Texas Press, 1984.

Atlas de la Republica de Chile, Santiago, Chile, *Instituto Geográfico Militar,* Chile, 1982.

Aylwin, M., et al., *Chile en el Siglo XX,* Santiago, Chile, Editorial Planeta Chilena, 1990.

Bonar, Ann, *Herbs: A Complete Guide to the Cultivation and Use of Wild and Domesticated Herbs,* New York, Macmillan, 1985.

Chile, Atlas Geográfico, Vols. 8 and 10, Santiago, Chile, Editorial Antártica S.A., 1981.

Coe, Sophie D., *America's First Cuisines,* Austin, University of Texas Press, 1993.

Echaiz, Rene Leon, *El Bandido Neira,* Santiago, Chile, Editorial Orbe, 1965.

Faundes, Juan Jorge, *Bernardo O'Higgins, El Honor y la Gloria,* Santiago, Chile, Empresa Editora Zig-Zag, 1993.

Foster, Nelson, and Linda S. Cordell, *Chilies to Chocolate, Food the Americas Gave the World,* Tucson & London, University of Arizona Press, 1992.

Garay G., and O. Guineo, *Conociendo Torres del Paine, Flora y Fauna en Torres del Paine,* Punta Arenas, Chile, Talleres Instituto Don Bosco, 1992.

McGee, Harold, *On Food and Cooking, The Science and Lore of the Kitchen,* New York, Collier Books, 1984.

Moorehead, A., *Darwin and the Beagle,* New York, Harper & Row, 1969.

Mostny, Grete, *Prehistoria de Chile,* Santiago, Chile, Editorial Universitaria, 1994.

Neruda, Pablo, *Odes to Common Things,* Boston, Bullfinch Press, 1994.

Perrottet, T., ed., *Chile,* Singapore, APA Publications, 1991.

Petit, Magdalena, *El Patriota Manuel Rodriguez,* Santiago, Chile, Empresa Editora Zig-Zag, 1957.

————, *Los Pincheira,* Santiago, Chile, Empresa Editora Zig-Zag, 1962.

Subercaseaux, Benjamin, *Chile o Una Loca Geografia,* Santiago, Chile, Editorial Universitaria, 1992.

Sutcliffe, Serena, *The Wine Handbook,* New York, Simon and Schuster, 1982.

Timothy, D. H., et al., "Races of Maize in Chile," from *Races of Maize,* Vol. II, No. 847, National Research Council Publication, Washington, D.C., National Academy of Sciences Press, 1961.

Vicuña, Alejandro, *Inez de Suarez,* Santiago, Chile, Editorial Nascimento, 1941.

Villalobos, S., et al., *Historia de Chile,* Santiago, Chile, Editorial Universitaria, 1980.

INDEX